# BECOMING A MODERN HEALER FROM THE ANCIENT WORLD OF AKƆM

This book is a publication of
Diasporic Africa Press

New York | www.dafricapress.com

Copyright © Nana Kwaku Sakyi 2024

All rights reserved. No part of this publication may be reproduced or distributed in any form or by any means, or stored in a database or retrieval system, without the prior written permission of the publisher.

Library of Congress Control Number: 2023946722

ISBN-13 978-1-937306-76-2 (pbk.: alk paper)

ISBN-13 978-1-937306-77-9 (ebook)

# BECOMING A MODERN HEALER FROM THE ANCIENT WORLD OF *AKƆM*

**NANA KWAKU SAKYI**

DIASPORIC AFRICA PRESS

NEW YORK

*When you offend God, he makes you an ɔkɔmfoɔ*

# ACKNOWLEDGEMENT

This book took many years of deliberation before I finally decided to publish it. In retrospect, I am glad I did not rush it. The question may be why did it take me so long? I could have done so after my first journey to Ghana, but did not. For the past thirty years I've wanted to publish the book, convincing myself that it would only be a reference for the one who would inherit my ɔbosom. I thought about it and found another excuse, making me indecisive. But it was the voice of Nana Kofi Effa coming from both my past and future, reminding me of what I promise to do, "remember their names."

I would like to thank my mother and father, Maize and Kenneth Blackman, who gave birth to me, because without them this book would not be possible. I would also be remiss if I did not thank my father's mother Rita Blackman, who indirectly laid the foundation that shaped my spiritual outlook.

I would also like to thank to my wife Kiah Asabea, who stood by my side and supported over the last twenty years always, with love and devotion. My children, Khalil, Khamisi, Etosha, Yaw and Yaatia, I did this for you all so you can know what our culture looked like in this ever-changing world, with the hope that you will pass it on to your children. Remember, we share the same ntɔn spirit, whereby you will have access to this worldly dimension as I do.

My journey also owes a great debt to my late friend and martial arts teacher Nganga Y. T. Tolo-Naa, who lifted the veil and directed me in discovering my African lineage, forever setting me on this path. I thank Assane Konte, my former dance teacher, for bringing into reality what my journey would look like through his dance teachings.

I much appreciate Osunyoyin Alake, my former wife, who kept her fingers on the spiritual pulse in Washington D.C. and introduced me to Bokor Nana Kwabena Brown, who had a profound influence on making me aware of the Akan spiritual world. He inspired to go to Takyiman, Ghana.

There are many parts that must come together before a book is published, and I would like to extend a special thank-you to Nana Dr. Kwasi Konadu. Without his support, this book could not be published. I am certain his efforts and directions in publishing this book could not be possible without his patience and contribution in helping me to settle on the title of this book. My original title was *The Flies of Takyiman are Powerful*. Thank you for your role as editor of my manuscript and the realization of my intent to write this book.

Finally, I can never fully express the impact and influence three human beings had on my life's purpose. Nana Kofi Effa, you answered my call and started it all by giving me the opportunity to choose how my destiny would unfold. I can't begin to convey how much you mean to me, showing me so much love, compassion and understanding. You selflessly took me in and brought me home and made me realize what Akan/Bono culture is all about by introducing me to our father, Nana Kofi Dɔnkɔ, who adopted me and gave me his name. Papa, you laid the foundation for me that would last a lifetime. As you said, when the medicine penetrates your bones, it lasts forever. I owe you so much. Your patient knew no boundary. How can I, in such a short lifetime, enlighten my readers of the gratitude I owe you. You are my spiritual teacher, fashioning me into the very being into which I have evolved.

Nana Akumsa, you set the bar very high and taught me that not all *Akɔm* is *Akɔm*. You taught me how to be an *ɔkɔmfoɔ* and about the *nsuman* we wear along with their songs. You gave me *Bɔngan* and made the third human being to acquire it.

Afia Monofie, my mother, you fed and took care of me as though you gave birth to me. You did everything a mother would do for her son. Never did I feel as a stranger, but as a true son.

Nana Kofi Kyereme, thank you for your wisdom and contribution, and clarifying the significance of *Kɔmpan Adepa*.

Nana Kwam Froɔ, our time was short, but memorable, for you opened doors for me. Thank you! Everyone in Takyiman knows me as Akoawoaduru, especially the dear ones. This name is forever fixed on my soul due to Nana Kofi Nimo, who first gave it to me, Akoawoaduru, thank you.

I thank the Bono people of Takyiman, who welcomed me into their embrace and nourished me in the Tano waters.

My brother and confidant, Nana Kwao Sarpon Kumankuma, you were more than a voice of wisdom, but a true brother as well. You are my right arm; nothing would have been clear without your voice. I am eternally beholden to you.

Last but least, my spiritual friend and supporter, Nana Kwame Nsowah. You are my dear friend who, like Nana Kumankuma, is my anchor, keeping me updated with your wisdom and knowledge, like an unbroken chair in our journey I sit upon. Kwadwo Owusu Kusuprem, thank you as always for your unwavering support. A special thank-you to Akua Takyiakwaa for your timeless support.

I hope I have not forgotten anyone, and if I did, please forgive me.

# GLOSSARY

## AKAN/TWI TERMS

***ɔbosom (pl. abosom)*** – spiritual forces of nature considered "children" of *Nyame*.

***ɔbrafoɔ*** – in Akan societies, an executioner, enforcer of law, and a healer's assistant.

***akɔm*** – the ways of becoming *akɔmfoɔ/abosomfoɔ*, expertise in rituals and medicines, working with spiritual forces and their celebration through dance, drumming and song.

***ɔkɔmfoɔ (pl. akɔmfoɔ)*** – one who does *akɔm*.

***ɔkyeame (pl. akyeame)*** – speech intermediary; one who invokes the *ɔbosom*.

***(a)boatia (pl. mmoatia)*** – short spirit creatures of the forest with great knowledge of herbs.

***abusua (pl. mmusua)*** – matriclan, lineage group or family organization.

***adae*** – a celebration occurring every 42 days on the Akan calendar, revolving around an *ɔbosom*, ancestors or *suman*. It is a day of rest for the *ɔkɔmfoɔ/ɔbosomfoɔ*.

***aduro (pl. nnuro)*** – medicine, including (in)organic materials and therapeutic methods.

***aduto*** – harmful medicine used to harm or injure.

***agyenegyenensuo*** – a horsefly or cleansing fly.

***akwasiadae*** – major celebration occurring every 42 days on the Akan calendar.

***aseda*** – an offer that expresses thanks and gratitude for (healing) services rendered.

***atanɔ*** – any *ɔbosom* fashioned and placed in a brass pan, such as a Tanɔ *ɔbosom*, whereas a pure Tanɔ *ɔbosom* derives from the Tanɔ river.

***dufa*** – herbal medicine with added ingredients that has been pounded and made into a hard rectangular or round shape and is applied by rubbing on a stone.

***kwasea*** – a fool.

***mɔtɔ*** – composite, black powdered medicine.

***nana*** – title of respect for the *ɔbosom*, ancestors, elders, leaders, and healers.

***pito*** – a beverage brewed from fermented millet or sorghum.

***sipe*** – a psychological disease cured through spiritual cleansing.

***suman (pl. a/nsuman)*** – minor spirit whose power comes from an ɔ*bosom* or the medicines and objects from which they are made. As talismans, they are for individual use.

***sumanbrafoɔ*** – a minor spirit that catches and punish offenders of law and custom.

***yawa (pl. nyawa)*** – brass pan.

# TRINIDADIAN TERMS

***cocoyea*** – spine of coconut tree fronds made into brooms.

***jockey*** – a childhood game involving tree bark shaped into a surfboard, insulated with candle wax, and then sailed down canals.

***jumbee*** – a protective or guardian spirit that keeps negative spirits in check.

***laglee*** – a sticky resin or sap from a tree placed on the cocoyea to trap or catch birds.

***lota*** – waterborne bacteria or parasite that gets into the skin, creating discoloration.

# A NOTE ON TERMINOLOGY

When I began reviewing my journals for publication, I found some inconsistencies in my spelling of Akan/Twi terms. Of course, this is to be expected, since I was not familiar with these words or their spelling and sounds. I ask for the reader's patience, as you witness my acclimation to a new environment, language, and culture.

I am by no means complete in my understanding of the Akan/Twi language, though my competency has grown over the years. *Anɔma de ɔkɔ ne aba na nwene berebu*, states the proverb, which means, "by going and coming the bird weaves its nest."

# FOREWORD

## KWASI KONADU

Indigenous healers deliver sixty to seventy percent of health care and healing in modern African communities, especially rural ones. In 2020, sixty percent of Africa's inhabitants lived in rural areas, despite ongoing urbanization. Whether rural or urban, indigenous medicine remains the dominant healing system, often the preferred mode of treatment by healers and recipients. From Ethiopia to South Africa to Cameroon and Ghana, indigenous healing systems persist as not only alternatives but the first option for many. Similarly, African diasporic peoples in the Americas also deploy Africa-based indigenous medicine and therapy. Healers in diasporic communities, like their counterparts in Africa, transform therapeutic knowledge into social and cultural practice, under the headings of Vodun, Candomblé, Santería, Palo Monte, and other Africa-based spiritual cultures. Having trained as a healer in Ghana but hailing from Trinidad, Nana Kwaku Sakyi's story fuses the ageless wisdom of African healers with the modern worlds of Africa and its American diaspora.

I first met Nana Kwaku Sakyi as a graduate student planning to do research on indigenous medicine and healers in the town of Takyiman, central Ghana. We did not meet in person, but through a common friend and elder, Nana Kwabena Brown. Without knowing me, and having only spoken on the phone, Nana Sakyi wrote me a letter of introduction to the family of Nana

Kofi Dɔnkɔ, a famed healer and his teacher. That was 2001. Since then, our friendship, then brotherhood, has grown in proportion to my relation to the healers and people of Takyiman and Ghana. As I have conducted research in this part of the world over the past two decades, Nana Sakyi had amassed a unique series of experiences, documented in his journals, under the guidance of healing savants now ancestors, including Nana Kofi Dɔnkɔ, Nana Adwoa Akumsa, Nana Kofi Effa, and Nana Kwadwo Bɛkɔɛ.

The first diasporic African to train as an *ɔbosomfoɔɔ-ɔkɔmfoɔ* in the ancient market town and spiritual center of Takyiman, Nana Sakyi's lived experiences under those elders' guidance forms the substance of this book. A memoir of the years under training, *Becoming a Modern Healer from the Ancient World of Akɔm* chronicles more than a decade of learning, practice, and relationships that marries Africa and the African diaspora, the spiritual and the temporal, and the realities of modern life with the healing knowledge of old and new. Over the two decades I have known Nana Sakyi, I have only gathered some of Nana's insightful story incrementally, but for the first time I have the same privilege and excitement as you the reader. Nana Sakyi lays bare, with perception and care, sacred and never-before-revealed details about the training of healers, especially in a special place like Takyiman. *Becoming a Modern Healer from the Ancient World of Akɔm* will stand as a timely and remarkable, yet accessible, memoir for a planet always in need of healers and healing.

# INTRODUCTION

## AGYENEGYENESUO
## / CLEANSING FLY /

As I look back on the events that changed my life forever, I can say they were all beyond my control. It all started with two life-changing experiences, the first as a young child in Trinidad in the early 1960s followed by a dream in 1987. When I first attended school as a child, I used to take a shortcut through a cemetery called the poor man's cemetery. I was often advised not to go through this place because something bad could happen to me, but I never listened. One day, as I disobeyed the warnings, I encountered a being dressed in what looked like a raffia skirt brandishing a cutlass, and he asked me, "What are you doing here?" This being was a spirit we call *jumbee*. It is said that a *jumbee* is the spirit of a bad or an evil person, but this one that confronted me was more a guardian or protector that kept the bad spirits of the dead in check. I became speechless and very afraid. He asked me again, and I was mute. I became even more terrified with panic and ran. The spirit chased me. I somehow managed to get out of the cemetery and ran home. I hid under a box we as children would often hide under while playing.

I was born at home in a small town called St. James in Port of Spain, Trinidad. The road I grew up on is call Upper Bournes Road; this road intersects a street call *Quamina* (*Kwabena*) street. This street will be significant later on in my life's story.

I had a normal, compact and adventurous childhood growing up in Trinidad. My earliest memory is of me sitting at the foot of my parents' bed and drawing, imitating my father, an amateur artist who loved to draw and paint. I felt so alive and free, exploring my environment, not like an adventurer, but being the adventure. I lived in harmony and was a part of the seasonal changes flowing with the pulse and rhythm of the time. My partners in these adventures were my cousins, Terry Marshall and Robert Taylor. I am called Keith, Kitos or Kito by my mother and other family members. We three did everything together except attend the same school. We made kites during the kite season to fly on the hill, pitched marbles, made tops to spin, made *jockey* from tree bark, which we insulated from water with candle wax for racing down the canals and competed with delight. We played with dry ice, spitting on it as we covered the can and lit a match to see and hear its Boom and watch with delight as the can lid became a projectile. We spent the majority of our time on the hill, a place full of excitement and danger.

On that hill, we observed many things: the cemetery, which we called the hangman cemetery, where you could witness the execution of prisoners; my school, Mocorapo Boys School; and the adults flying a big kite that we called mad bull. I recall my aunt's husband, Uncle Herbert, procuring a sap called *laglee* from a tree and putting it on a coconut branch, which we call *cocoyea,* to catch birds. This is where you could find us when we were not gallivanting in the ravines, hunting for the sweetest mangoes and *pomsetay* fruit that all who did not live here on the island would call exotic fruits. Pelting stones at each other on the hill was a game of daring the other not to move until the last second. It was by far our most dangerous game. One time during our pelting session, my sister encroached on our territory, yelling, "Keith, Mommy is calling you." I told her to move; pelting stones was not a game, and you could get seriously injured. But she had a mission to accomplish and so did I, for this was a battle of daring. "Keith, Mommy is calling you," she shouted again. The next thing I realized was that my stone took a turn for the worse; it hit my sister in the head, blood flowed, and I was in deep trouble. I rushed toward my sister to console her and take her home, but no consolation would appease my mother, and I got a beating.

Everyone knew that I loved to catch fresh fishes and keep them in a glass bowl. After school, I would pass by Fatima College and go by the river, take my shoes off and have fun catching fishes. Later on, I found out this river was dammed, and when the rains were heavy, they would raise the dam to release the overflow. These very dam waters led to the part of the ocean called the slipway. Many souls caught in the river at that time lost their lives and were never found. I developed a skin rash we called *lota*, which had to be cured using a sulphur ointment. I did not like it because it burned a lot.

One day my cousins wanted to go by the sea and swim, and they tricked me to go with them by saying they were going to catch fish, and that was all the coaxing needed for me to follow them to the ends of the earth. They knew me better than I knew them, or perhaps they were a little older and wiser.

After what seemed like hours, we arrived by the sea. By the way, we did not tell our parents. Robert and Terry walked to the pier and jumped into the sea. They must have done this before. I was coaxed into the waters, and off the pier we three went. In a little while I came to my senses, realizing I could not swim. I panicked, and my cousins had to save me from drowning. We were away too long not to be missed, and on our way back we dried our trousers by sitting on the hot pavement, hoping our parents would not ask the obvious questions. All I recall is that we three got a beating and were sent to shower. Boy, did the shower sting. We had no idea about the worry we'd caused our parents. Sometimes too much freedom has… well, let me not go there. My mother had her adventurous side too, and perhaps I inherited that from her. She traveled a lot in the early days, to Canada and then to the United States, seeking something I was too young to comprehend.

Sometime later, I had another interesting experience. My mother had arranged that at lunch time I would go to my *Nenen*'s house. *Nenen* is whom I would call my godmother. One day I took my usual walk to her house for lunch. It had been a rainy day and I was sitting near the window. While eating I heard the sound of thunder and saw the flash of lightening and felt a shock of electricity through my spoon and dropped it. I lost my appetite and could not eat. When I was about to go back to school my Nenen asked me why did I not eat all my food. I just told her I was not hungry. I had more similar experiences, but I think I illustrated my point that something was at hand in my destiny.

Let me take some time and mention some of my *abusua*. I lived in a house that was built by my grandfather. In this house, my grandparents lived, of course, along with my mother, father, two sisters, and myself. My eldest sister died at an early age, I believe at the age of three. I was too young to remember her, except one day my mother was going to the cemetery to visit her and asked me if I wanted to go and I said, "No." Why I said no, I do not know. My aunts, Tantie Melvina, Janet, Cynthia and her husband Uncle Michael and their eight children, Maureen, Ann Marie, Muriel, Robert, Marilyn, Michael, Kelvin and, of course, Rudolf. Rudolf was her eldest son whom I looked up to and admired, and I wanted to be just like him. Then there was Tantie Joycelyn and her husband Uncle Herbert and their children, Terry, Donna, Yvette, and Wayne. Her eldest daughter Margaret lived in Diego Martin and would come from time to time to visit. There was also my cousin Grace from Tantie Gloria who lived in Woodbrook, and Cousin Ruby on my grandfather's side. My aunts, Tantie Cynthia and Joycelyn, did not always live with us. I remember the elders, which is funny for me to say, because they may have been in their early twenties, digging the foundation for their homes, and killing snakes that were found. Most significant was my Tantie Joycelyn, who came later on. She evokes so many strong memories; she passed away in 2015, and I am saddened by the thought of her departure. What I want to say is when they were adding her addition to the house, a song "Our Day Will Come" by Ruby and the Romantics was playing on the radio. Whenever I hear this song, it transports me back in time to the very day they were building her house.

I enjoyed a lot of freedom as a child and ventured as one who did. I My father felt that we would be better off staying with his mother, so he took us to live with her in Gonzales, not realizing that experience would have a profound effect on my future spiritual journey. It was at my paternal grandmother's house that I began to be exposed to West African practices cloaked in Christianity. My father's mother was a staunch Catholic, but at the same time she exhibited strong West African retentive traits. In spite of it all, my father's mother was overly protective and concerned about our well-being, so much so that she did not want anything to happen to us for fear of being blamed for it. With her overprotectiveness, she would make sure we did not come into contact with anything supernatural that might bring harm to us. For example, whenever we came home after midnight, we would have to walk backward into the house so that *jumbee* would not follow us into the house. It was believed that evil spirits roamed about after midnight, and you did not want them following you into your house. We would turn around and walk backward into the house, looking forward so that they would not follow us. She even went as far as not to allow us to pick up coins or anything on the street, fearing that our hands would rot off. She would also not allow us to kick bones, fearing that our foot would rot off. If we did anyway, she would take this liquid that smells rather peculiar and wash our hands. This was how it was at my grandmother's house.

Most interesting was what happened when there was any thunderstorm; we would have to cover the mirrors for fear that the mirrors would attract the lightning, and we did not want this in our house. When the church bell rang at 6 p.m., we could not lie on the bed, nor could we sit in any doorway for fear that if *jumbees* were in the house when the bells rang, they would rush out of the house and run over us or blight us. As a young boy, I was not permitted to allow girls to jump over me for fear that they might blight me and stunt my growth, nor could I allow anyone to walk or cross over me.

The time came when my mother sent for my sister and me to come live in the United States. We had to get photos taken for our passports and also get tickets in preparation for our journey. This was all another new adventure for me, going to the airport, getting on a plane, and traveling to the United States of America. A friend of my mother named Irma accompanied us.

The plane ride was interesting. We experienced air turbulence, and it was challenging at the same time, but we managed to get through it and arrived in the United States safely. We landed in New York, and then I don't recall if we traveled by car to Washington, D.C., or took another plane, but eventually we were reunited with our parents.

Life for me in America was totally different from the way it had been back in Trinidad. My mother enrolled us in a private elementary school, and I began to experience a cultural shock and division. Even though I was of the same color as my classmates, I was picked on because I was considered a foreigner or an alien because my mannerisms were different. It was rough.

I spoke differently, I walked differently, and the boys would say that I walked like a girl because I didn't have what I call the "broken leg" walk. I behaved differently, and all of this was a problem for me; even though I was of the same color, they would not accept me. Girls would also pick on me, squeezing orange juice down my back, pushing and shoving me. One day, I had enough and pushed back. They refused to relate to me, and because of that, I was never given a chance to make friends. But fighting back was not a solution. I decided I had to change. I began to practice in the mirror, changing and trying to get rid of my accent, feeling ashamed of who I was, a person from the Caribbean with apparent African mannerisms. I wanted to talk like a Black American, so I would purposely begin to speak like them, wanting to lose my identity and be accepted, to be absorbed into the Black American experience. But no matter how much I tried, I remained different because my spirit was different and because I grew up and had a worldview and experiences so different from theirs. I looked for friends who would be American, not West Indian, but no matter what, I stood out like a sore thumb and I could not deny my heritage. My time in D.C. was challenging.

One white teacher whose face I will never forget saw my sadness and must have overheard and seen students picking on the way I spoke. He said to me, "Do not worry, you sound beautiful." That made me feel comfortable. I had not begun to understand the politics of being Black in white America. How could I? I could not understand why there was so much hatred, something I had never experienced growing up in Trinidad. I may have been naive, but if I had role models, they looked like me; if I had enemies, they looked like me back home. They never made me feel like a foreigner or that I was competing with them or trying to take away their resources. Eventually, I began to get close to some of the students but not close enough to have a relationship outside of school. These friendships remained in school only.

As I approached my high school years, I began to open up a little more. In 1973, there was a significant change in my life. It was the era of Bruce Lee and the martial arts. Remembering how I became hooked, I would have to give credit to my mother and sister, for they were the ones watching the martial arts movies. I learned to keep to myself as a form of self-preservation, but they convinced me that I should go and check out these kung-fu movies. So we went to the movies together, and my sense of adventure swept me up in the wave of the kung-fu world.

I took a serious interest in learning martial arts, but I did not know where to learn. I asked my father for a martial arts book, and one day he brought home a book by Masutatsu Oyama titled *This is Karate*. I studied this book intently and practiced as much as I could comprehend. I took a delight in my new martial arts experience. I practiced until I was soaking wet with sweat, kicking and punching out candles. I eventually bought some more books on karate forms and began to practice them, but I found I was getting nowhere fast this way and I needed to seek out professional teachers in order to study seriously. I went about town searching for schools, and I would visit them and watch them practice. In my mind, I had a vision of what type of style I wanted to study, but I did not find any that were right. Then one night I was watching a TV series called *Kung-Fu*, which I watched with excitement, anticipating that one day I, too, would be studying martial arts. Just by coincidence, I saw a commercial for a kung-fu school. I watched it intently and with joy, and said to myself, this is where I want to study. I looked it up and found out the school was in my neighborhood. Lin Kung-fu school was the name; I visited the school and immediately felt that this was where I would be accepted and connected. Indeed, this was where I belonged.

I approached my mother and told her that this was what I wanted to do. I said that I wanted to study martial arts, but I don't think she took me seriously enough. I would ask over and over but to no avail. Eventually, I decided I needed another advocate and enlisted my sister; we both approached her, and my mother finally agreed.

After I had studied with him for two years, Mr. Lin decided to open a branch at another location with his chief instructor, Dennis Brown, who was also my teacher, as the head of that school. I was fortunate to be chosen by Dennis to be an instructor at that school. Dennis always had great ambitions and decided one day to put on a martial arts demonstration, inviting other martial arts experts. One of the visitors was a teacher named Mfundishi Tolo-Naa, who demonstrated his skills for us. When I saw him, I immediately knew that he would one day be my teacher.

After a while, I felt stagnant and wanted more development, so I enrolled in the school of one of Mr. Lin's classmates, Teacher Liu. I eventually began to explore my independence in the martial arts, and one of my former classmates approached me about opening up a martial arts school. One student of mine, and who eventually became my wife, knew a traditional priest named Nana Kwabena Brown, and she invited him to bless our space. My classmate, who also happened to be studying with Mfundishi Tolo-Naa in Chicago, invited him to our grand opening. He was also my mentor. Talk about destiny; mine was beginning to unfold. The school didn't last long, and eventually it closed, and I began to teach on my own. My mother worked at Washington Hospital Center, and she told me they were hiring unit clerks, so I applied and got a job there as an ICU clerk.

A couple of years later, I resigned because I had the opportunity to move to Chicago and study with Mfundishi Tolo-Naa. I eventually became one of his principal instructors. He taught me about my African heritage and made me reflect on who I am as an African person. I had the opportunity to study African dance and how it was related to African martial arts. I met pioneers such as Mfundhishi Maasi and Kilindi Iyi. Then the time came when I decided to move back to Washington, D.C. I had gotten married, and the move was inevitable. I was told that I was a natural dancer, and if I wanted to continue with my dancing, I should study with Assane Konte of the KanKouran West African Dance Company. It was here that I began to truly explore African culture and etiquette while learning to dance. I was learning more about African customs and traditions, and in time, I became more involved with African traditional spiritual practices through dance. My wife at the time had her hand on the pulse of the Yoruba and Akan spiritual world, and since we both were curious, we began to explore this world. She was having a hard time with her pregnancy, so we decided to seek Nana Kwabena Brown for his help. Meanwhile, we visited him often and joined him on Sundays, learning shrine protocols. This continued for a couple of years.

Needing to support a family, I reapplied for my former job as a unit clerk at the Washington Hospital Center. It was here that things really took a turn down the path for me to become a traditional priest. I worked the evening shift from 3 p.m to 11 p.m. During this time, I began to have severe headaches to the point that I wondered if I needed brain surgery. This went on for a while, then one night my wife called me to check and see if I was still at work and was surprised that I answered the phone, for she thought I was at home. I told her no, I'm still here at work. She then said someone is in the house, and I heard a scuffle and called the police immediately and gave them my home address and I told my supervisor I had to leave. When I arrived, the police were there. They had dogs sniffing the house, trying to find the tracks of the man who had broken into my house. This disturbed me greatly. I coincidentally was teaching Tai Chi Chuan to a new training priest named Ama Nwotwewaa, and during class I confided in her what had happened. She advised me to ask her teacher Nana Nsiah to look into the matter.

I thought that was a good idea. I made an appointment for the consultation. During this consultation, all she spoke about was me and my headaches, and the fact that my head felt big. I said yes, but all I wanted to know was why someone had broken into my house and attempted to do harm to my wife. However, she only spoke about me, saying, "You have headaches, your head feels heavy and big, and something is coming." I listened intently, but I was somewhat disappointed, for my worries were not appeased. She said I needed to take a spiritual bath and do a sacrifice to open the way. I reluctantly agreed, but I had no intention of doing the work, for my concerns had not been addressed. The day came when Ama Nwotwewaa was graduating as a new priest, and she invited me to the ceremony. Nana Nsiah possessed her ɔbosom and, through an ɔkɔmfoɔ who acted as a translator, reminded me that something was coming and I should do the work. Well, you did not have to tell me the same thing three times, and so I decided to do the work. I took my bath each day before I went on my evening shift at the hospital.

Time passed, and the time came when Ama Nwotwewaa, who is now known as Nana Ama Nwotwewaa, was celebrating her forty days *adae* as being a graduate of an ɔkɔmfoɔ. She invited me to her *Akwasidae*. Everything was proceeding as normal; the evening went by quickly, and things were wrapping up. It was time for me to go to work, and as I was about to leave, Nana Botwe arrived fashionably late. No sooner had she arrived than she possessed her spirit. I decided to hang around a little. I recall her ɔbosom looking at me; she grabbed me up and placed her head against mine, and spun me around in a circle. Something unfamiliar was happening to me. I had never felt like this before, but before I got the chance to come to my senses, she grabbed me and spun me around again, and that was all I recalled. I would come in and out of possession with an uncontrollable feeling of not being myself. Every time I thought I had regained my normalcy and attempted to go to work, I would go into possession again. I recall my wife saying, "I don't think you can go to work," and she called my job to notify them that I was calling in sick. I inquired about what happened, and everyone had a story to tell. What stood out is that I was told that the spirit had said, "God first."

I eventually made the decision to train under Nana Nsiah, since the spirit would not leave me alone. I would possess this spirit every moment, and Nana Nsiah asked me what I was going to do. She was moving from where she was living, and we were looking for a house in the D.C. area, since the officer advised us to move from the house where the break-in had taken place. We decided to have Nana Nsiah come and live with us. The day arrived when I was to be initiated. In 1987, Nana Oparebea of Larteh visited the United States and stayed at my house. She was going to initiate me as an ɔkɔmfoɔ. Her stay in the United States lasted for about three months, and when it was time for her to return to Ghana, she left Nana Nsiah in charge of continuing my training. Before she left, she made what was called a training pot for my shrine. What stood out the most was that every time I sat in front of it, I wanted to pick it up and put it on my head. I confided this to Nana Nsiah, and she cautioned me not to do so. I would also see a hand coming out of the pot, holding what looked like a very large cowrie shell the size of an egg. I became a little frustrated, wanting to put something on my head and being told not to do so.

*It was around this time that I had the dream about a spirit sitting against a wall of light. Later on, I had the dream of being in Ghana flying over a flowing river.*

The date, to be exact, was March 31, 1987. In my journal, I wrote:

*I had a very interesting dream this morning. I guess it was between the hours of 4 and 7 a.m. I dreamed that I climbed into a room of pure light. I could not distinguish between up and down, left or right, just an open space with a figure of a man, somewhat muscular, not too tall, and not too dark in complexion. His build, in fact, reminded me of a friend and ɔkɔmfoɔ Nana Kwabena Brown. He was dressed in dark colors, wearing a circular hat on his head that was somewhat woven in red and rust in color. He was wearing a shirt-like outfit that had straps on the shoulders that came to the waistline. He was sitting on what looked like the floor, and yet not a floor, with his back against what might appear as a wall of light. The figure's head was resting on his forearms, which were on top of his knees, hiding his face, and in his right hand he held a cutlass. As I approached the figure, I had a sense of anxiety that the figure of a man, in fact, was ɔbosom waiting for me. His presence, in fact, startled me and I exclaimed, "Oh ghost!" and I woke up from my dream.*

*The next dream was about me in Ghana somewhere. I was flying over a river path that meandered and was calm. Off to the side of the river, I could see women dressed in white living with their children and families on these tall trees. I continued to follow this path as if searching or being led.*

My teacher could not fully decipher these dreams to my satisfaction.

At that time, I was one of the dancers for the KanKouran West African Dance Company, first as an understudy, then as one of the principal dancers for about four years. It gradually became difficult for me to continue dancing, due to the fact that I would possess my *ɔbosom* during rehearsals.

The *ɔbosom* would speak to me in my head about leaving and going to his town, which caused even more frustration for me. The dreams I had intensified this frustration, and they were part of this message to leave. There were many factors that led to my decision; I eventually made the choice to follow these urges and go.

Now I was without a benefactor and a teacher, but my possessions did not stop. I would still possess the ɔbosom, but now I had no one to guide me. I visited and consulted Nana Kwabena Brown on what to do. He said that there was Tanɔ in Surinam, and I contemplated going to train there but was discouraged by a friend who was familiar with the politics of that place, and he advised me not to go due to the civil war. In addition, Nana Brown gave me a flyer about a documentary he had seen titled *Bono Medicine*. What struck me about this flyer was that it contained the names of priests and a town in Ghana called Takyiman. Now I had names of people to talk to and a town to go to, but no address. I called the Ghanaian Embassy and inquired how to get an address to write to them in Takyiman. The representative asked me why I wanted to go to that old town, telling me there is nothing there but gods. I insisted, and then he asked me if I wanted to go to old Takyiman or New Takyiman. I thought and concluded that what I have is old, so I want old Takyiman. He said I have only one address, and it is of a secondary school. On this flyer were the names of Nana Kofi Owusu, Nana Kofi Dɔnkɔ, and Nana Kofi Effa. I quickly wrote my letters and patiently awaited their response.

℅ Sachi K. Daniel (#1)
Post office Box 85
Techiman B/A
Ghana - W/Africa
16/2/1989

Dear Kwaku,

I received your letter dated on December 1988 safely with maximum satisfaction and anxiety. I hope my reply to your letter will meet you in goods condition of health; if so I thank the Almighty God and the Tano gods and ancestors.

Kwaku, as to your problem it will only materialise if you could possibly offer me some means to come to your residence so that I can give you some herbs to uphold the equinoctial points. Thus as you begining possessing Tano shrine you need assistance both spiritual and physical medicine to make you strong enough to withstand everything. I mean a ticket to washington.

In other words if the above cannot be fulful then you need come to me personally so that I can give you all the essential training. You have been given two opportunities for your welfare.

I am ever ready to help any body who wants my aid to become prespertise fetish priest, because I devoted all my time to help people and service my gods.

Furthermore I thank the Tigare priest for kindness of given you broschure where you were able to come across me name. Also sorry for Dr. Kofi Asare Opoku of the University of Ghana who disappointed you.

Here are Nana Kofi Donkor whom you ask had asked for his address; ℅ Kingsford Amoakohene Box 47 Techiman B/A, West Africa and sad to tell you that Nana Kofi Owusu whom you had been requested of has had expired quite recently.

Again asking you to introduce yourself to me. I would like to know precisely your the name of your home town. Send me your telex number so that we can

establish communication to each other.
At this juncture I only give you a bit about my background. I am native of Techiman born and breed there. About the age six, I was sent to school. I could not complete because gods [Tano] possessed. Later I got dwarfs (mmoatia) with whom when any time I am playing they help me to display wonders.

In 1984, I was selected to attend "Healer Conference in Washington D.C. as Africa Spokesman. My second attendance failed me due lack of poor communication at that time. Mike Warm and Sister Linda who took are Seminal ethnomedical works in Ghana (Techiman-Bono) both are medical anthropologist will bear me up. They are in America.

Once again assure you that I will do all that I can to help you in all ways.
I hope to read from you soon.
yours affectionately

Nana Kofi Effa.

Techiman Secondary School
P. O. Box 85
Techiman, Brong-Ahafo
Ghana, West Africa
27th March 1989.

Dear Sir,

I am glad to receive your telegram quite recently. I have also send you a telegram and writing to confirm to it.

I am once again happy to admit you into my service. You asked me to advise you of any needs in your preparation toward Ghana. However you may not need so much things to bring from America.

You need to come along with the following:
1. One brass and umbrala.
2. Three piece of cloths 8 yards each one should white (calico) and the other different colour. You will use the white one to wear during in occasion.
3. Strong alcohol.
4. Bring me please a camera and shoe.
5. Three or Two note books for keeping records.
6. Tape and cassettes to assist keeping record and notes.
7. Bring money to purchase the minor ones here.

I will educate you also to become a herbalist. So if you have your own car you may bring to enable us to go to various place where we can get in touch with many other herbs. I am saying this because if I cannot find kinds of herb at the same place. If you have none do not worry because I have not got one but do manage to get them (herbs).

Please may I know if you really know Techiman well? How can you locate my residency? If you do not know use the above address

...he is my junior brother. He can help you to know my house. OK write him to meet you at airport during your arrival.

I am serious about this because I do not want you to be wanting before you may locate my house.

I wish you my compliment and good prospect

Your faithfully

(Nana Kofi Effa)

Time moved ever so slowly; it had been three months with no response. Nana Nsiah had moved back to New York after I notified her of my decision to stop training. One day, she called and informed me that she was coming to D.C. on that weekend to get the rest of her belongings. She noticed that I was in a stagnant state and asked me what I was going to do. I needed training. I, too, realized that things could not stay this way. I told her that I desired to go to Takyiman and train. She also told me that it was an old town and far away, and she wanted to know why I had decided to go there. She pressed me about what I was going to do, and I told her that I would make a decision soon and let her know. I knew she wanted me back as a trainee, but I was hesitant about returning to her. That very Monday, I received a letter from Takyiman, Ghana, and I was so elated and relieved. Nana Effa had responded to my letter and introduced himself; he said he could help me in one of two ways. Either I could send him a ticket to come to the United States and train me, or I could come to his town in Ghana. I wrote him back and told him I would come there.

As I reflect back on my experience in training with Nana Nsiah, I have no regrets. Yes, circumstances led me to walk a different path, but that sort of thing happens in life. We must listen and follow our hearts. Nana Nsiah took me under her wing and taught me sincerely from her heart. She took me on journeys to watch her do spiritual work in the D.C.-Maryland-Virginia area and to Rhode Island, where there is a vibrant Ghanaian community. She made me realize what was important to me as far as my spiritual quest. I had been a vegetarian for sixteen years when I began training with her, and one day when she was traveling home to Ghana, she did not want to leave me here spiritually vulnerable. She prepared a sacrifice and cooked *mɔtɔ* in it for me to eat. She approached me and said, I know you do not eat meat, but this is the only way I know how to prepare this for you. I did some deep-down soul searching and asked myself what is important. Was it my principles regarding spiritual attainment that had been influenced by Indian and Western thoughts on diet, or achieving my goal of becoming an ɔkɔmfoɔ? I thought I might get very ill if I ate it. With all of this racing through my mind, I decided to protect myself, because this is who I am, an African searching for his roots. By the way, I never got ill, and this also primed me for my stay in Takyiman, Ghana.

Finally, I would like to say that I owe a debt of gratitude to Nana Nsiah. I learned a lot from her. She was sincere about making me the best ɔkɔmfoɔ she could, but my destiny was on a different path. Still, I must say thank you, Nana Nsiah.

Now my journey begins.

# CHAPTER ONE

## 1989, THE WORK BEGINS

On May 11, 1989, I arrived at Heathrow airport in London at 1:20 a.m. I caught what is called a speed link to Gatwick airport, where I was scheduled to leave later that night to arrive in Accra early in the morning of the following day. On my way to Accra, I had a series of interesting dreams on the plane.

*I dreamed of a house that Apisha (my name for my wife) and I owned or rented, and then later on we purchased. We decided to pick up the old carpet and put down a Turkish rug. My friend Wayne Chandler was there. The ceilings, walls, and all parts of the house were renovated and painted.*

*The next dream was about an old woman who owned a candy store and I wanted to eat some candy.*

*The third dream was about Hevioso. I came upon a woman or young girl who thought I was Hevioso or perhaps possessed him. But I did not possess* him. There was an open space, and I could hear a chant about Hevioso repeated over and over again. Later on, Kwame, the son of Nana Nsiah and Nana Kye, her husband, whom she divorced, was in the dream. Kwame was talking to me while his mother Nana Nsiah was in another room. I am a bit fuzzy here, but I recall I had possessed my Tanɔ ɔbosom who greeted Nana Nsiah by pouring gin on her hand. She sat down, and not too long after that, Nana Kye came by, dressed in ntoma. He greeted my ɔbosom by bowing and extending his right hand, and the ɔbosom poured gin over it while Nana Kye's head was bowed. Nana Kye then extended his left hand and the same was done, and then he sat down next to Nana Nsiah. The ɔbosom was going to ask them a question, but he looked at Nana Nsiah, then at Nana Kye, and said he knew. I believe this was in reference to the fact that they were no longer together. All the while, some universal phenomena were taking place, something about the stars. At this point, the girl who thought the ɔbosom was Hevioso came by and sat next to the Tanɔ ɔbosom. She began talking about someone who brought a shrine down (Hevioso?) being some kind of royalty. She said he had to go through some kind of initiation by killing a bull with one punch. Nana Kye said he knew this and confirmed that this person was back home living in the mountain areas. The ɔbosom held something in his hand, but I cannot recall what it was. The ɔbosom's face was covered with white clay.

The plane landed in Ghana early in the morning of the next day. I went through customs and proceeded out, whereupon I was swarmed by several young men wanting to help. They will grab your bag and if you do not stop them; they will take it to a cab and you will have to pay them. I insisted on carrying my own bag. I did not get used to this, but found myself needing help anyway. I found someone who spoke English to help me get to Takyiman. I was told that I had to take a taxi to a station and then a bus to Kumase and from there another bus to Takyiman. On my journey to Kumase, the driver let us off for a bathroom break and to get some refreshment. I followed the crowd to familiarize myself with their rhythm. I bought a soda and then was about to get back on the bus when the attendant of the store stopped me. At first, I did not understand why he insisted on stopping me, since I had paid for the drink. But I came to understand that he wanted his bottle back, so I finished my drink before I got back on the bus to leave.

Fortunately for me, when I arrived safely at the Kumase station and inquired about how I could get to Takyiman, there was someone who happened to be going there. He overheard my conversation and came to my rescue. He told me to follow him and he would lead me there, so I put my trust in him. I did not feel the need to be concerned or worried. I was accomplishing my destiny.

After what took over 8 hours, I arrived in Takyiman that evening after a long journey. Nana Effa was not there; he had traveled somewhere, and someone went looking for him. I was welcomed by those around and was asked to wait. After some time, Nana Effa finally arrived. He told me that he had somewhere to go, but he cancelled that obligation because of me. Going through the formalities of asking my mission and giving me a drink, Nana Effa poured libation at his shrine, then asked me to pour libation so that I might call my *ɔbosom* and give him a drink. Soon after, Nana Effa possessed one of his *mmoatia*, Kofi Asante, whom I found to be extraordinary. This *boatia* started to sing, which I recorded. He rang a bell with his left hand and was constantly reading while looking into a mirror surrounded by a frame. Not long after, I, too, began to possess my *ɔbosom*. After I came out of possession, Nana said he asked the *ɔbosom* his name, but the ɔbosom did not speak. Nana, realizing that the mouth of the ɔbosom has to be open, begged the ɔbosom to leave and told him to come again tomorrow. Then I was back to normal. The spirit of Kofi Asante did not stay long and eventually left.

Nana possessed another spirit called Mossi, which I would describe as a happy spirit and greedy at the same time. He is very amusing and entertaining. His full name is Kwaku Mossi. You can call him Kwaku or just simply Mossi, which is how most people refer to him. Mossi informed me that his purpose for coming was that when a stranger comes to visit, he must come and greet them. He came to see me because yesterday he had known I was coming. When I arrived, he stopped everything he was doing to come here to visit me. He looked for me but found out I was not at one place but here and there. I also remember the same thing that was said earlier. I continually observed this spirit and concluded that he really does not like to share. He sits on an animal skin placed on the floor. He loves to eat kola nuts, and after he has satisfied his appetite, he will hide the rest in his pocket from you, hoping you would not think of asking for any of it to eat. If you do ask, he will incoherently look at you, almost shocked that you would be asking for some. If you insist on pressing him, he will pinch off a small piece, look at it to make sure it is not too much, and hand it to you. Sometimes we would beg for more and get it. Mossi made us laugh.

As for his favorite drink, *pito* is number one. (This is a local beer made from millet grain. Its first brewing is considered as food, and it does not have the alcohol content as when it ferments as the hours go by.) You can forget about tasting this brew. If you dared ask Mossi for a drink of his beer, he would put some into his mouth and spit it out into the calabash, and if he suspected this did not deter you, after he looked at your eyes and saw you were not daunted, he would hack and spit into it then offer it to you all with the hope you would say no thanks. If you were still audacious enough to reach out to receive it, he would pull it back and call you *kwasea* (fool). I realize all this is in jest, a sort of game they play with Mossi. Since he is Muslim, alcohol is of course taboo. Mossi will constantly insult people, talking bad about them, but all in an amusing way, a sort of playing of the dozens. Mossi would see something about you then look at your face and ask you a question about what he saw and observe how you respond. You cannot help but be charmed when you are around him. He will tell funny stories, making you laugh.

It seems to me that Mossi puts you at ease to study your nature and lulls you into the traps that he sets. This spirit is what is called here a *sumanbrafoɔ*, an executioner, a witch catcher. He catches and punishes witches and bad people. He will even kill them if their crimes are too great. This is his job, and therefore he puts you off and at ease by being amusing. In this way he is making you easily forget his seriousness, and when you have committed the offense, you are trapped, because you did not realize your entertainer is also your executioner. Overall, I would say that everyone here knows the nature of Mossi; he is very gregarious and is just having a fun relationship with you. Later on, Nana Effa said that the holy days for his *ɔbosom* are Fridays, Sundays, and Tuesdays, and these are the days the *ɔbosom* possesses on him.

Some time later on I was taken by Nana Effa to go and greet the elders; Nana kept saying that he could not do anything without their consent. When we arrived, I was introduced to Nana Effa's father, Nana Kofi Dɔnkɔ, and his mother, Afia Monofie. I was told that Nana Kofi Dɔnkɔ was *ɔbosomfoɔ* to the *ɔbosom* Asubonten. I was asked my purpose. All this was translated through Kofi Sarpon, Nana Effa's younger brother, who was a secretary.

He was now acting as my *ɔkyeame*, and he spoke on my behalf. I stated that I came here for help and went on to explain that I was training under an *ɔkɔmfoɔ* from the Larteh shrine and had difficulties with them training me; I was shown this town in a dream by my *ɔbosom* and decided to come here. Nana Dɔnkɔ poured libation and asked for a blessing to be upon me. I noticed and found it very interesting that all the elders and people of the compound turned out to witness, greet, and welcome me. It was getting late, and I was shown where I would stay.

I came back to the big house, and the elderly women welcomed me by singing songs. These songs introduced me to the world of *akɔm*, the *ɔbosom*, and what kind of relationship I would have with them. I was amazed at how harmonious the singing was; there was a lead singer who was supported by other females singing the refrains. When I looked back on it, it felt like I was on a grand tour. My helper Kofi Sarpon was interpreting the meaning of some of these songs for me. I realized that they were very proverbial and explained their reality of life and *akɔm*. In between these songs, he would inquire about my world back in America. He wanting to know about where I came from would ask me if we had chickens there and wanted to know if my world was similar to his. The elders were also fascinated by someone like me who loved their *abosom*, and they were unaware that there were others from back in the United States who loved the *abosom*.

I became curious about a song I heard and asked Kofi to explain it to me. The song said that when the river rises, it means that the chief Tanɔ is coming. Another song said that if you are coming, we welcome you. This of course refers to when they are calling the spirit to come and possess them, and yet also to me, who has come to accomplish something. I noticed a young priest there; what caught my attention were the beads on his left wrist. I asked Kofi what was the meaning behind them, and he said that maybe today was his worshipping day, because *ɔkɔmfoɔ* wears them on his *ɔbosom* worshipping days. Being curious, I asked Kofi who was his *ɔbosom* and he inquired, and he said it was Boabuduro. The next song describes when someone tells an untruth about you and you could not bear the weight, you would say "do not cut fresh firewood and put it on my head." This means that if you weigh wet and dry firewood, the wet would be heavier, like an untruth, and it would be too much weight for you to bear. All this was captured on a cassette tape.

On May 13, I had my first consultation, when I saw the *ɔbosom* Nana Tanɔ. What can I say? I never expected or dreamed what the possession of this kind of *ɔbosom* would be like. I arrived at Nana Effa's place early in the morning, and the others were there as well. Nana began to prepare for possessing the *ɔbosom*. He poured a little alcohol on a flat stone and ground a *dufa* (ground plants shaped in a rectangle, cube or cone, and left to dry). He used his left pinky to pick up the potion, waved his hand horizontally then vertically three times each, and wiped it across his eyes from his right ear to the left ear. He proceeded to do the same thing, except he motioned his left hand vertically then horizontally three times each. Then, he came down vertically in the center of his face. He again poured some more alcohol on the stone and grounded the *dufa* to release and mix the potent fusion in the alcohol. This he smeared on his joints, first at the shoulders, then elbows, knees, and ankles. Nana then poured more alcohol on the stone and ground the *dufa* again, except this time he poured the elixir into a bell; he passed the bell under his left knee and then drank it. He dressed himself with a special *nsuman* to carry the *ɔbosom*.

The same thing was done horizontally and vertically to the pad called *kahyire*, which was placed on his head for the pan to sit on. Next, the leaves of a plant were kneaded between both palms and clay added to it. He bit some off and chewed it, then pressed the rest of this kneaded plant in the center of the pad, passed the pad under his knee, whispered into the pad, spit on it three times, and slapped it three times with his right hand before he placed it on top of his head to carry the pan. Everyone was in place and the pan was lifted off its platform by an assistant and placed on Nana Effa's head. The *ɔkyeame*, sitting to the left of Nana Effa, petitioned the *ɔbosom* by citing *mmrane* (appellation), but he would not come that easily. After a while, Nana Dɔnkɔ began to summon the *ɔbosom* with new appellations. He spoke in a symbolic and metaphorical language to the *ɔbosom* as sweetly as one would speak to their lover. Suddenly, Nana Effa possessed his *ɔbosom* Asuotipa, a son of Asubonten. The women in attendance began to sing a song, "Mema wo akwaaba oo, Asuotipa, akwaaba," welcoming the *ɔbosom*, and calling him by his name. The *ɔbosom* was given an egg, which he took and threw on the ground. If the shells landed up, that meant that all obstacles were removed so that the *ɔbosom* was free to stay. Now that the path was cleared, the *ɔbosom* began to greet everyone one by one, asking, "How are you doing?" and each would respond, "I'm doing fine." The *ɔbosom* spoke a proto-Twi language, which the *ɔkyeame* translated to Bono Twi.

Asuotipa would only speak through his *ɔkyeame,* and before my concerns were addressed, Asuo (as he is affectionally called) took care of the family matters that were pressing. I found it very interesting that everyone contributed to solving the problem between the husband (the *ɔkɔmfoɔ*) and his wife. When everything had been solved, Asuo left, and Nana Dɔnkɔ poured libation to inform him that there were no more issues between the couple. Nana Effa then carried Asuotipa again, and he began to address my training. He said he could help me, but it would be disrespectful if we did not consult his father Asubonten before he did anything. He told me to see his father the next day. When Asuotipa was finished, he tilted his head forward, motioning that he was about to leave, and the helper lifted the pan off his head. With the pan off his head, Nana Effa bent forward, allowing the pad to fall on the floor. If it lands up, it means there are others with concerns preventing him from leaving. They will place the pad back on Nana Effa's head to carry Asuotipa again. This process would repeat itself until it lands face down to indicate he was fully gone and the session was over.

The next day, I visited Nana Dɔnkɔ and consulted his *ɔbosom* Asubonten. The preparation was the same as I'd observed with Asuotipa. I sat intently awaiting the arrival of the *ɔbosom* as the elder women began to sing. The body of Nana Dɔnkɔ began to quiver as if caught like a fish on a line. As the songs and the *ɔkyeame* reel him in, they are careful, like a fisherman, not to break or snap the line. Little by little the line of songs pulls the *ɔbosom* to earth, until finally he's here and we hear the sound uttered by the *ɔbosom* that breaks the cosmic silence: HUH. The women sang of joy and exhilaration. There was happiness in their voices, like seeing an acquaintance you are always glad to see. Asubonten motioned to be given an egg, which he threw down on the floor and was accepted.

The *ɔbosom* slaps the *yawa* three times to greet all, for this is a way he greets, and meanwhile the women sing songs greeting and welcoming me, saying I have come home, and if Asubonten sees anything he should tell me. Nana Dɔnkɔ possessed the *ɔbosom* and spoke through his *ɔkyeame* Nana Kofi Boɔ. When an *ɔbosom* is called to communicate, you are seldom alone, and everything is done in the open for all to see. Family members are always flitting around, in and out of the shrine room. In possession, I observed that the son (Asuotipa) and the father (Asubonten) acted in a very similar manner.

Asubonten spoke to his ɔkyeame and my ɔkyeame Kofi translated, telling me that Asubonten said the ɔbosom was given to me by Nyame from infancy, but it did not want to possess me then; he waited until I was grown up. Asubonten said my ɔbosom was happy and smiling to see that I have grown up fine and what I have is pure Tanɔ. I was delighted to hear this, because it explains my dreams and why it brought me here. This is where I belong.

Asubonten asked me, "Now that I have come here, what did I want them to do?" I said I would like them to train me in akɔm. Asubonten said, if he gave me *aduro* to bathe in would I bathe in it? I said yes. And if he gives me some to drink, will I drink it? I said yes again. Asubonten instructed me that before anything is done, I should go and see another ɔbosom, Ɔboɔkyerewa (also called Kwaku Adaku). Asubonten said he and Ɔboɔkyerewa are brothers, and they would come together to help; they are family, and they will work together in helping me with my training. Therefore, he would like me to go and visit him. Ɔboɔkyerewa is the ɔbrafoɔ for Taa Mensa and the protector of Takyiman and the Tanɔ river.

Asubonten said I should give him a cock and drink and he will share it with my ɔbosom. They will call my ɔbosom, inviting my ɔbosom to come from the first place I possessed him, back in America to Takyiman to eat, and welcome him and then talk to him so that they will know what is to be done for me. Through my ɔkyeame I was told that Asubonten said I should be patient, for after I see his brother, he will tell me everything. He went on to say after he, Asubonten, consults with my ɔbosom, I should come back around the 30th of this month and they would carry him again, and he will discuss how they will proceed in helping me. This meant a lot of waiting.

Asubonten asked me for my beads and talisman that I brought with me from when I was training in America. I quickly went and got them and handed them to the ɔkyeame, who in turn gave them to Asubonten. He asked for an egg and read it spiritually, then threw the egg on the floor and said now he sees everything and knows all my problems and *aduro* (i.e., the spiritual power that was put on me back home). After the egg was accepted, Asubonten welcomed me again and then the women broke out in songs welcoming me as well. Asubonten then went on to give a riddle: when a hunter is hunting and he doesn't see prey, does he shoot? Now that he has seen my problem, he can help me.

The Almighty gave this to me in my infancy. I now can reflect upon my encounter with the *jumbee* spirit, for I cannot in truth say if it was a dream or if it really happened.

I find it very interesting that the people here think I am a white man. Never in my life would I have thought that I would be called that. It has taken me three days of trying to convince them that I am not a white man. I would ask them to look at me, and yet I am not certain that I have convinced them of this. Some were surprised that a white man likes their ɔbosom and would ask me if we all worship them abroad. Naturally, I felt insulted and defended myself and said look at my skin, my hair, and compare me to a real white man like Mike Warren (who they all knew, as he lived here for some years and still visits the town) and see the difference. I realized it would take me some time to gain acceptance as one of them.

My translator and I went to the capital Sunyani to visit the immigration department to extend my visa without consulting Nana Effa. When we arrived back, Nana met us on the way. The fact that I, who was in his charge and care while I was there, had left to go somewhere without informing him, disturbed him very much. He had no idea where I had gone. Nana said the *boatia* (I assumed Akua Bɔmmɔ) came and was asking for me and I was nowhere to be found. The *boatia* informed them where I had gone and would accompany me there and back. I am amazed by the wonders of things here.

Nana Effa told me, and so did Nana Dɔnkɔ, that if Nyame was willing, they would tell me everything, but until then they could not. Nana Effa, in particular, emphasized this to the point of saying he is very serious about this, and if I do not obey and follow his instructions, I will be lost. He also counseled me to be patient, because he was not a well-educated man (meaning he did not complete school) and could not speak and explain everything properly to me in English, so I should learn his language, and he also would inform everyone around me that they should speak Bono to me, not English. To me, Nana Effa seemed more educated than those with college degrees. He knew and understood the culture and how to maneuver through it. Thanks to people like him, those doing fieldwork and who want primary resources can get the necessary knowledge from people like him to write their dissertations to earn their degrees.

*Today I took the opportunity to tell* Nana Dɔnkɔ *and the elders about the man I saw in my dreams. Nana laughed and said that the man I saw in my dream was* Ɔboɔkyerewa, *and that I would go to see him and all the places I had seen in my dreams.*

After almost a week, the elders finally settled on everything for my initiation. The fee was 200,000 cedis and I needed to help them get a car. I was told that this was very cheap, for one student was charged 400,000 cedis, but I am sure they were not charged a car. I still think they believe that I am rich. They started the preparation with my *nsuman*/beads, fitting me with them and everything else. A ram was decided upon. I put down a payment of 100,000 cedis, promising to pay the balance when the *ɔbosom* helps me to get it. After the fitting, I went to Nana Effa's house to buy something. I had so much going on, I do not remember if this happened before or after the fitting.

Nana Effa made my *mpesempese* with a special plant called *ntum* and a bath, but first I had to offer a sacrifice to his *ɔbosom*, then take the special bath made with a kind of thick vine that he called *humatre*. I went into the woods and bathed three times beside a big tree, air-drying in between each bath. I got dressed after the last bath. Nana said this vine would talk to me as he does. This plant *ntum* was used to create the locks or twists in my hair. After all this, I proceeded to Nana Dɔnkɔ's house, where food was given to my *ɔbosom* to eat, like peanuts, banana, and some other food that I do not recall, then they sacrificed the ram.

Libation was poured, and the ceremony of putting the beads on me began. On this day May 20, 1989, I sat upon a stool like a bride, and one by one the old women fitted me with the appropriate beads on my wrists, knees, and ankles, saying each one's name and singing the song (if it had one) that accompanied that bead.

When they were finished, I was told to call my *ɔbosom* and possess him, but they never come when you want them to. *Ɔkyeame* Kofi Boɔ had to pour libation for the *ɔbosom,* beckoning him to come, because only after it possesses me will the marriage be consummated. I recorded everything, but as I was writing from my journal on my computer, I lost this tape. What a treasure I lost.

After the possession, the ram was cooked and given to the *ɔbosom,* and the rest was eaten by everyone, including me. As a newly initiated *ɔkɔmfoɔ*, Asubonten instructed me not to go anywhere, and told me that I should not accept things from anyone except from those in charge of me. Nana Effa had explained all the rules to me earlier, emphasizing that I should be very careful because the witches here are very powerful, so I have to take care. I was given the name Sakyi after Nana Kofi Dɔnkɔ, whose real name is Nana Kofi Sakyi. He is called Dɔnkɔ because his mother gave birth to him after she lost a previous child at birth or soon after. My official name now was Kwaku Sakyi.

With this name, I became part of a family and the second son of Nana Dɔnkɔ with the name Kwaku Sakyi. Nana Dɔnkɔ and his wife Afia Monofie are now my parents. Their children are Kwame Amponsa, Amoakɔhene (aka Kingsford), Sewa, Kofi Effa (who is one of my teachers), Kwaku Sakyi, Kofi Sarpon, and Yaa Badu in that order. They were all my siblings, including the other children from Nana Dɔnkɔ's other wives.

My older brother Amoako, who, by the way, speaks perfect English, had a conversation about my coming here. He said the headmaster got my letter and did not know what to do, so he gave it to him. He, too, did not know what to do and sat on it for a while. Nana Kofi Owusu had just passed, and he knew the family politics of his father and did not want me to go directly and get embroiled. So, he elected to direct or lead me in a back way to Nana Dɔnkɔ through his junior brother Nana Effa, and hence my introduction to

Nana Dɔnkɔ.

I started bathing in *aduro* (herbal bath) three times a day at 5 a.m., 12 noon, and at 6 p.m. I did not use any soap or other water, and after each bath, I rubbed onto my body the scraped and ground bark of the tree roots used for my bath, along with *famwisa*, and let it dry. This mixture lasts a few days in the warm weather of Ghana before it begins to ferment and go sour.

I was now beginning to feel somewhat unwell. The water, *pito*, palm wine, schnapps, and food were all giving me a hard time, not to mention the fumes from the lamp and burning wood used for cooking. All of this upset my elimination; I had diarrhea for two days, and sometimes I did not feel like eating. I truly missed my wife's cooking.

Even though I was having a difficult time adjusting physically, the people were the most courteous I had ever been around. Of course, not all people are good, since witchcraft is said to be so powerful here, but those with whom I interacted became like family to me. They all tried so very hard to please me and make sure I did not want anything.

There are some taboos, which they call *akyiwadeɛ*. I had to observe them all while I was training. Most of the taboos were when I was eating, such as a person passing or carrying things behind me. Others involved food, sound, and what I saw.

From this time on, since I have been initiated, the *nsuman* that I have to wear have songs associated with them, but I also have to mention they do taboo water, though I could bathe while wearing them. These *nsuman* were given to support my character and educate me in terms of the Creator and *akɔm* life along with its challenges.

## LIST OF *NSUMAN* WORN

- **Abia:** Small black seed used to remind me not to tell lies.
- **Sedeɛ:** This is for hearing the *ɔbosom*. It is also the *ɔbosom* money. It stops people from laughing at me.
- **Atobia:** A brown seed put on the end of *nsuman* worn on the left wrist. This is to protect me from *bayi* ("witchcraft"). When they see you, they will bow down, for they cannot look you in the face.
- **Ntwerema:** Glass beads with white stripes. They will bring people to me for help. *Ntwerema* means to pull. Song: *Nkɔmmoa yɛbrɛ oo*—we are calling *akɔm* helpers.
- **Ntontonton:** This prevents me from being extravagant. It teaches me to economize. These are assorted or leftover beads from what has been used.
- **Ahunu/Akoko *fufuo*:** White beads that will help me to see and become a seer. Represents *ɔkɔmfoɔ* should not hate one another. Song: *Akoroma kyere ma ni dadaada*—do not hate other *ɔkɔmfoɔ*.
- ***Akommere*:** A red flat bead worn on the right wrist. This is so the *ɔbosom* will love me. Song: *ɔhene aniwa a, akɔmmere wɔ no*—eyes of the chief…
- **Samando nkuruwa:** A spherical white bead used for the *nsamanfoɔ*/ancestors who loved me so that I can get the *ɔbosom*. It is worn on the right wrist and is for my protection, and to make sure that I do not ignore them even though I have a *ɔbosom*.
- **Ason wote:** Ason means the ear. These are shells and beads worn near the ears for hearing the *ɔbosom* and other spirits.
- **Kahyere:** This is a pad for the *ɔbosom*. Because I do not have a

real pad, this takes its place so that the ɔbosom can rest on me.
- **Sedeɛ nson:** Cowrie shell worn on the left knee. This *suman* has a song that goes like this: *Mo sre no ne ho bɛ ho / yɛn sere no ada oo, yɛn sere no ne ho bɛ ho oo / osuo aboro asɛnsɛ e*—let's not laugh at him for he is wet, for he shall surely be dry.
- **Nim oo, Nim oo yee:** No one wants a bad name.
- **Awuroko:** These are small bells worn on the left knee for telling people to be aware that the ɔbosom's wife is walking and the sounds warn people to be aware.
- **Ngyeraa:** Two blue beads on the left knee. When the ɔbosom akɔm should help me to dance well.
- **Dɔ:** Meaning love, whoever sees me will love me.
- **Asase gye me tata:** Blue string with shells worn on both ankles. Now during training, I am regarded as a baby who is crawling, so the ɔbosom will help me to stand on both feet.
- **Asase gye me tata kuma:** This is the junior and has raffia and is worn at both ankles. This is to prevent those who wish my downfall or wishing my ɔbosom to disgrace me by not possessing me.
- **Gyebunu:** Green round cylinder beads with white stripes and gold at the end, also called venetian melon bead.
- **Onyamyo amyo:** White beads with blue stripes.

Nana Kofi Effa and I have developed a very close relationship. He feels that if I go back home without anything to show, it would be a bad reflection on his name. He is extremely cautious and is constantly saying if the ɔbosom is willing, he will teach me everything, but I must first finish with the Old Man (Nana Dɔnkɔ) and let them do everything for me. I should keep notes on everything they teach me and give him a copy of them. I promise I will.

Yesterday a football player died, and lots of people were coming by to mourn, give respects and condolences to Nana Dɔnkɔ, who is the elder here and is somehow related to this young man, so the mourning goes on today. Nana Effa reiterated that there are lots of evil people here, some good, some bad, and that they are using this time of mourning to come and see me. He cautions me to be very careful, do not take anything from anyone except him and the Old Man. Nana shared with me that he had studied *akɔm* with four different teachers and learned a lot; he also speaks different languages.

The people here are jealous of him; some respect him and others do not, but because his *ɔbosom* catches bad *akɔmfoɔ* this is why they fear him. Nana said he wants to teach me a lot of things if the *ɔbosom* is willing, but it must be in secret. He does not want anybody to see and try to spoil things and that I must obey his and the Old Man's instructions. Nana also expressed that he has some reservations about me keeping these recordings and notes. He says, "What will you do if you should lose them"? I said I would also depend on my memory. Nana insisted that I must give a lot of attention to the herbs, for without them I am useless, and I would not be able to help others. I should also learn the language so that he can teach me more things.

I came back to the big house, and as soon as I had gone to bed, as I lay down to sleep after a full day, I heard the beating of *dawuro,* a gong, and women singing. Following the singing voices, I was led to Fie Kɛsem and, after realizing what was going on, I returned to my room to retrieve my tape recorder. On my way back, I met Kwadwo, the son of Nana Asantewaa, the *ɔkɔmfoɔ* of Asubonten, and the niece of Nana Dɔnkɔ, who also trained her.

I asked Kwadwo what the occasion was. He said the event happening was the Adapa preparation for Asubonten Kwabena' da tomorrow. Present were Nana Akumsa, Nana Dɔnkɔ's elder sister, Nana Asubonten, another sister, Nana Dɔnkɔ, and Nana Asantewaa. The focus of the attention was on the *ɔkɔmfoɔ* for the *ɔbosom* Asubonten, and lastly present were a number of elder women and men. The youths, of course, were present in full force.

I do not think anyone was left behind or absent. As I was not yet familiar with what was happening, I asked Kwadwo if anyone was possessed, but there was no indication of that yet. The singing took on another phase, and I had a premonition of something about to happen, a sacred event about to unfold. They were pulling something from somewhere, and yet it felt as if it were in my gut. The songs intertwined and weaved patterns to allure Asubonten into a net if he was nearby. You could hear them sing, *bisa ntwerwa, ntwerewa w'adeɛ okɔ*. Each woman took turns, as if to say, "I will fill in the void with a song"; all this was orchestrated in an orderly fashion to entice the *ɔbosom* to come into the *ɔkɔmfoɔ*. And if the baited trap did not seem to spring fast enough, they reached deep to pull out songs that would give meaning to the occasion.

Every now and then you could hear the voice of Maame, Nana Dɔnkɔ's wife, singing and beckoning to Asubonten like she has so many times before. After nearly half an hour of singing a different song, Asubonten finally arrived. He came fully and began to introduce songs that were masterfully carried on by the singers. This was done for several songs until Asubonten settled down on the *ɔkɔmfoɔ*. I found it noteworthy that he would introduce a song that was picked up, and while they were in the middle of that song, he would start to converse with them and they would stop, listening and responding to him, sometimes verbally or with songs.

This went on for a while. I could tell that we were in for a long night. I soon began to realize that song was a conversational method of communicating thoughts, not unlike the drums that communicate in their own language.

I have observed that Nana Akumsa would reply to something Asubonten said by responding to him with a song, with keen precision, not disrupting his flow. From time to time, Asubonten would say something amusing enough for others to laugh, which made me realize how much I was missing by not understanding the language. There never seemed to be a lack or shortage of songs. It was at this moment I realized that I was truly experiencing something I had never seen before. I was witnessing the depth and retention of songs these elders possess. I would say their knowledge of songs is as vast as the knowledge of their history. Asubonten seemed to be discussing some intimate concerns about someone specific with the elders. This spilled over into an intense conversation with Nana Dɔnkɔ, and all the while there was a plethora of songs, so much so that the *ɔbosom* asked for Ntumpane to be played, but there were no drummers around.

Whatever the discussion was about, it seemed to be a serious matter. The feelings I got from all that was going on was like watching a musical drama, except that I was a part of it. Their dialogue and songs made no distinct separation. This is what *akɔm* is all about: only at certain intervals music was added to the spoken dialogue and you flowed with it. This situation seemed to involve someone being distracted by a woman or women and they should not allow this to happen at this phase of their life. The time approached for Asubonten to go and sleep, and the sequence of songs connected me back to the beginning when they were invoking him to come. The only difference now was the reversal, for they were petitioning him to leave.

Last night, Nana Effa and two of his companions came by to greet me. During their visit, Nana Effa possessed one of his spirits that did not speak. I was told later that this was Asuo, but I was a bit confused about that since I have seen Asuo before and he talked. Anyway, this spirit left my quarters and disappeared into the darkness of the night. People were searching for the spirit, but they could not find him. The ɔbosom eventually ended up at Nana Dɔnkɔ's house, and suddenly he started to pull at the support that held up the roof that Nana Dɔnkɔ happened to be sitting under. I must admit, when I first saw this, I was a little wary of its structural integrity. The young men tried to stop the spirit from bringing down this column, but the spirit ignored them and continued banging against the column, all the while gesturing his disapproval.

Next, the spirit went and turned over a barrel of drinking water, which they quickly picked up, and he began to jump up and down in the puddles, splashing water everywhere. And if you thought that was enough, the spirit then tried to scale the very same column to get up onto the roof. Everyone was saying *dabi* (which means *no*) to the spirit, but again, he did not listen. Then one of the young men tried to restrain the spirit from behind by holding him, and the spirit would turn around and raise his hand to slap the young man, who would duck, of course. When the young man would back off a little, the spirit would try again, and the young man would restrain him, and the spirit would try to slap him again. The spirit, realizing that he was getting nowhere fast, turned over the barrel of water again and proceeded to stamp in it, splashing the water everywhere. Some happened to splash upon me, causing me to possess my ɔbosom.

I do not recall what took place when I was possessed, but after my possession, I retired to my room, with some help of course. Then, when I thought all the excitement was over, I heard the banging of a gong they called *dawuru*. Out of curiosity, I got up out of my bed to explore what was going on, and as I approached closer to where the sound was coming from, I heard women singing chants. I thought I should go back quickly to my room and get my tape recorder, for I could not miss this momentous occasion. I have it all on tape.

I was most impressed with how everyone assisted in bringing about the possession of the *ɔbosom* Asubonten. They all cooperated to accomplish one thing, which was calling their family *ɔbosom* to come and be among them. The *ɔbosom* showed a high state of being and character while possessed upon the *ɔkɔmfoɔ*, Nana Asantewaa, whom I documented earlier, not to mention how wonderful the *ɔbosom*'s dancing and singing skills were. I am eternally grateful to have captured it all on tape.

I was late getting up this morning, and Nana Dɔnkɔ sent someone to call me. I got up and prepared myself to pick up from where I had left off the previous night. They were preparing for Nana Dɔnkɔ to carry the *ɔbosom* Asubonten. Nana's *ɔkyeame,* Kofi Boɔ, was pouring libation at one time and Nana Kwabena Kranka, Asuotipa *ɔkyeame* can be heard talking in the background. So could Nana Effa.
An elder whose name escapes me was drumming, and others were singing. It is all on tape. I will not get into too much detail about what happened since I am not aware of all that was said, and this journal book has to serve me for three months. I will skip to my part, where the *ɔbosom* spoke to me. I will make it brief. Asubonten, through my interpreter, said that the *ɔbosom* I possess is from Takyiman, and when they open the mouth of my *ɔbosom*, they will know more. He will tell them all that they should do for

me.

After Nana Dɔnkɔ finished carrying Asubonten, they prepared for the *akɔm*. Nana Asantewaa would possess Asubonten for the session. I have observed how both Nana Dɔnkɔ and Nana Asantewaa shared responsibilities in possessing the *ɔbosom*. He took on the male role, possessing only by carrying the brass pan called *yawa* placed upon his head, and she the female role, possessing Asubonten freely and anywhere. The drummers and singers positioned themselves for the event to take place. The *ɔbosom* Asubonten possessed Nana Asantewaa. The drumming was very professional, even though these drummers were very young, but they were highly experienced in drumming. The *ɔbosom* sang and danced accompanied by the drummers. As I am listening to the tape, I am reliving the whole day. In all, it was a most enriching day to experience the pulse and rhythm of Tanɔ *akɔm*.

My body is finally adjusting to being here a day ago. I no longer feel nauseated or have diarrhea, but I will see what the future brings. I am still not happy at the way the people here are always referring to me as a white man. This, of course, is due to their isolation from world events and lack of interaction with Africans from the diaspora who were enslaved and brought to the so-called new world. They are innocent and unaware, but my presence here is changing their perspective. I, too, suffered from a type of isolation and naiveté about what it takes to be African.

I had come here to receive, to claim, and align myself with what I believe is historically and ancestrally my destiny from birth. I was always told, even back in D.C. by other *ɔkɔmfoɔ*, that I was born with this *ɔbosom*. My lack of having what is called an African worldview has made it difficult for me to fit in, and therefore I have become a bit cynical about some things here, which I just do not understand. I assume it is my ignorance and due to my misunderstanding of the culture here that present too many challenges and cultural barriers for me.

I came here in western clothes, with their money, customs, language, and most of all education and socialization. There has to be a change in the education of the people here about people like me in the other parts of the world, as well as an education of people like me in the western world who think that our melanin automatically allows us to be accepted as African without knowing anything about the African language, customs, and culture.

Last night, they increased the number of times I took my baths, starting at midnight, then every four hours. This has disturbed my sleep cycle adversely, but like everything else here, I have to make significant adjustments. This advancement of my bath schedule is due to the fact that my stay is short, so they want to get as much herbal *aduro* into my body as quickly as possible. Today I am going to the Ɔbookyerewa shrine.

I was having disturbing thoughts about things back home and I am thinking about consulting Nana Effa to divine for me, but I discussed my concerns with Nana Effa, and he assured me that as long as I was here nothing bad would happen, so not to worry.

On a different matter, I consulted Asubonten, and he assured me again that the *ɔbosom* I am possessing is from Takyiman and that it is truly an *ɔbosom*, not a *suman* (minor spirit), and if I trust them, everything will go well for me. He assured me that when the ears and mouth are open, the *ɔbosom* will tell them more; he instructed me to get an egg and tell it all my needs, then place the egg under my pillow at bedtime, and in the morning, I should travel to a road and repeat what I said last night and put the egg down and leave. Asubonten advised me again to go and see his brother Ɔboɔkyerewa on the 30th and consult with him so that they could work together to help and protect me.

*I had a dream that I possessed my ɔbosom, who was sitting on the edge of a chair anxiously with his hands on the arms of the chair calling for Ateokɔsaa. He wanted Ateokɔsaa to help him with something or do something for him.*

Two days ago, I was confronted again with the problems of my dreams. Later on, that same evening, I went to visit Nana Effa. I gave him a drink to pour libation for me. Soon after, it started to rain and he possessed his spirit, Kofi Asante. Kofi Asante is quite an *ɔbosom*, and I asked him about the dream I had. He laughed and said everything was all right and that my dream had nothing to do with my family back home and I should not worry. He then switched the conversation to talk about a letter I mailed and asked why did I not inform his *ɔkɔmfoɔ* Nana Effa so that he could have assisted me. I said that I took this responsibility upon myself and did not consult Nana Effa, because his elder brother Kwame Amponsa offered to mail the letters for me.

Kofi Asante said to me that I would suffer very much here (I already feel this) but I should not give up. That evening I had an in-depth conversation with the elders about why they call me *boroni*. I first tried to explain, as I always do, by telling them about slavery and the devastation it had upon people like me in the Americas and West Indies, and how it has created a cultural divide between us. I implored them to look at my features and skin color and at someone like Mike Warren, who is white, so they could sincerely know and compare us. They said they understood, but I wonder if they really do.

The next day I went to Accra, and on our way there I asked Kofi about a white image of a Jesus Christ I saw. I said to him, "Do the people here believe that he is an *ɔbosom*?" Kofi said, "Yes, and they think white skin is beautiful too," to which I replied, "I do not believe he is my *ɔbosom*." To think that I am here to learn about African *abosom* creates such a juxtaposition with them learning about Christ as a European *ɔbosom*. The purpose of my trip to Accra was to receive money that was sent to me by my wife and to change the dollars into cedis.

I wanted to also call my wife, but the fee was too expensive, as it would have cost me 7,000 cedis. I also went to British Airways to check on the cost of a ticket to the United States for Kofi. It was $1,800 US dollars, a bit too expensive for me. This trip, I found, was costing me a lot of money. The custom here is that you have to pay the expense of the person accompanying you and I neglected to mail the letter I had with me to my wife Apisha. This trip was not successful.

I have not yet adjusted to how people look at me here. I feel as if I am so foreign and removed from them. I finally questioned Kofi about this *boroni* label they have placed upon me. Kofi seems perplexed and did not seem to have a satisfactory answer for why I am called *boroni*. He does not seem to understand why they do this and why am I so bothered by this word. I get the feeling that I am someone they have never interacted with, someone like me from abroad whose ancestry was and still is affected by the aura of post-slavery.

Kofi, for example, called a certain girl white who to me looks like a Ghanaian or someone of African lineage. To my surprise he calls a man whose skin tones does not look as dark as the former woman black. I just had to question his logic and asked him why? Kofi replied: it is because she, the light skin one, speaks the language and have ethnic markings on her face. Then he looks at the man, who appeared as African as can be to me, and called him white because he was fair skin. You can tell those whom I referred to are not a product of race or I should say white race mixing. I am beginning to see that if you are not as dark skin you are considered white, but does that mean if you have ethnic marks and speak the language you are Ghanaian?

Amusing myself with Kofi, I said, "Now that I am getting much darker, what will you call me?" He said, "A black man." I was in a sarcastic mood, and I asked Kofi how could I become something if I did not have the potential of being that in the first place? Kofi just laughed and said, "Oh! I see." I realize that no one I have encountered has an adequate answer to this *boroni* problem as far as I am concerned.

My presence here seems to have given birth to the question of who is a *boroni* and who is not, with respect to people like me coming from abroad. Being the first of my ancestry to come here and live among the Bono people in the capacity of learning *akɔm* and the culture has allowed me to step into a world that has never been explored by anyone like me. I have come back home to suckle from the *ɔbosom* of my forebearers. You could not expect the white researchers and doctors to understand this issue. Their sole purpose here is to do their field research to get the knowledge of the indigenous people and then to go back home to their respective countries and get their degrees. They get prestige, recognition, and money in their country and around the world, but they do not share the money and acknowledgements with their African teachers, who remain poor and anonymous. I hear them complain a lot about being forgotten.

Of course, there are a few exceptions to the rule, and in time that must change completely, but by and large, we cannot expect or depend on non-Africans to educate the African people, making them aware of what Europeans did by snatching us before we were weaned off our forebears and transporting us to distant lands to serve as an economic product for their coffers. That obligation and responsibility falls upon us to help educate ourselves and our lineage in the remotest areas of the continent; we must make them aware of our history, which they are a part of.

Kofi accompanied me to Nana Effa's house, and as I passed the house, I heard children singing a greeting song calling me *boroni*. I questioned Kofi about where they learned this song. Kofi said, "They learned it from their parents." I said, "Yes! Children do not have the mind to conceive of such things unless they learn them from their parents and elders." The question of how can we change this.

The next day, I was very ill and still remained a bit weak; my head ached, my skin was painful to rub, my joints ached, and my stomach ached. I felt cold all the time and hot to the touch. When I stood up, I got vertigo and felt absolutely miserable. I complained to Nana Dɔnkɔ about my feeling ill, and he gave me some pills that helped a little, but I still clung to my bed. Later on, he gave me some herbs to drink that made me feel like throwing up, but nothing came up. I would just sleep and sleep. People showed great concern for my well-being, but it was difficult communicating with them.

Some said my illness was due to my being exhausted from my trip to Accra.

Kofi Sarpon showed me a photo of Nana Kwasi Opoku, a friend back in the United States who was murdered under strange circumstances and whose case the police were unable to solve. His death has touched me deeply. He must have stopped through Takyiman on his way to a town called Bredi to collect shrines such as Ati Mframa and Tigare. Looking at his photo I reflected back to this unfortunate incident. I can still remember sitting on the top of the stairs at my home in D.C. talking to Nana Opoku when our conversation ended abruptly. He told me that he had to go, someone was at his door knocking. I believe that I was the last person who spoke to him just before his death.

I first found out about his death from Nana Kwabena Brown, who called me not too long after Nana Opoku left. I was told by Nana Brown he was shot and bled on his shrines by the doorway. I can still see myself sitting at the top of the stairs in my house on the phone, stunned while talking to Nana Brown as he broke the news to me. I believed that I was the last person who spoke to Nana Opoku just before his untimely death. The memory is still fresh on my mind. National attention was given to the case on a television show called *Unsolved Mysteries*. I told Kofi I would like to find out the circumstances behind his death and why he died the way he did. Kofi said he would inquire for me.

I think about my wife all the time, and sometimes I feel sad. I miss her so much and our daughter, Etosha. But I know this sacrifice will benefit us all in the future.

Kofi Sarpon felt it was not good for a married couple to both be *akɔmfoɔ/*

priests. I have heard this before, and the reasoning behind this was, who will take care of the ɔbosom and the children when both individuals possess. He also said the power would go to one of the couple and the other may die. He advised me that if we were both to be priests, my wife should wait until I was finished so that I could help her. I tried to reason with him that it could be done, but I do not know if he understood me.

People here would ask me in conversation to take them back with me to America. They, of course, expected me to pay for their travel expenses. They all seemed to think that I am rich or have the means. I have witnessed that people here are not striving for the same understanding of spirituality as we do in the United States There is no separation of church and state mentality. The fundamental difference in how they live their lives, it is very simple and uncomplicated, and something I am not accustomed to. They do not have to separate themselves from God and the community by going to temples or other such places to seek a meditative state or connection with the divine. They seem always connected to the divine. Everything seems to be provided for them within their culture and by the way they live their lives. I heard many times Nana Effa and his father Nana Dɔnkɔ say to me that they can do anything for me if it is the will of Nyame or the ɔbosom. I know this because it has been interpreted to me many times.

Nana Effa has a friend named Aduma; he is a well-educated police inspector, and he speaks very good English. We have had in-depth conversations about many things, which led me to the conclusion that he understands the fundamental problems that rural Ghana is facing. Surprisingly, we have talked about the Rosicrucians and the mystery schools. I would never have expected to engage with someone here in the middle of Ghana in discourses about Manly P. Hall. The inspector is a fascinating man. Even though he worships the *abosom*, he shows a lot of interest in what I would call African-based Western-influenced mysteries. He understood my situation and knows that I am not rich, as others think I am. At times like this, I missed my home very much.

Sitting here in my room reflecting and writing about my daily events, I am accompanied by a faithful nine-year-old companion named Yaa Tua, who visits me all the time. She would sit for a long time saying nothing, and not that we could engage in any deep philosophical conversations, but she makes the time go by much more quickly.

Nana Dɔnkɔ came by to inquire about how I was doing, and I told him I was feeling a lot better. He said it was the *aduro* (baths) that made me ill, adding that if he had told me that would happen, I may not have wanted to do it. (But like I always say, I would not have come all this way if I were not serious). Nana encouraged me, saying that the *aduro* has to get into my blood, and I will get much stronger later on.

Nana Effa also came by to greet me that evening. He also mentioned that my illness was due to the *aduro* and this is what had given me the fever. He advised me since I was feeling so cold, I should not bathe anymore for the rest of the evening and at night, and like Nana Dɔnkɔ said, eventually as the *aduro* gets into my skin I would feel a lot stronger.

I have observed that the people here carry enormous loads on their head. They carry heavy buckets, foodstuffs, and all odd stuff on their heads with expert balance, from the young to the old. What is even more amazing is the tremendous load of firewood that men and women carry. I see that some (as I was writing, Nana Dɔnkɔ just came by to greet me) do suffer from such loads on their head. I recall one man in particular came by to see Nana for treatment; he was carrying a heavy load and fell, injuring his spine. He was an elder, and I felt he should not have been carrying such a load. Nana Dɔnkɔ's visit was a social one. He came by to see how I was doing.

I did feel a lot better the next morning. (But I did wonder if what I wrote was true. As I was transcribing my notes on my computer, I noticed how bad my handwriting had become. It did not flow, and the letterforms looked very uneven. Comparing this writing to how I normally write, it would certainly be an indication that something was wrong with me. Anyway, I will continue).

After I took my bath, I went to greet Nana Dɔnkɔ, and I noticed that he was in preparation to make an *aduro* bath with herbs. Later on, after the greeting formalities, Nana poured libation into the bath. Maame, Nana Dɔnkɔ's wife, came and told me that we should go and visit Nana Effa.

On the way there, my *ɔbosom* wanted to come upon me but did not fully possess; it was halfway in and out. When we arrived at Nana Effa's house, he told the *ɔbosom* to go and sleep, which it did. Nana then poured libation and asked me to do the same for my *ɔbosom*. Nana Effa possessed Kofi Asante, and after the greetings and formalities took place the *ɔbosom* spoke to me, telling me I should give my ancestors food and drink so that they can help me to stand strong. The *ɔbosom* stressed that I should be a man and stand strong, stating that back home someone had challenged me, and my *ɔbosom* killed him.

I began to wonder if I knew anyone who had died. I thought that the only person I knew who had died was Kwasi Opoku, but I doubted that the ɔbosom was referring to him. Kofi Asante said that (which appears confusing to me now and may be due to a lack of in-depth understanding of English by my translator, Kofi Sarpon. I think that it was not him, but when I get back home, I will know everything). He said if anyone challenged me, they will die, that the person who challenged me did not know my ɔbosom was from Takyiman. Even if my mother, father, or anyone challenged me they would die. Asante said I should get a cutlass, a knife, and drink, tie them together with a red cloth and present it to one of the *abosom* and ask them to protect me. Kofi Asante then looked at me and asked if everyone back home in my town loves me. I said, no! Asante went on to say if anybody says that everybody loves them, they are a liar.

If a person is sitting down and a thief comes by and steals something near him, who do you blame? I said, the thief. Kofi Asante said the *aduro* in my bath will prevent anyone from throwing bad *aduro* at me and the ɔbosom will show me everything. Asante said to me that I had come here to get something, but I would have to suffer to get it. He asked me if I was prepared to go all the way, knowing that the ɔbosom is like this, or do I want the ɔbosom to go only halfway with me? I said all the way, then he stressed that I should be careful because there are powerful people back home who want my downfall. But I should not use the ɔbosom only to kill; leave this decision to the *abosom* alone, and go away if I am challenged.

Kofi Asante inquired about my dreams, and I told him about the one I had about my ɔbosom and Ateokɔsaa. Asante told me he would come and see me while I was sleeping. He must have, because I recall making the sound "HUH" as he also does, and it woke me up. I also recall him telling me not to worry too much about money, mentioning that I came here to Takyiman with a purpose, but one of them I put aside. I must say I was a little lost about what it could be. I contemplated, maybe he was referring to the fact that at first, I thought about making plans to go and see Nana Oparebea, but now I did not desire to go and see her. He said no, and that he did not want to expose everything publicly.

I then went on to ask if it was concerning Sarpon and the fact that I do not have the money to take him back to America with me. The inspector interjected, "Don't worry about money, the *ɔbosom* will not tell you to go back home because you do not have money." Asante supported this by saying not to worry about money. I said I should ask my wife for help. At this time, Asante said he would send a messenger to my home to inspect things. It was not clear if this was to investigate if my wife had the money or not. Asante continued by saying that when the messenger returns, he will tell me everything. He specified that I would have to feed the messenger six times for the journey and that he would show me a vision, not while I was asleep but awake, and I should not get scared and run away. This is where the inspector told me to "be a man and fear nothing." I went back home and got 1,000 cedis and gave it to Sarpon to give to Asante to feed him. I also bought a drink. My little friend was here all the while I was writing in my journal.

Next, I need to explain about why I was in the hospital and how it came about that I was released from the hospital. On Saturday May 27, after I visited Nana Effa and consulted with Kofi Asante, I returned to get the money to pay his messenger. I took Nana Effa's bike to return home, and after I arrived, I began to feel very ill again. I went to the pharmacist, and he said I had malaria and gave me an injection and some pills, but that did not help me in any way. Finally, after a trying weekend of not sleeping well and just feeling bad, the family became very concerned about my well-being, and realizing what bad shape I was in, they decided I should go to the hospital and get treatment. A taxi was flagged down and brought to the compound. Amoako, our older brother, picked me up and took me to the taxi, since I was in no shape to walk. I have never before felt so sick and dreadful at the same time.

When I was talking to the administrator at the hospital and describing my symptoms, he added, "You feel like you want to die." I said yes and was admitted immediately. I recall family members coming to visit me; Maame came by every day, and Yaw, the son of our eldest brother Kwame Amponsa, stayed with me all the while. Nana Effa's wife brought me food, and Bɔɔ Yaw *ɔkɔmfoɔ* came by and looked at me with so much concern and put money or something in my hand. I think it was cedis, but I cannot recall how much. This was very same *ɔkɔmfoɔ* Nana Kwadwo Bɛkoe whom I met when I first arrived in Takyiman. Soon after I arrived Nana Effa took me around to greet people and, most of all, the *ɔkɔmfoɔhene* Nana Kwabena Mensa, who is Taa Mensa *ɔbosomfoɔ*. Nana Bɛkoe was there; he looked me up and down, and inquired if I truly possess an *ɔbosom*, to which Nana Effa promptly replied, "Yes!" His curiosity must have been running strong, and Nana Bɛkoe asked me if I could possess my *ɔbosom* so he could see it, and to that Nana Effa replied, "Not today." That was my first impression and memory of Nana Bɛkoe.

I remember one day when Kofi visited me, but again with malaria you are not thinking straight. That day I suddenly felt cold and started to shake so uncontrollable that even the bed was moving, and he quickly went for the nurse, who immediately came and gave me an injection in my thigh, which abated it. I had never felt so out of control before. This, I was told, was brought on due to my high fever.

The diarrhea I am experiencing has left me very weak at times, and it was excruciating to walk, which I could not accomplish without the help of Yaw, who was always there to keep me company. One night, in and out of sleep, I felt like someone was playing with my toes. I would wake up and see no one there, but this happened again so strongly that it woke me up each time. I often wondered if it was the *mmoatia* of Nana Effa. The day finally arrived when I was well enough to be released from the hospital. It was a long-awaited moment. I was hospitalized for almost eleven days, from May 27 through June 6.

Ever since I was released from the hospital, I have not been completely well, and was unable to keep up my notes. I got so far behind. The day after I was released, I visited Nana Effa, and he consulted his *mmoatia*. I never expected she would speak with a high-pitched voice that was understood. Nana was not possessed, but engaged in conversation with the *mmoatia*, constantly rattling a bell. Coming out of his shrine, an audible voice could be heard. If I had known this was going to happen, I would have brought my tape recorder. Nana Effa told me I had to clean up due to my illness and my stay in the hospital. I was given three eggs, a plant called *dwera*, and seawater to purify myself. Facing a wall, Nana cleaned me off with the plant and seawater. When he was finished, I ate the eggs, but I was still very weak.

Mossi informed me that the priest who was training me in the United States was trying to stop me from training here in Takyiman. She does not want to lose face by me leaving her and accomplishing my training here. Mossi said that knife can cut a knife and that if I bring him a turtle and a cat, he would make *aduro* for me to eat. He said that this was because he knew

I would not eat *opete* (vulture). He also added that with this *aduro* my ɔ*bosom* would talk and say everything and I should not worry. I realized that I was far behind in the spiritual work I needed to do. Mossi must have seen what was on my mind, because he said everything would be okay. He said my general weakness was due to having been sick, and I wouldn't be healed in one day, saying "when you get cut it does not heal all at once." He notified me that he would catch a witch for me to see before I went back home. That evening, I restarted my *aduro* baths again. Nana Adwoa Akumsa told me to bathe four times a day.

The *mmoatia* came and spoke today, and again I was not prepared to record her. Last time she asked me if I would be afraid if they took me to the bush. I said no, and she just laughed and laughed. By the way, the *boatia* who speaks is called *Akua Bɔmmɔ*. I asked if she would come back home with me, and she said no! She does not like all the noises. She likes it quiet but would send one of her brothers with me. She repeated, once you have visited someplace and you do not like it, you will not go there again. This is true; Nana Effa came to the United States to promote the documentary *Bono Medicine* in the mid-80s. I recall him saying that he possessed one of his spirits during a showing.

I was still very tired; having to walk that distance to Nana Effa's house and back exhausted me. Also, I do not get adequate rest when I am there, and that does not help. The *abosom* comes plenty on Nana Effa, so he is always busy. Mossi said I should hurry up and do the work quickly; time was short. I had already informed all the people who needed to know, so I was waiting to do the work. I alerted Nana Dɔnkɔ, and he said he would do everything tomorrow. Nana Effa wanted me to go and see Ɔboɔkyerewa, but because the roads were not good to travel, that journey was cancelled.

My digestion is still giving me difficulties, probably because of the diet here. I must be patient with the people; I realize I am a foreigner to them and how strange that sounds to me. I, who pride myself as an African of Ghanaian ancestry because of the *ɔbosom*, have had to reevaluate who I really am. I feel like I am a sideshow at times, with everyone looking at me as something odd, new, different. I do not get a sense of belonging yet. Everyone still calls me *boroni*, and how I dislike that word when it refers to me.

A woman definitely much lighter and redder in complexion called me *boroni*. I said to her, "*Dabi boroni*," which means, "no white man." I found myself becoming more and more outspoken about this, and I realized that if I was not careful, feelings might get hurt. This did not seem to be a problem with the *abosom*, at least I did not think so. I realized that I needed to search for a deeper understanding of what they are seeing and thinking when they see me. Maybe they do not mean any harm. Maybe it was just their way of responding to something unfamiliar.

All this raises in me the question. what is it to be African? I know one thing: it is not about skin color. Africans are somewhat colorblind. Everyone they interact with for centuries looks like them, so they relate to each other from an African cultural or Afrocentric perspective, not a colored window. I was new, different from them in many ways, and had lost that cultural perspective because of living in America. Living there distorted me in that sense. Even when I was around my West Indian family, I had lost my commonality with them; in certain terms, I had forgotten the meanings of my West Indian roots, which are closer for me, and I had to search for remembrance. In Trinidad, they refer to those who have gone away and come back acting differently as "freshwater Yankee."

Yaw, who stayed with me during my entire stay at the hospital, is very dear to me. In gratitude, I gave him my favorite bracelet I had brought with me from America. This young man was with me every day and night, tending to all my needs. He washed me and supported me every time I had to walk to the toilet. I am so grateful to everyone who visited me, Maame, Nana Effa's wife and daughter, and all of the others.

The *mmoatia* came, and she spoke to me again. One day I will capture her on tape. I also had the opportunity to witness and accompany Nana Effa doing shrine work. A woman came by for help; someone had used *aduro bɔne*, which is bad spiritual medicine, to take her husband away from her, so she came to the shrine for help. Nana Effa used this occasion to teach me how to pour libation before we left. I do not fully remember what I said right now. The way knowledge in *akɔm* is assimilated is that you have to be attentive while things are being done and remember everything. Nana asked me to pour libation. I was a little lost for words at first because of the language barrier, but I managed. Nana then took a stick with a mirror that was covered in animal skin off his shrine area, and we proceeded to the woman's house, with her leading the way. At her house, Nana then told me to hold the stick briefly, he then showed me the bad *aduro*, sprinkled some *mɔtɔ* on the area, poured libation, took the stick from me and threw it down where the *aduro* was, then picked up the bad *aduro* and said "Bye-bye." Soon after, he picked up his stick, licked its base, took a drink, then left. I realized that I needed to get a stick like this.

The next day was a fruitful day, and I was very happy. I must say that when I first arrived here, Nana Dɔnkɔ had graduated one *ɔkɔmfoɔ* and kept him on because he was considered too young to be sent off. He also was training Abena *ɔkɔmfoɔ* along with me. Nana Effa also graduated Afia, about whom I will speak. Some people I had not seen since my hospital stay had traveled and returned last night. Afia *ɔkɔmfoɔ* was graduated, and they accompanied her to her town. When an *ɔkɔmfoɔ* is training, they live with the Master *ɔkɔmfoɔ*, who trains them for a period of three years or more, and a lot could have happened in their town during their absence.

The newly graduated *ɔkɔmfoɔ* must demonstrate that he/she has the power of the *ɔbosom* by revealing what took place in their town during his/her absence. And so, the Master *ɔkɔmfoɔ* who trained the *ɔbosom* would accompany the newly graduated *ɔkɔmfoɔ* to their home to witness that the *ɔbosom* had functioned properly. This also demonstrates to the new *ɔkɔmfoɔ*'s family that the *ɔbosom* can truly function on its own.

Nana Effa, who trained Afia *ɔkɔmfoɔ*, did not accompany her due to my illness. Therefore, the witnesses he sent to accompany and support her came back to inform Nana of how the *ɔbosom* performed in her town.

Mossi possessed Nana Effa and urged me about the work I had to do. I informed him that I was waiting for Kofi Sarpon, who was currently busy representing someone who had gotten into some legal problems for his mishandling of someone's check. I was a little frustrated about not being able to get the work done quickly, but I had no choice but to wait on Kofi.

Finally, Nana Effa, the inspector, and I decided to do the rituals. I had to get a cat to be sacrificed to one of Nana's *suman* called Yansara. This *suman*, I was told, tricks people and can get you whatever you desire. After the sacrifice, a drink was presented for libation. The inspector sold me his cutlass for half the price, and the work was done. Now all that was left was for me to get a turtle, feed the ancestors, and do something with an egg. Mossi also informed me that my past teachers were working hard to stop me from succeeding, but he assured me that their doings would be unsuccessful.

I used this opportunity to inquire about my friend who died mysteriously back in Washington D.C., Nana Kwasi Opoku. This man wanted nothing more than to acquire the whole lineage of the Tigare pantheon and possess the spirit, but no matter what was done, he could not possess any *suman* or *ɔbosom*. I asked Mossi, why did Nana Kwasi die? Mossi replied briefly, if you take money to buy something and you did not or would not give as promised, but pretended you would give all that was promised, this is not right.

I surmised from this that Nana Kwasi promised something and he never intended to live up to it. He tried to fool someone or people. Anyway, it comes down to an *ɔbosom* or *nsuman* pulling their blessings from him and allowing the tragedy to happen. I still feel I do not know everything and will ask more questions later. I recall visiting Nana Opoku before his demise one Sunday at his residence after my wife and I came from visiting Nana Kwabena Brown. He was in the middle of sacrificing chickens to his shrines in his basement. You could see about half a dozen chickens dead on the floor and he was still sacrificing more. I asked him what he was doing, and he told me he dreamed of seeing someone throwing dead chickens across the water (maybe he meant across the ocean) at him.

Nana Effa stressed to me that I should write a book and remember their names. That is all they asked of me—remember their names. That day was truly a blessed day. After the cat was sacrificed, I came back home to rest while they prepared the herbs to cook with the cat meat. The herbs that were used to cook the meat were explained earlier to me by Nana. They were *Taamenwu* (if you hate me, I will not die), *Gruo* (the usage escapes me as I am writing), another plant whose name cannot be mentioned as it is being used, *Kekaduro* (ginger, a substitute for pepper) since I could not eat pepper right now, and some others. All these herbs are used for protection. I came back to my room in Nana Dɔnkɔ's area to rest and see what he had in mind for me.

Sometime later, Nana Effa came by my room to take me back to his place to eat. On the way, we stopped by Nana Dɔnkɔ and got a turtle. As we proceeded to his house, I took the lead. The meat was dished out by Nana. I had to eat the head, jaws, brain (which tasted mushy), the paws, the intestines and who knows what else. I had to drink all the broth and was told that if any witchcraft was used against me, because I ate the head it can never touch me. I was not permitted to wash my hands after I ate. I began to wonder what else I would have to eat after the turtle is sacrificed.

Later on, after I finished eating, I had to take a bath with a vine called *humatre*. I was supposed to bathe in this *aduro* earlier but did not due to my malaria illness. I bathed in it three times behind the shrine house. Nana told me this plant would talk to me like a person. When my bath was finished, Nana commented on how strong the *aduro* was. I possessed my *ɔbosom*, and he spoke, but Nana said he did not understand the *ɔbosom*. He, too, possessed one of his *moatia*, Kofi Asante.

I was told that Asante said my *ɔbosom* was near, he is coming, and the inspector added "I am lucky Asante said my *ɔbosom* is old, one of the oldest ɔbosom and most powerful. He is near and wanted to come fully, but because they did not have any drums, he could not, but will come again tomorrow." He also mentioned that Asante said I should go and see Ɔbookyerewa tomorrow. I was so happy to hear all this wonderful news that my ɔbosom was near, very near, and was coming soon. Now I was able to train. The inspector said he was happy for me and my ɔbosom. He said he felt cool or cold chills when it was coming on me. Nana Effa said something like that also. The inspector said he wished the ɔbosom had come all the way so he (the ɔbosom) could tell him something.

That evening the inspector and I discussed my situation and said it would be Nana Effa who would go with me to display the ɔbosom back home. He would help me. This made me feel very happy, if the ɔbosom permits this to happen.

Nana Effa told me that about a year before I arrived, the ɔbosom were saying that a stranger was coming, but they thought it was from another country on the African continent and he (Nana Effa) would go if people did not treat him kindly. I am not sure what he meant by go. One day after the ɔbosom had left Nana Effa and we were all chatting in the shrine room, he commented that someone whose name I will not mention had tried to kill him. I could not believe it at first because I had seen this person around and he was always assisting Nana Effa. They would all laugh and said yes, he tried to kill Nana Effa because he did not believe anyone so young should have so much power. Yes! It is true, I was amazed that the priests and priestesses do start training akɔm at a very young age. They are proficient and seasoned ɔkɔmfoɔ by the age of twenty-five. The ones I have encountered, most of them are so young.

I went to visit Ɔbookyerewa, whose appellation name is Kwaku Adaku as Kofi Asante instructed me. I found this place to be very interesting indeed. To get there, you have to travel on a difficult, long road. After we arrived at the *ɔbosom*'s town, which is called Traa, we went through the usual formalities and greetings before we proceeded. The main shrine was about a mile walk away, near the Tanɔ river. The shrine is built upon a stone or rock on which the Tanɔ river flows perpetually. Upon this rock or stone is another large stone that sits upon it. It is this rock that the *ɔbosom* was found to be sitting upon. No one steps on it or he will be punished. This shrine place is unremittingly busy with people who have come from a long way for help.

After more formalities and handshakes, it was time for the *ɔbosomfoɔ* Nana Kofi Asamadu to possess the *ɔbosom*. This *ɔbosomfoɔ* is somewhat hyper, and they say the *ɔbosom* act that way too. A stool was placed facing the Tanɔ river, and all you could see is in the back of the *ɔbosomfoɔ*. He placed a string with seven *nnufa* around his forehead. The *ɔkyeame* sat behind him and began to call the *ɔbosom* through *mmrane* (incantations) and proverbs. After observing the ritual for possessing the *ɔbosom*, I discerned the only difference is that the *ɔbosomfoɔ* does not put the pan on his head like the other Atanɔ in order to possess the *ɔbosom*. The *ɔkyeame* petitioned the *ɔbosom* to come for a long time, but Ɔbookyerewa did not come, and as the singers were singing *ɔbosommerafoɔ* songs to call the *ɔbosom*, I began to possess my *ɔbosom*.

All this was recorded on my cassette. I was told that the *ɔbosom* is like that; he is unpredictable. Sometimes it may take more than ten visits before you ever see the *ɔbosom* possess.

Since Obookyerewa did not come, a female *okomfoo* possessed her *obosom* and informed me that I should bathe in the river seven times, and Obookyerewa gave me a cock to welcome me, further saying that when you have a guest, you first must feed them before you ask them to talk. I was instructed to return on the 24th. After my bath, clay markings were smeared on my joints and around my neck. I took a picture after my bath. They say Obookyerewa does not belong to anyone; he resides in Traa and is the chief *obrafoo* for Taa Mensa and he looks after the Tano river and Takyiman. We left the shrine and proceeded back to the *obosomfoo*'s home. We found there a man waiting for the *obosomfoo*'s return with a chicken, drink, and eggs. Obookyerewa had caught him, and he was here to pacify the *obosom*.

Back at Nana Donko's, I did the sacrifice for my ancestors, and it went well. I gave my *obosom* the cock Obookyerewa gave to me to welcome him; this too was well received. Later that day, I went to Nana Effa, and I sacrificed the turtle and we ate it. It was pleasant, not strange as I thought it would taste. When we were finished, Nana Effa asked me what I would give in thanks after his *obosom* catches my *obosom* for me. I said I will give a ram, but the inspector said I should have said a cock and drink. Nana interjected and said all the work was done, so what I said was right. Now all I have to do is sleep with an egg under my pillow.

I went back to Nana Donko and they made me aware that they will give me new *aduro* for my *obosom* to wear, but they did not ask me to throw away what I had gotten from my previous training. They also mentioned that at the end of the month I will get a *doso* (raffia skirt), and they said that they will only do what my *obosom* asks of them and not the way my past teacher did things. I like that very much. We had a conversation about my purchasing a brass pan, because the one I brought from the United States is too heavy and big. There was also talk about opening the mouth of the ɔbosom so that he can speak. All this was interpreted by Kofi Sarpon.

I have noticed with the onset of the rainy season, the sun does not shine as much, and when it does it is not as strong and the weather stays cool. This all has an effect upon the people here; young adults and the old all seem to have symptoms of colds and getting sick, even me. I have even developed a sore throat, but I suspect it was due to my bathing seven times in the Tanɔ river at Traa. The water there was very cool and so was the weather. The next day I noticed I had a sore throat.

I observed that the diet here had an effect on the people's digestive systems even though they all had an appearance of normalcy. Everyone day in and day out ate primarily two types of dishes, *fufuo* (pounded yam) and *ampesi* (boiled yam) and meat. I would never entertain the idea or notion that they practice any form of vegetarianism, but some vegetables are ground into a somewhat thick paste and added to the soup. They do consume a few fruits. I have discerned that the men who frequent the communal toilet have a free and loose bowel movement. What I am saying is that constipation would be a rare thing for people here. All this is due to their diet and the water. I cannot speak for the women, but I might deduce that their system may respond in the same way. Due to my diarrhea, I had to go all hours of the day and night, and I have met others at the toilet as well. Fortunately for me, I am now on a rice water diet, and my symptoms have subsided considerably. My hope now is that I do not get constipated. I must say the diet here is rough on me, and it is taking time for my stomach to adjust to it. How I do miss my wife's cooking! I would like to conclude that there is no normal time here for visiting the toilet.

The cold weather is making it difficult for me to feel motivated to take my baths. It is cold in the morning and the water is so cold. After bathing, you can see steam rising off my body like an early mist. I am not exaggerating, but I manage somehow during the daytime and can't complain too much because, at night, bathing is a mental discipline. I do miss home.

The following day was uneventful. Nothing of any significance or importance happened, except for a certain woman accompanied by a man visited Nana Dɔnkɔ for treatment. This woman annoyed me like the others who insisted on referring to me as *boroni*. I ignored her because she kept calling me *boroni* and would converse with others, laughing and saying "*Boroni bra* (to come), *boroni bra.*" I did not understand all she was saying. I ignored her to the point I could take no more and I finally responded to her "*Dabi boroni!*" It was then, Nana Dɔnkɔ perhaps sensing my annoyance, intervened and said "*Bibini,*" which I later understood to mean black man. When she was leaving, she said to me, "*Boroni*, bye."

This type of playing a person as a thing reminds me so much of how we were treated by white people. Some people do not even ask for your name. They just start calling you *boroni*, like I do not have a name. They would never treat each other like this. The social custom is to ask for your name and purpose. I do not like this. Back home we are called niggers because of our black skin. Here you are called *boroni* because of your skin. Enough! Both are wrong. I know I should be more understanding because they do not know the history; they are the product of a historical disconnection. It is a matter of knowing the history and what happened to Africans as they were enslaved and taken to the West. Education is the key, so I hope by being here I can bring awareness to this reality.

Amoako, an older brother to Nana Effa and one of Nana Dɔnkɔ's sons, came by to reassure me that he had spoken to Nana Dɔnkɔ and Nana Akumsa about expediting things for me because my time was getting short. He said he told them to get started and not to delay, that my time now was precious and everything should be finished before I leave in August. He indicated that they would have gotten started and taught me more, but they needed a translator.

The next morning, I traveled to Nana Effa and we visited Mframa *ɔkɔmfoɔ*, a woman in her late thirties or early forties, and after the formalities, she went to Asuo Yaa and divined. I was dazzled by the sheer brilliance of the brass pan of Mframa; something about it captured my attention. At Asuo Yaa, she mentioned some things, but what stood out was that she said that my *ɔbosom* liked it there and would remain with Mframa for a few days, but not to worry, he would come back to me. When we were finished, Nana Effa and I returned to his home for him to take care of family matters. We used this opportunity to discuss my needs and the time I had left. Nana discussed with me that he divided the work he had to do for me into two parts between what Nana Dɔnkɔ would do and what he would do for me. He told me Nana Dɔnkɔ said he would make the shrine, *nsuman*, and all that the *ɔbosom* will wear. I would have to buy gold for him to put into the things he was going to make, and he (Nana Effa) would catch my *ɔbosom* for them to put in the brass pan.

I recall that this morning before I left, they discussed sending Kwabena to Oboase to buy gold for me and about my being certified after training. I was also encouraged by this and found out that not too many *ɔkɔmfoɔ* get certification from the government; it is a rare thing. They say they will try to do this for me. On the other hand, Nana Effa will provide me with a *Boame suman* and a *ntrama*, a stick like the one he used at the woman's house to protect against bad *aduro*. It will cause the evil to fall to the ground for me to see, and a *suman* worn at the wrist (*bansere*). Kofi said since I was now part of the family, they would not charge me like a stranger. Nana Effa promised to give me the stick free, and the *Boame* would be made from the turtle shell I had sacrificed. This *Boame suman* is like *Yansara*. It will get me anything I want. Nana Effa said these are the things he wanted to give to me, and they would see what else the ɔbosom would like me to have.

When I returned home at Nana Dɔnkɔ, I went to the shrine room to greet Nana Akumsa, who was divining for someone. After she was finished, she said her ɔbosom said my stomach was much better and now they could begin the work. The ɔbosom also mentioned that my wife is doing fine and I think too much about home. Something was said about when I get back home to be careful that I do not get ill. I am not certain of Nana Effa's translation.

Yesterday, I witnessed a very sad state of affairs. A young woman in her mid- or late twenties behaved as abnormally as you can imagine. She paraded herself around the compound, decked in all sorts of beads in her hair, wrists, legs, and neck. At first glance, I thought she was a strange ɔkɔmfoɔ wearing lipstick smeared on her face and lips. When she spoke to the people around, I inquired what she was saying and nobody seemed to understand her. She sang a song of what was supposed to be in English, but I did not understand a word she was singing. I probed into what was wrong with her, and the story went like this: she went to Abidjan (Ivory Coast) with the intention of marrying a man, but she took his money, and left. The man, realizing what she had done, either did or had someone do spiritual work against her. Now all her money is spent, and she does not have any more to go back for help. I was told that there is a big river that is very powerful in Abidjan and it can harm you.

The other story is perhaps she was training and broke some taboos, like chasing men or having sex for money, and her ɔbosom made her mentally abnormal. I inquired where she had come from, and no one seemed to know. I also asked can the ɔbosom (Asubonten) help her? They said the ɔbosom cannot unless she has someone to represent her, and she may be too far gone for help. Who would take responsibility for her and spend the money to help this woman, I pondered. She would just ramble on, talking about ɔbosom and asking for alcohol to pour libation. If no one would give her a drink, she said water would do. They gave her water, and she splashed it here and there, left and right. She asked me if she had a festival would I come and dance. She begged for a cigarette, soap powder to wash her clothes, and for money. She took off her clothes right there in front of everyone. The children, adults, and I stood affixed watching her. Nana Effa, realizing what was going on, told the children to go and help their mothers. Finally, the woman left as suddenly as she came. I felt so sad for her. I asked, "Where does she stay, where does she sleep, how does she eat?" They said she begs for food and a place to sleep and people do help her.

*Kofi related a dream he had about me this morning. In the dream, I was leaving and he was chasing after me. Still in this dream state, he told me that when I got up from my sleep this morning to use the bathroom, and as I was closing the door, he heard me and he jumped up from his dream and tried to run after me to stop me from leaving.*

Of course, this led to a discussion about my needing his help in translation.

I mentioned that there were times when I needed his assistance and I could not find him, and therefore I had no one to speak on my behalf. A lot of things needed to be explained to me and there was work to do, but I could not get them all accomplished since he was not there. Kofi said he understood and would be there for me.

We saw Ɔboɔkyerewa ɔkyeame and informed him that we should expedite things so I would not have to wait till the 24th. We planned to travel there on Monday, but Kofi had the intention of walking there. I do not know about that. Traa is pretty far away for me, and the road is rough and long, plus added to that a long walk to the shrine. I am not walking.

Nana Effa collected 5,000 cedis from me to begin the work, and I hope everything else goes well and very quickly. I wanted them to open the mouth of the *obosom* so that he would tell us everything he needs; this is what I want so that they could really begin to train me. The female *ɔkɔmfoɔ* who possessed at Traa when Ɔboɔkyerewa did not come and said Ɔboɔkyerewa welcomed me and gave me a cock, was also present, along with the *ɔkyeame*.

That night I put the egg under my pillow, and the next morning I traveled with Kofi to Sunyani, some two hours away, and deposited it. Yesterday, Kofi and I went into the forest to collect a particular plant that grows only in a specific area. This plant, whose name I am not allowed to mention, was ground into a paste and cooked with egg for me to eat. This *aduro* was to make all my dreams come true and whatever I say when I possess would be so. I cannot go into details about this particular ritual. We also went to the farm to get another plant and harvested the roots of this plant, which is a very large vine. I first had to offer a sacrifice of an egg, and mention my name and reason for collecting it. Most important I could not let my shadow in anyway fall upon this plant while I was cutting it. When I had finished and separated part of its root I noticed water dripping from the severed parts. Kofi quenched his thirst with its water; I am not sure if I did also. I was told that it would protect me from any bad *aduro* and make my enemies fear me. Kofi carried the plant on his head, and once we arrived back home, because of this plant, Kofi could not speak and I had to do all the talking. I was told this plant is said to kill people if the rituals are not done properly. Kofi said that he was indeed very surprised at all the *aduro* they were giving me. He added that he had learned a lot since I had been here. They have done things for me that they have not done for other ɔkɔmfoɔ.

A man that they call Africania came by to visit Nana Dɔnkɔ. He was dressed in a white Muslim outfit, and I was informed that he was the head of the Africania Mission. He seemed to be a good friend of Nana, and gave me a couple of their small pamphlets. He spoke good English. He taught me their song called *Sankofa*, which I recorded.

Later that evening, Maame told me to get ready to go to Nana Effa. It is June 18, the night of his *Aburoo ne Nkateɛ Adapa*; the *adapa* is the day before the *Adae* on which Nana will celebrate his festival. When we arrived, everything was set. The drummers were warming up, with Nana Effa playing the lead. We started singing a greeting song, *mema woadwo*, to Asuotipa, Akua Bɔmmɔ, Kofi Asante, and others. We sang songs that put me in a good mood and made me so happy. I have recorded it all for posterity. People will be able to hear this historical recording. In a sense, I am preserving my own historical experience.

Nana and others sang songs that were outstanding; his mother, Akosua, his wife, and some of his children made it an occasion to remember. I even got the opportunity to chime in, singing here and there, with plenty of drumming to accompany our singing. The next song was truly noteworthy. It is by far the most beautiful and moving tribute to the *akɔm* world. Nana, his wife, and mother would each take turns singing *Agya mo oo, aye ee*. This tribute displayed vocal polyrhythm to its apex. The music became so exciting, we all took turns dancing to the accompaniment. We sang songs congratulating the *ɔbosommerafoɔ*, and the *mmoatia*, that took a young girl for *akɔm* training and so much more. Another song that stood out was *Bo bi yɛ, bo bi yɛ afa,* meaning how *Nyame* created you whether you like it or not you have to accept it.

It was all a matter of time before Nana eventually became possessed by Kofi Asante, his messenger, followed by Kwaku Mossi, the *sumanbrafo* for Asuotipa. Mossi is very funny and does not speak Twi with any fluidity like his other spirits, and they teased him jokingly by saying I speak Twi better than he does. They say they have difficulty understanding Mossi because of his northern Mossi accent and he does not pronounce the words properly. This I have witnessed and have observed them asking him to repeat at times what he says. When they tell him he does not speak proper Twi, he gets insulted and calls them fools.

After Mossi left, we got ready for bed to pick up tomorrow where we left off. I slept in the shrine room with Nana and others.

The next morning, the day of the festival, Nana was going to carry his *ɔbosom*, and I quickly made haste home to wash, change and return. The *ɔbosom* was summoned by the *ɔkyeame*, and he did not take long to come.

He was welcomed and greeted with a song, *Ee me ma wo akwaaba oo*. In return, Asuotipa slapped the pan, greeting and asking everyone how they were doing. He took care of some family issues, then addressed a woman being bothered by Bronsam that had come to her, and he advised her that she should not delay in getting the work done. In response to the woman asking for help, Asuotipa began to sing a song *Boa me, Atanɔ boame, boame Agyeman Tanɔ boame*, a song that is asking Tanɔ to help you.

Now, it was my turn. Asuotipa, seeing that something was worrying me, inquired. I told him how it bothers me that people call me *boroni*, and everyone burst out in laughter. Asuo said I should not let this worry me, because I came from abroad and that is why people call me that. I said that if I am part of the family, then why do they call me that? They say I may be one of the children that have come back, and if this is so, then why do they call me something different?

So many people were chiming in that I did not get a clear interpretation of what Asuotipa said during all the chatter, and then he left. After a few minutes, he was called again, and he asked me why he was not informed after we visited Ɔboɔkyerewa. He said if I want things done quickly for me, I, too, must be quick. I was told to make the sacrifice of a ram with two knives tied to its belly with red cloth and present a drink. This sacrifice is so that when my *ɔbosom* comes he will speak properly.

After the *ɔbosom* was consulted, they presented the *aburoo* (corn) and *nkateɛ* (peanut) for the *ɔbosom* to eat, and then we ate. Sometime later, after Nana Dɔnkɔ and the others arrived, the festival began in earnest. The drumming and dancing became hot, and Nana Effa possessed Asuotipa. They took the *ɔbosom* to the shrine to get a dress with his *doso*; in his hands he held long raffia, and a spear. Now the *ɔbosom* was decked out and ready to perform. The *ɔbosom* called me up to dance.

After a while, Nana possessed another of his spirits, Kofi Asante. Kofi Asante grabbed me to dance with him and I, too, became possessed with my *ɔbosom*. When I came out of possession, I noticed I was dressed in a *doso* and raffia. Being back to normal, I was still required to dance a lot. I recall that one man called Atta Kwaku helped me a lot with my dancing, but I found him too boastful about his dancing, to the point that he annoyed everyone with his insistence about helping me to dance. My older brother, Kwasi *ɔkɔmfoɔ*, a teenager whom I am right under, also helped me to dance. Kwasi *ɔkɔmfoɔ* possessed his *ɔbosom* too, and his *ɔbosom* also tried to injure him severely. I reflected back on the time when Nana Akua Asantewaa possessed Asubonten and he was the topic of conversation. He must have committed some offense. That is why his *ɔbosom* was punishing him.

The *ɔbosom* tried to stab him with a knife, burn him with fire, knock him around, drag him through the mud and throw a *konte* stick into the air and step under it to crack the *ɔkɔmfoɔ* on his head. If that was not enough, he would take the club and beat the *ɔkɔmfoɔ* body with it all. This was a reoccurrence, but today it was more severe. After the *akɔm*, I asked Nana Effa why was this happening to the *ɔkɔmfoɔ*. Nana said it is because of a girl he would not leave alone until after he finished his training. Before I forgot, Nana Effa possessed Mossi, who is petrified of cars. People would scare him, telling him a car was coming. I found this to be hilarious. A spirit afraid of a car! Mossi would run and hide. It was too, too funny. I could not help but laugh.

Mossi did mention to me that my ɔbosom was coming and not to worry about money. It was during the festival that I had to go and greet the ram by patting it three times on the belly before the ram was to be the sacrifice. I had to stand over it like before and speak and say all that is on my mind. Nana Dɔnkɔ poured libation and did the first cutting of the ram's throat, and it was finished by Nana Effa's ɔkyeame. When the blood was drained, I was told to go and pick the ram up, speak, and throw it down forcefully to the ground. I spent the rest of the evening and night at Nana Effa's shrine.

My assessment of the difference between akɔm at Nana Effa's place and Nana Dɔnkɔ is not that much different. Nana Effa displays a more youthful akɔm, very energetic and exhilarating, but getting the job done, while Nana Dɔnkɔ represents that same as Nana Effa but more of the older ways it was done and how it has matured with age and wisdom. Nana Dɔnkɔ's approach is slow, methodical, and in no rush. Akɔm is like a forest that is seen from afar. All the trees from afar appear together like a cluster, but the closer you get you, you see each individual tree. This, too, is reflected in a constellation seen with our unaided eyes, but with a telescope, we can see individual stars.

*I had a dream on June 19th that Nana Nsiah was greeting me; I am not sure, but I think I was sitting on a stool and she was standing. She wore a white cloth around her waist. I was a bit hesitant about shaking her hand at first, but I did.*

The next day, back at Nana Dɔnkɔ, I began my bath of protective *aduro*. Ɔboɔkyerewa ɔkyeame came by again and informed Nana Dɔnkɔ that Ɔboɔkyerewa would not show today and I should come on Saturday, a holy day.

Sometime during the night, I got up to go to the bathroom and felt something crunchy under my feet as I came back in. I shined my flashlight to see what was on the floor, and to my astonishment, I noticed a mass of swarming movement on the floor. I woke Kofi up and asked him what this mass of movement was on the floor. He inspected it and said it was termites. They were all over the floor and everything. I had never seen anything like this before. It covered the ceiling, on the books, chairs, and tables; everything was covered with termites. I am amazed we were not covered by them. My room had to be exterminated.

I stayed at the home of Nana Kwabena Kranka, Nana Effa ɔkyeame, in the meantime until my room was exterminated. I believe I developed an allergy. I did not know if it was from the dust or what. I also had a sore throat, and my sinuses were congested. My nose was constantly feeling itchy, and I had a slight cough. Kwabena went to Oboase to buy the gold. Nana Effa said that he finished the *nsuman* and he would get all the other things today to begin the work and the rest tomorrow. Nana said he wanted me to see everything he was doing for me so I could know how to make them.

I finally had time to sit down with Nana Dɔnkɔ and have a conversation; the problem had always been having an interpreter to translate. Amoako is one of his elder sons, and my older brother who served as an interpreter for us. I had a lot of questions about the *ɔbosom* Ɔboɔkyerewa and his personality. My first question was obvious. Why did the *ɔbosom* turn his back to people when he was talking to them? Nana said this was so that he did not sympathize with them. If he looked at your face, he might be compelled to forgive. I reflected back on the dream I had of him a while ago, and now I understood why he did not allow me to see his face as to show me who he is. This made him very distinct from others. I was also curious as to why Ɔbookyerewa did not come every time he was called. Nana's response was that he travels a lot, even overseas at times, so he was always very busy catching bad people.

*I dreamed that I was putting a ring (the type the ɔkɔmfoɔ wear) on my index finger. I am not certain if it should have been on my thumb or the index finger, since most of the ɔkɔmfoɔ I see wear them on their left thumb.*

Yesterday, Nana Dɔnkɔ, with the assistance of Kofi, began my herbal studies. We started with infertility problems. There seems to be a little strain between Kofi and me. I am sure Nana Dɔnkɔ may have suspected it. Later on, Kofi and I went to visit the nurse, Sister Nyamekye, at the Holy Family Hospital, who was so helpful to me in the hospital during my illness. She did not feel well and complained of headaches. I thanked her so much for taking good care of me. I will always remember the good nursing she gave me. After our visit, we returned and greeted Nana Dɔnkɔ. We went to my room, and Kofi began my Twi lessons. It was after this session I told Kofi that Nana Oparebea sent some of her *ɔkɔmfoɔ* from Larteh to America to assist others and promote *akɔm*.

Kofi asked me if the people that go for help are white people. I told him I have not seen white people involve themselves like that in African spiritual practices back home. They may attempt to embrace it, but they can never truly represent African spirituality. I muse at the presumption that people here think I am a rich white man who gives Kofi things and may one day take him back with me to America. But no matter how others may feel, the family here does not look at me like that. They understand my circumstances and have done a lot for me.

The termites were still a problem for me in my room, and because of them, the night before I had to sleep somewhere else, while Kofi exterminated the room again. Now I was back sleeping in my room. I got up around 3 a.m., and like before I felt like I was walking on something crunchy. The termites were all over the place again. I began to wonder if this issue with the termites would go away any time soon due to the heavy rains, which does not help. It was raining copiously almost every day for hours. The rain and mud also made traveling very difficult, and you had to be very attentive while navigating through the mud so that you did not slip and fall into it.

Kofi and I decided to travel to Wankye to purchase a brass pan, so we planned to stop off at Nana Effa's house first. I recall Nana telling me last week he would travel to Oboase on Thursday. A certain female ɔkɔmfoɔ from that town came to visit him and had been staying at his residence for a week now. She wanted him to go back with her to help her in some way or another. Nana Effa said he would not travel that day because the next day was Fofie and he could not travel, but he would travel on Saturday.

I developed a close friendship with Nana Effa's sister-in-law Abena, who is also called Rose. Abena and I spoke about a situation I have been contemplating. She advised me to speak my mind and address my concerns straightforward, but how can I? It is a little too complicated to speak my mind at this juncture, so I elected not to do so.

Rose confided in me a story about the birth of Nana Effa. She said when he was born, he held a gift from the ɔbosom in his clenched right hand. The family attempted to open his hand but could not. They put fire to the back of his hand and the heat burned his hand, and when they did that, he opened up his hand and the gift flew away like a bird. This was the second time I had heard this story. I asked Nana about this story, if it were true, and he showed me the scar on the back of his hand as proof of the story. Rose went on to say with more resolution that because of the family, Nana had to go away to the Ivory Coast to train. They wanted to stop his power.

Rose flatly stated Ghanaians love witchcraft and its intent is not always to kill but to spoil the other, so that they do not prosper more than you. As she begins to warm up, she educates me about how the ɔbayifoɔ hide their deception well and are extremely jealous of their neighbors. Abena spoke of the wonders Nana Effa used to perform back in the day before his accident. After he came back from training in the Ivory Coast, he could dance on a rope and was the best dancer in Takyiman. His ɔbosom could materialize things out of thin air, but people became jealous of him. His drinking problem stems from people wanting his downfall, so when Nana Dɔnkɔ passes over, he would be useless to fill the position. She told me about the accident where he fell from a tall tree and almost died. I have heard two different versions of how Nana Effa fell.

Our older brother Amoako said Nana's fall was a result of his always traveling out and drinking too much. His *mmoatia* did not like this, and Nana Effa would go to other towns and drink. One day his ɔ*bosom* called him home, and Amoako recalled seeing Nana on that very same evening. Nana told him that his ɔ*bosom* was calling him home and on the way, he became possessed by one of his *mmoatia*, who took him up a big tree. Nana was still intoxicated when the *mmoatia* unpossessed him up this tree. Nana, being in such a state, had no balance and fell. Both Abena and Amoako agreed that as a result of the fall Nana almost lost his life; rumors abound everywhere that Nana was dead, and it was Nana Dɔnkɔ who interceded and pleaded with the *mmoatia* not to kill him. The *mmoatia* wanted to kill him but spared his life. This would explain to me why Nana slurs his speech at times and cannot use his left arm nor stand erect properly. I was told all this took place about a year and a half ago.

The next day was Fofie. I started collecting plants to take back home. I purchased some small bells for the belt that is tied around my chest when I am to carry the pan on my head and was told I will have to acquire more for the *doso*. Since we were in Takyiman and they have the largest market, I found it ironic we had to go to the Wankye market to look for these items, but we did not find any that were reasonably priced. All that we saw was far too expensive. Kofi planned to go to the Takyiman market and look for the brass pan and cowrie shells.

I began to take more notice of my body; my definition was beginning to come back, and I was feeling much stronger, even though at times my stomach still pained me, but nonetheless I was pleased with my progress. My body and my legs were looking stronger, and my arms were regaining the definition they once had. I accomplished this by exercising after my baths, and in bed before I got up, and it was all paying off. I bought a photo album for my herbal collection.

Kofi and I went to the market, and I ran into a man who sold Nana Effa some *akommere* beads. Kofi and I greeted him, and during a conversation Kofi referred to me as *boroni*. Then he caught himself, and said: "He is not a *boroni*."

Sometime later in the market, I met another man who just happened to call me, and I turned around and approached him. He reminded me of a martial artist I knew back in America. He wanted to know if I was Ghanaian. He asked me where I was from, and I told him I was born in Trinidad but live in America. This man was a little lighter in complexion than I am, but not much. We chatted briefly and bonded. I commented that we were similar in color and he acknowledged it. This man did not assume I was a *boroni*. Most of all, he did not call me that name. He seemed to understand who I was. It made me very happy to see there are some people here who do not look at me that way. I respected this man's spirit and mind, and we shook hands as I was leaving.

The day finally came when I was going to Traa to see Ɔboɔkyerewa, but due to the rain, I was not sure if we would be able to make the trip. We were supposed to leave at 3:30 a.m. from Nana Effa's house. The day before, Mossi had told us to come here and have Nana pour libation before we traveled to Traa. The purpose, he said, was so that Asuo could talk to Ɔboɔkyerewa to assist in helping me. Mossi reassured me that my *ɔbosom* was coming, and that he would try to possess me at Ɔboɔkyerewa shrine. When the time came, I should also hire some drummers to assist in calling my *ɔbosom* so that Nana could catch him. Mossi also wanted to tell me a lot of things, but since I was there without an interpreter, the language became a serious barrier to our conversation.

Today I witnessed Mossi treating a baby who could not straighten his joints. This child had some birth defect with his joints. Two sacrifices had to be done for the child. Mossi killed the first one himself by holding the chicken down on its back with its wings folded around its legs, and the chicken eventually died. I sacrificed the second chicken by cutting its throat. Mossi said he wanted the blood to flow onto his mirror, and I allowed it to do so. He drank some of the blood three times and put some into the child's mouth three times as well. Finally, Mossi massaged some of the blood all over the child's arms, legs, and joints. All this was a part of me learning how to do work.

Ɔbookyerewa ɔbosomfoɔ visited Nana Dɔnkɔ, his teacher, yesterday and instructed me to bring a notebook to document what the ɔbosom would tell me at Traa.

Later that evening, Kofi came in and did not speak, but went straight to lie down. I was eating, and I asked him if he had been successful in acquiring the pan. Kofi said no, he had gone to three places but had no success. I reminded him that Nana Effa said he should go to Kumase since he had informed us he did not see any in the Takyiman market. He reminded me that Ɔbookyerewa ɔbosomfoɔɔ said we should come to Traa at 4:30 am. I said that was too early, since I had to do work at the Nana Effa shrine. I mentioned to him that a lot was said at Nana Effa and I had no one there to translate. By this time Amoako came by. I told him I felt caught in the middle of everything, having to accomplish both recommendations from Asubonten and Mossi of going to see Ɔbookyerewa. Both are important to me in being able to fulfill my training requirements. I expressed to him that Mossi also said after I return from Traa I should do immediately what Ɔbookyerewa advised me. If I put more effort into doing what only one recommends that I do, I will suffer, and either way, I will lose something. I said I know in this world life is full of choices and I heard Amoako laugh. Amoako agreed with me, but I hope Kofi understood me well.

June was almost finished and I had not heard anything from Apisha. This concerns me very much. Maybe she had written and the mail was taking longer to get here, or maybe she had not written to me. What was she doing? I needed to hear from her; I needed her support. This phase of my life that I was going through was the most important stage; either I would become a success or a failure. At night, when I was feeling sad, I would go outside and look up at the stars. I felt that I could almost touch them, it was so quiet and clear. When the difficulties in adjusting got to me, I would do this frequently and talk to the stars, telling them how difficult learning *akɔm* was for me here alone. At times, tears would flow from my eyes. I do not think anyone understood this more than I did.

# CHAPTER TWO

## 1989, THE WORK CONTINUES

The rain finally ceased, and we decided to go to Traa and consult Obɔɔkyerewa, even though Nana Dɔnkɔ claimed the *ɔbosom* would not come; he would say it rained on my mirror. Nana Effa, on the other hand, advised us to go, since he promised us that he would come and if we did not show up and went another time, they could fault us by saying we did not come as we had agreed. Therefore, we decided to go. We took the lead, and Nana Effa decided to come later. When we arrived at the shrine, we saw the effects of the heavy rainfall. The rock, which is so important for the *ɔbosom* divining, was flooded. They said the river was polluted due to the heavy rain. We were at the shrine for a while, and Kofi insisted that we leave at 2 p.m., but I said we should wait for Nana Effa.

It was taking too long, and Nana Effa had not arrived, so I said to Kofi, let's go. As we were on our way, we received news that Nana Effa was on his way, so we turned around and went back. Nana Effa arrived late because he had to pour libation for me as he had agreed. He also possessed his ɔbosom on the way, and the ɔbosom would not leave, even as others tried to send it away. His ɔbosom wanted to take off his clothes and *sebe* (talisman). Arriving possessed, it took Ɔbookyerewa *ɔbosomfoɔɔ* to make the *ɔbosom* or *suman* leave, but Nana was never fully himself because the *ɔbosom* had not completely left him. The *ɔbosom* came back again fully, and while running around (since the area was wet and slippery) he fell and hit his head on the ground, then someone broke a bottle of schnapps, and pandemonium broke out. I just stood by for a few seconds looking for the opportunity to go and assist Nana Effa. Things eventually calmed down, and Ɔbookyerewa *ɔbosomfoɔɔ* left and we all followed him back to the house. Nana Effa still kept possessing his *ɔbosom* on and off on the way. Ɔbookyerewa has two shrines, the main one near the river and the second one located at the house near the road. Ɔbookyerewa *ɔbosomfoɔɔ* suggested that we come back on Monday, and we left for home.

We informed Nana Dɔnkɔ what happened, and he said Ɔbookyerewa *ɔbosomfoɔɔ* did something wrong. He did not call the *ɔbosom* before he did the sacrifice to feed him. Nana repeated that the protocol is that you go early in the morning and call the *ɔbosom* to possess, then go back a second time and offer the *ɔbosom* the sacrifice, but the *ɔbosomfoɔɔ*, being young and lazy, did the sacrifice the first time so that he would not have to leave and come back a second time. Nana reiterated by doing so the *ɔbosom* would not come. The *ɔbosom* will not possess nor speak while eating, as one does not talk and eat at the same time.

Nana Effa came by this morning to greet me and inform me that we would go to one *ɔkɔmfoɔ* shrine. Nana and I left for his home, where he had clients waiting for him. He consulted with his *boatia*; first he would pour libation, then ring bells held in both hands. I tried on many occasions to record the *boatia* speaking but never succeeded until this time. This *boatia* is the senior of all his *mmoatia*. She is called Akua Bɔmmɔ; we consulted her for a while. What was interesting is that the spirit spoke in a high-pitched voice, like a whistle, and in proverbs and metaphors. Even more interesting is that the voice of the *boatia* came from within the shrine. At first, I thought Nana was throwing his voice like a ventriloquist, but after scrutinizing, I could not tell if that was the case. I guess my suspicion comes from living in America, where this form of entertainment exists. It was difficult at first to believe that this was not a parlor show and that such a thing could really exist. Now, I began to wonder if the ventriloquist is a western parody of this African reality. I was both enthralled and inspired by our spiritual reality and how it benefits us. Songs were sung, but not just randomly. Something in the conversation or what someone said led to a song that referenced and revealed what was said. Unfortunately, I could not understand most of the conversation between Nana and Akua Bɔmmɔ. Nana's wife served as the *ɔkyeame*, and she helped me a lot. From time to time, Nana would refer to the *boatia* by saying *Mullah*. There were times Nana did not understand what Akua Bɔmmɔ said and would ask for her to repeat herself. Bɔmmɔ told me my things are coming and I should try to prepare myself for their arrival. I interpreted this to mean she was referring to my *ɔbosom* and I should not worry too much about if I have enough money for things like sacrifice, eggs and wine for a drink. She uplifted my spirits by saying when my *ɔbosom* comes he would tell me what he likes and doesn't like. Bɔmmɔ stressed that I should not be late in my preparations, the thing is coming, and not to be afraid.

Following Akua Bɔmmɔ's departure, there was a female *ɔkɔmfoɔ* who came to Nana for help. He was originally to go to her town, but she ended up staying a few days at Nana's home. Due to my situation, he could not immediately go to accompany her and help her possess her spirit. I think her spirit is called Atia Kwaku. She possessed her spirit, and Nana stood in as her ɔkyeame and told me Atia Kwaku told him to bring a chicken, eggs, and gun powder for sacrifice because Atia Kwaku wanted to do something for him, but they should wait until the nighttime. He also told him that he should get a plant called *nsamensa* and send it to Tanɔ to make a *kahyire* (a pad) for him to carry his *ɔbosom*. I recall many times I had to ask Nana Dɔnkɔ for his pad for Nana to use when carrying Asuotipa. Since Nana's English was not that clear I got a piecemeal understanding of what he was translating to me. This plant is pounded to sit the *ɔbosom* upon, and if he was going somewhere he would pour libation so that no one would trouble him. Atia Kwaku also told Nana that I should get a drink and go see Tanɔ (Taa Mensa) and offer a drink before I left to go back home. Nana riddled if I come to a house, but I do not see the house number, how can I be sure I am entering the right house? I was cautioned that when I go back home, they will see that I am very strong, and they will become jealous and challenge me. Part of the problem is that they will see that I am different from them. A song of praise was sung to this spirit. *Boa me Atia Kwaku boame*, which means "help me Atia Kwaku help me." Atia Kwaku told me to do a special ritual with a padlock and a duck for sacrifice. I am to write down all that worries me, close the lock and put it at a place on the ground where rituals occur called *apaso* and where the *abosom* alight, and the last sheep that I sacrifice, take the head, the neck, and legs as well. This is difficult for me to translate right now and, hopefully, I will get it done in the future and offer the sacrifice; I am not to tell anyone what I have done.

Nana Effa clarified and said to me we do not do that, but if you are my wife and you see that this is the custom people do, you have to say it because if you do not and you get ill with something like a stomach problem, then it is your fault. Here Nana seems to hint at an *ɔkɔmfoɔ* dilemma. He has to say it even though he knows we do not do that kind of spiritual work.

Atia Kwaku told them that he was afraid of me and there was laughter. I asked if it was because of the way that I looked. They said no, he is afraid of me because of where I came from. She is afraid of that person. They explained that she means I will come and catch her. I laughed and said no! I wondered if this is a historical memory of slavery when the Europeans were enslaving our people.

Atia went on to say if you dislike a situation where people are crowded and they want a seat (to get ahead), and they push to move you over, you do not like that because you can't get a seat. The spirit was revealing its insight into human nature and what holds them back from progress was revealed to me again by saying if a person wants to say something and you laugh at him or her, they will not speak. Atia Kwaku advised that I should keep some things in my mind and not say everything, for someone whom I depend on may not say it correctly to others and try to confuse me. Overall, I should obey the *abosom* and not worry about things. It is because of them I was here so I should not worry. They will look after me. When you are at work, you have to listen to your supervisor to do your work properly, not just to anyone here and there. I was enlightened about the character of this *ɔkɔmfoɔ*. Atia said if you have an *ɔbosom* and someone comes to you for help, they do not call the *ɔbosom*'s name but yours, so you have to be careful and not spoil your name so that people who want to come to the *ɔbosom* avoid you because of your bad name. If you spoil your name, you spoil your *ɔbosom*. If I know that you have come to learn something, you have to obey the instructions to learn it well, so when you go no one can challenge you.

The spirit on the ɔkɔmfoɔ reminded me of Mossi; it was also left-handed. Perhaps it was a family member. The difference was that, unlike Mossi, this spirit liked Akpeteshie and beer. The spirit reiterated, too, that my ɔbosom was coming soon, and when I got back home other akɔmfoɔ would be jealous of what I had because it was so different, and would challenge me. The ɔbosom said that if Kofi was around, he would instruct him to be more supportive of what I was doing.

After the ɔbosom left, we prepared for the journey to see the ɔbosom Boɔ Yaw. The ɔkɔmfoɔ was called Nana Kwadwo Bɛkoe. Now my life would take a major turn. He was the same ɔkɔmfoɔ who had wanted to see me possess my ɔbosom when he first saw me at Taa Mensa, and he also visited me in the hospital and put some cedis in my hand. I will never forget his kindness.

When we arrived at TaaKofiano, the town of the ɔkɔmfoɔ, we went and greeted him, and he welcomed us. We had some time before they called the ɔbosom on him, and we waited in the yard. Nana Effa went to the drums and was calling me on the *Ntumpane*, the talking drum, but I did not understand the drum language. He kept trying to get my attention, but to no avail. He would drum out my name and say *Kwaku Sakyi*. He drummed out saying, *me fre wo wante*, which means "I call you, but you do not understand." I was failing my lessons miserably. This was all part of my training, but Nana always had a good disposition and a sense of humor and would laugh and repeat for me to hear. He then would say in English, "I am calling you." Then he would play some *Ayan* text and repeat the Twi. The more I listened, I found my ears becoming more in tune with the drum language.

The ɔkɔmfoɔ called us in for a libation. It is all on tape. I presented him with a drink, and he poured libation to his ɔbosom for me, mentioning my place of birth, who I am training under, and so forth. The shrine room was crowded. No women were allowed in the shrine room because it is taboo for them to be there. After the ɔbosom was invoked and came, he greeted and began to sing a series of songs one after another. He used a mirror for seeing and copiously applied *hyire*/clay on his face. It was absolutely incredible to listen to the sweetness of his voice and the empathy. When speaking, this ɔbosom spoke different from the Tanɔ ɔbosom. To my surprise, the ɔbosom spoke in long phrases, which are not the domain of Atanɔ ɔbosom. The ɔkyeame is incredible with his retention skills. I also came to understand that the ɔbosom spoke in the dialect of the Ivory Coast. Like Nana Effa, I surmised he was also trained there. This is a popular dialect for those trained in the Ivory Coast. I hear the same in Kofi Asante.

The ɔbosom took care of others before it was my turn. Abena ɔkɔmfoɔ, who was also training along with me by Nana Dɔnkɔ, was there to solve some problems she had with her ɔbosom. The apprentice ɔkɔmfoɔ had serious problems with her family, and the ɔbosom and Boɔ Yaw spent a long time consulting with her. At one point, the ɔbosom sang a tribute song to Akua Bɔmmɔ. To me, this links and unifies everything in *akɔm* as one.

The ɔbosom told me that my ɔbosom sometimes wanted to come, and sometimes he did not. I said yes. He told me that the person who directed me to come to Takyiman, when I get back home, I should thank him. He said the ɔbosom loved me from birth before he came to me. He mentioned it was not the old ɔbosom of my town that loved me and wanted me, but a new one that has come to me. Through the ɔkyeame, he said that my parents thought maybe I had done something wrong, and that is why I look worried, but he said it was not so. It was because a new *ɔbosom* was coming to me. When I was young, I went places with my parents. He said I have two sisters; I said yes, but one died. The *ɔbosom* exclaimed, Oo yoo! and thanked me and left. Then the *ɔbosom* came back, and said he went to my town and began to describe my home, books, and the place where I read. He said my mother did not know that an *ɔbosom* had come to me and therefore she was afraid of what I was doing. I said yes again. He asked me that when the *ɔbosom* came I was searching for my father. This question I did not understand. The *ɔbosom* asked more questions, but I will not go into details, since I have it all recorded and I was trying to save paper. He said I worried too much, day and night, about my *ɔbosom* and I should not. He mentioned again that the *ɔbosom* I possessed was not the *ɔbosom* of my place or family, and this *ɔbosom* was for me. When I possessed the *ɔbosom*, my family thought I did something wrong, and it worried me. I was told to come back.

After the *ɔbosom* was finished, he left. Everyone began to socialize and chat. Then Nana Effa and Boɔ Yaw *ɔkɔmfoɔ* got into a dispute over where I was staying. The *ɔkyeame* told me the *ɔbosom* said if I listen to my *ɔbosom* and I go to my town, I will prosper. He also said I want to know everything about the *ɔbosom* now and when I go to sleep, I think a lot about it. The *ɔkɔmfoɔ* pulled me aside and questioned me as to where I was staying. I told him at Nana Dɔnkɔ's house. He then said to me, Nana Effa lied to him. I then said I stayed with Nana Effa. Next, the *ɔkɔmfoɔ* asked him how old I was? I told him and he said he would like to help me, but because Nana Effa lied to him, he could not. I begged him to help me and said I could not do this alone. He then agreed to help me. Not too long after that, they got into it again. The *ɔkɔmfoɔ* again came over to me and inquired as to where I was staying. I told him like before, and added I visited Nana Effa almost every day. He asked who I had come to see? I said Nana Effa. They continued where they left off. I asked Kwabena what they were arguing about; he said the *ɔkɔmfoɔ* accused Nana Effa of lying to him. I then told Kwabena to beg the *ɔkɔmfoɔ* to forgive Nana Effa and help me, and he said he would.

I awoke very early in the morning to prepare and go to Traa to consult Ɔbookyerewa. There was no sign of rain, so things looked good so far. Kwame Adu, one of our brothers, planned to take us in his taxi, Nana Effa, his *ɔkyeame* Kwabena, Kofi, and I. We arrived at Traa and went to the shrine and found out that the *ɔbosomfoɔ* would not possess the *ɔbosom* until a sacrifice was done at Tanɔboase three miles away. After much discussion, Kofi and I decided to return home, while Nana Effa and his *ɔkyeame* stayed. On the way home, Kofi and I talked about my challenges that were keeping me from seeing the *ɔbosom*. When we arrived, Nana Dɔnkɔ was surprised to see us back so soon. Kofi told him what had happened, and I got the opportunity to get more clarification on what had taken place. Kofi told me that Nana Akumsa said Ɔbookyerewa asked for a knife and ram. Upon hearing this, the *ɔbosomfoɔ* should have begged the *ɔbosom*, for this was a sign that the *ɔbosom* wanted to kill anyone who offended him. It looks like the *ɔbosomfoɔ* still needs guidance.

As I was relaxing in my room and writing the day's events in my journal, Kofi came by to speak with me. He told me Nana Dɔnkɔ said not to worry, they could still do everything for me, even though I had not consulted with Ɔbookyerewa. I reflected that this was the third time I had tried to see the *ɔbosom* and always something happened that stopped me from seeing him. I could see curiosity was getting the best of Kofi. He was subtly trying to see what I was writing in my journal. I have on two occasions asked Kofi to write the two names of the herbs I collected and the songs I have recorded, but he has not given me anything as yet.

Amoa, the girlfriend of Kwabena, surprised me when she came by to instruct me on Twi. She was accompanied by Yaa and her friend Richard; they came in to see what I was doing and then left.

I returned as I had been instructed to continue my consultation with Bɔɔ Yaw. Kofi accompanied me this time. Nana Bɛkoe attempted to possess his ɔbosom, but he did not come, so we spent time listening to him sing songs and explain them. We also had time to snack on some food.

The ɔbosom was called a second time, and this time he did come. The ɔbosom said since I have come my ɔbosom has not been possessing on me. I said yes. He asked me where I went to train before I came to Takyiman. I told him I was initiated by Nana Oparebea. The ɔkyeame wanted some clarification on who she was, and we told him she was from Larteh. The ɔbosom asked me if I had informed her that I was coming here. I said no, but I am sure she knows. He said that Nana Oparebea is very serious. Every time she pours libation, she asks her ɔbosom to stop me so that I will fail and have to come back to her. I was still amazed by the retention of the ɔkyeame. The ɔbosom spoke for about three to four minutes nonstop, and the ɔkyeame patiently listened. The ɔbosom gave me a ritual to do that consisted of a white chicken, cowrie shell, and a bath. I should get a plant, whose name I shall not mention, that shakes in a river while others do not. When I am finished with this ritual, my ɔbosom will come big. The ɔbosom sang songs for about half an hour.

*The night before, I had a dream that I was at a riverside and the Asubonten shrine was there. There was a river that bends and seems to have concrete blocks with sharp pronounced grooves that separated these blocks. Water at times would flow along with the blocks following its course like a tide when it comes in.*

*The next dream was about a woman who fell and injured her back. I was wearing dark-colored socks. I was helping her into a room when I, too, fell and injured my back.*

Kofi and I went to a riverside to fetch water for my bath and pick up any plants that were found to be trembling near the riverbank. But first I offered an egg to the river and prayed for its help. I asked that those who stood in my way would desist and be stopped with their hands bound, so that my ɔbosom would possess me no matter what, all in accordance with what the ɔbosom Boɔ Yaw specified.

There was a young woman here in Nana Dɔnkɔ's compound that bleaches her skin every single day. I know, of course, why someone would do such a thing to their beautiful black skin, but I wanted to hear it for myself, so I asked Kofi why she did it. Kofi said it was because she wanted to be white, and added further, look at her sister; she has done the same thing. I sarcastically responded, is she all right? You will see people here with Jheri curls, just like they do in America. They are all suffering from their tragic colonial past. I do worry about the state and affairs of black people everywhere.

I began bathing in the *aduro* with a chicken tied to my leg, as Boɔ Yaw recommended. The plant I found trembling near the riverbank and whose name I cannot mention was also used in the *aduro*. A white piece of cloth with a cowrie shell strung through it was tied around the chicken's neck, and another piece of cloth was tied to one of my legs and the chicken. I bathed with this chicken and slept with it for three days.

I took some time to visit Nana Effa, who was collecting *aduro*. One in particular is called *Adade dua* (this plant can hold onto and break a cutlass if care is not taken when collecting its bark), mahogany, Kyikye (a bark that bleeds), *Humatre* (a spiritual vine), any root on a path frequently traveled by people that stub their toes on as they walk by, and any root that travels or crosses a path. Back at Nana, I chopped up the *Humatre*, mahogany, and *Adade dua*. These would be cooked the next day for *mɔtɔ*. The night before, Maame, accompanied by Yaa, one of Nana Effa's daughters, visited me and sang shrine songs for me, which I had the privilege of recording. Yaa was too shy to sing along.

The next day, I went to Nana Effa and finished what we had started the day before. We burned the roots, stems, and leaves of the plants we had collected. I asked Nana to record the names for me on tape. Some new plants were added to my list of herbs.

I recalled that Nana Dɔnkɔ had waited for me to come and sing songs, but due to the heavy rain, I never went. Thinking back now, I should have gone. The *mɔtɔ* was overcooked and did not turn out right. Normally it is very black, but when overcooked it turns out looking gray and ashy. Nana Effa borrowed my tape recorder. I just hoped I had enough batteries to last, since I had one month to go and only had four left.

I was still somewhat concerned about it and still had not gotten used to people here talking about me. Maybe they were just curious or found me different. I noticed if I did not eat there was talk. I guess we just needed to get used to each other. I was even a topic of conversation to Maame.

Whenever I was around Nana Dɔnkɔ and Nana Effa, I enjoyed myself and learned a lot about the culture and people. I observed that there was an abundance of women around the compound and the men were often absent. The women took care of the children, it seemed by themselves, without the presence of a man. The *Akan* did not seem to publicly show a lot of affection. That is not to say I have not seen anyone displaying outward affection for each other; yes, some do, but I really did not see a lot of public displays of affection, or hugging and kissing like back home. Ghanaians are very private when it comes to the outward display of kissing and the sort. I noticed Nana Dɔnkɔ showing affection for children, but then again, he is an exceptional man.

An old man was caught by Kofi and Kwabena for stealing plantain, yam, and cassava from Kofi's farm yesterday. It is said that they beat this old man something terrible, and Amoako had to go to the police station to get Kwabena released from jail. The problem arose after the old man was beaten. He was taken to the police station by Kwabena. During the investigation, Kwabena was arrested for excessive abuse of the old man. To compound things, the old man denied stealing anything from the farm. When Kofi heard what had happened to Kwabena, he got scared and did not go to Kwabena's aid. I said to Kofi, if you are a man, you should go and face the consequences. Even his girlfriend, who was there, said he should go. Kofi would not, so this is how come our elder brother Amoako went to the station and got Kwabena's release. Sometime late that night, I heard Kwabena crying out of shame like a baby. He said the police slapped him for what he and Kofi did to the old man.

Nana Akumsa's son Nana Yaw Manu and I talked about my situation and my concern about what Nana Oparebea could do to me for leaving her shrine. He is an *ɔkɔmfoɔ* from Nkoransa and possesses *nsuman*. He was amused that I was concerned about her being a threat to me. He described her as a big woman who jumped around when possessed by her *ɔbosom*. He said he did not mean to brag, but he had more *aduro* than she did, and he planned to give me a *suman* that would protect me against enemies. He asked if I would like cutlass and gun *aduro*.

I have finished my three-day bath. I did the ritual and set the bird free. I went to an intersection, presented the bird to the four corners, and said I wanted protection, prosperity, good health, and wished no harm would come to me, and I asked my *ɔbosom* to come strong and that no one would stop my *ɔbosom*. Then I released the chicken.

As a training *ɔkɔmfoɔ*, I had to be around the shrine all the time, and I had the opportunity to see and hear a lot of things. A certain woman came to see Nana Dɔnkɔ for help. It appeared that Ɔboɔkyerewa caught her for cheating on her husband. Even though the *ɔbosom* caught her, she refused to confess. I guess things must have gotten very serious for her, and now she was here to see Nana. When I arrived at the scene, she had already thrown three eggs and now she was on her knees, begging Ɔboɔkyerewa to go and lean or rest on his wall. She got up and threw another egg, and it too did not break, which meant he did not accept her apology. The children and adults were all talking, making noises at what had just happened. Some were laughing in disbelief that the egg did not crack. Eventually, some semblance of order was restored, and she threw another egg, and this one you could hear the sound of it splitting when an egg is cracked, but it just sealed itself back together again. I, too, found this incredulous. Nana Dɔnkɔ, seeing the seriousness of this life and death situation, took the sixth egg and spoke to the *ɔbosom* with prayers. After a surreal time when it seemed like time stood still, he threw the egg and it landed with a thump and left an indentation that looked like a crater on the moon in the hard Ghana red clay. I was in disbelief. This egg, when it was looked at, did not have a blemish on it. There was a hushed silence, because we all knew this was a bad sign. The great *ɔbosom* Ɔboɔkyerewa did not forgive. Nana Dɔnkɔ returned the money, drink, and chicken to the woman, and she had no choice but to return home and accept her fate. This *ɔbosom* is serious. Everyone fears him, even me.

Last night, the sisters of Nana Dɔnkɔ, Nana Akumsa, Nana Afua Asubonten, who, by the way, is not a *ɔkɔmfoɔ* but knows a lot about the practice of *akɔm* and *aduro*, along with Nana Dɔnkɔ, were teaching me shrine songs. Most of the songs were sung by Nana Afua Asubonten, which I had the honor of recording for posterity.

*This dream took place on July 2: I went back home and was so excited about telling everyone how* Nana Dɔnkɔ *helped me. I spoke about how he taught me about herbs and their preparation, all about the abosom/ɔbosom and what a great man he is.*

*In the next dream, I was talking to Nana Korantemaa (who lives in Washington D.C.), who was lying on the floor. There were other akɔmfoɔ, mostly women. In fact, I do not recall any men being there. I spoke about the wonders of the abosom in* Takyiman *and what they have done. I spoke mainly of* Nana Effa. *But she did not believe me. She said they were just magician tricks that pass off as abosom working wonders.*

Preparations were underway. The day before, Nana Dɔnkɔ and Nana Kofi Owusu, Mframa ɔbosomfoɔ, had finished putting the cowrie shells and bells on my *abomu*, the chest belt that I will wear when possessing the ɔbosom. Another *aduro* bath was prepared for me; I presented gin and chicken to Asubonten, and he accepted the bird. I told Nana Dɔnkɔ about a dream I had.

*I was in* Takyiman *outside looking up at the sky and I saw what appeared to be a constellation. This constellation appeared to be a huge black cat with fangs and claws. The cat would show its fangs and claws and retract the claws, then show them again.*

I asked Nana Akumsa to interpret the dream for me, and she said the cat represented a witch or enemy who could turn into a cat. When it showed its fangs and claws, it wanted to harm me, possibly kill me. The retraction or withdrawing of the fangs and claws showed its passive state, because it was unable to harm me or act. Its stationary position meant it was unable to carry out its attack.

Nana said if it moved to harm me, my ɔbosom would kill it, because of the *aduro* baths I have been taking. No one can harm or throw bad *aduro* at me. I became curious about how long the *aduro* would last in my body and put the question to Nana Dɔnkɔ if I would have to periodically renew the *aduro* by taking more baths? Nana Dɔnkɔ said it would last as long as I live.

*I had a dream about* Nana Dɔnkɔ's ɔbosom Asubonten and a bent river.

I wanted to know what the relationship was between the two (i.e., Asuo and the bent river). Nana said it was about the *ɔbosom* Ɔboɔkyerewa. He elaborated that Asubonten and Ɔboɔkyerewa are the same; they are alike. If you possess Ɔboɔkyerewa, you can possess Asubonten and vice versa.

A few days ago, Nana Effa told me his *ɔbosom* Asuotipa is the son of Asubonten and comes from the Ivory Coast. He informed me that the Tanɔ river runs through the Ivory Coast, which I did not know.

I was concerned that Apisha had not written to me. Why? My mind told me not to worry. All this could be the workings of people who wanted me to fail, and all their machination could be a result of the bad dreams. I guess when you want someone to fail, you use all available avenues at your disposal.

I do not know if I wrote a follow-up about why Nana Effa could not go to Tanɔboase. A certain tree near his shrine had to be cut down, and he had to supervise the cutting. After this tree was notched and about to fall, it almost hit his shrine house. I felt the person who was cutting it did not estimate or calculate properly the angle of the fall. The tree was supposed to fall in the opposite direction. The cutter said it did not fall as planned, and if the winds were strong, it would have hit the shrine house. I guess we should thank the *ɔbosom* it did not, but it came so close I thought it had hit the shrine house.

Another time Nana was to go to Tanɔboase, and on the way, at Nkoransa, the car stopped and would not start back up, but when Nana got out of the car, the car started. When he got back in, it stopped, so Nana decided to return home. Nana went on to say the *ɔbosom* would not let him go because of me.

This morning I visited Nana Effa and he told me he had purchased some of the items I needed for the *suman*, along with a cock. I noticed he had a carrying bag from which he took out a beautiful kente cloth to show to me. I have been seeing this cloth for almost a month. He told me the man from whom he got the cloth was coming to collect 6,000 cedis and would like me to help him. He thought he would have the money, but the people he sold plantain to did not pay him. He said when they give him the money, he would pay me back. Nana also said someone owed him 70,000 cedis and agreed to pay, but changed the date so Nana would like me to give him the money. Even though I felt what money I had remaining was for the shrine work, I had to do what I could to help Nana. I was also expecting to get back the money Kofi owed me, so I decided to lend the money to Nana.

My money was getting short, and things were looking a little expensive, so I had to be careful. I had to itemize what I would have to spend for transportation, not only for myself but for others who were accompanying me.

The pulse of life here was not that different, and yet at the same time very different from back in the States. Someone would take a bicycle that did not belong to them and go away for hours or until the next day, leaving the owner to travel by foot. For example, when Kofi and I traveled to TaaKofiano to visit Boɔ Yaw *ɔkɔmfoɔ,* Nana Effa left his bicycle there, and Kofi was using it. A boy who saw the bike decided to take it and go who knows where without asking. Luckily, Kofi saw him just in time to stop him. I have come to the realization that cameras, radios, and cassette players are mesmerizing to the people here. I recall an experience with my camera and cassette player. People would just want to hold them to the point of taking them out of my hand to touch them. At times, it seems like a tug-of-war with them, with me always surrendering to them for a while. Then as I was about to leave, they would hand it back to me.

At Nana Effa's *Aburoo*/corn festival, one man wanted to hold it, listening to the drumming I had recorded. His friend teased him, saying you just listen to it and you want to hear it again. I was about to leave, and he insisted he would bring it to me later. I told him no, it goes where I go.

I overheard a conversation about one of the *ɔkɔmfoɔ* Nana Dɔnkɔ trained and graduated. He went to his town and invited some local a*kɔmfoɔ* to his festival. One *ɔkɔmfoɔ* in particular came to Nana Dɔnkɔ and asked if he had given this *ɔkɔmfoɔ aduro*. Nana said no, so this *ɔkɔmfoɔ* threw bad *aduro* at the newly graduated *ɔkɔmfoɔ* and this *ɔkɔmfoɔ* fell and had to come and beg Nana Dɔnkɔ's forgiveness, for the young *ɔkɔmfoɔ*'s *ɔbosom* almost killed him. This is what they call *akyingye*.

The night of July 3, we celebrated the *Kwabena Adapa* the same way Nana Effa celebrated his *Aburoo Adapa*, but the only difference was the support given. At Nana Dɔnkɔ's, the elders were all in attendance. I attempted to record the event, but my pause button was on, and I missed all the beautiful songs they sang. I managed to see my error and recorded the drumming at the tail end. Asuotipa came on Nana Effa all the while.

During this this *akɔm* I was in an extremely depressed state since I was not possessing my *ɔbosom*. Asuo possessed Nana Effa for quite some time and was about to leave. It is not too often that Asuotipa takes the center stage at the Big House, and that night he did. I was used to seeing Asubonten possess Nana Asantewaa here at the Big House with the elders singing for him. Now, it was Asuotipa. They sang songs to him and he brought forth a song that changed everything. The drummers began to drum, and the women were more inspired by the song. When the *Ntumpane* came on the scene, the *akɔm* was sealed and anything could happen. One has to be there to know what I mean. This was truly uplifting. You cannot help yourself, but feel you are in a place where you can experience an altered state of consciousness, but nothing was happening to me. Abena *ɔkɔmfoɔ*, who had difficulties possessing, possessed her *ɔbosom*, but not me, and I began to lose hope and thought of giving up and going home. What a sad, depressed state I was in. I was lost in my self-pity. As Asuo was about to go, he called me. I thought perhaps he took pity on me; I do not know. He asked me to dance and as I danced, I began to feel my *ɔbosom* descend upon me very strongly, like the first time I ever felt him, and he possessed me.

From this possession resulted bruises on my body, I must have fallen or was rolling on the ground while in possession. As I listen to the tape, I can hear myself screaming and shouting. I must say I am happy nonetheless, because before I was not possessing and now I AM. I recall after I came through, I did not feel balanced due to my *ɔbosom* staying on me off and on for a while. It would not leave me completely. He would partially go and come back for a while to the point I needed help and support in walking. After the event was over, we all prepared ourselves for sleep and went to bed, for tomorrow would be *Kwabena*, and the festivities would continue.

This morning Asubonten was to be carried by Nana Dɔnkɔ. Nana, as the male *ɔbosomfoɔ*, and his maternal niece Nana Asantewaa, as female *ɔkɔmfoɔ*, shared the *ɔbosom* Asubonten. I found the family relationship with the *ɔbosom* to be fascinating. I had never heard of nor seen such relationship between family members male and female *akɔmfoɔ* back home in the United States.

Now came the time for ɔbosomfoɔ Nana Dɔnkɔ to carry Asubonten, but before that took place, there was introductory drumming by a family member who is a master drummer. Ɔkyeame Nana Kofi Boɔ, who is the brother of Nana Asantewaa and of course Nana Dɔnkɔ's maternal nephew, poured libation before Nana Dɔnkɔ carried Asubonten. During libation he introduced himself to Asubonten and mentioned other *abosom*. He prayed for the blessing of all and the education of the children, and mentioned Kwaku Ɔbookyerewa. Someone presented two chickens and a drink to him. The *ɔkyeame* can do everything with the shrine except possess it or kill its sacrifice. This is the sole prerogative of the *ɔbosomfoɔ*. When it was time to carry Asubonten, the elder continued to drum to invoke and stimulate Asubonten to come. His drumming was like talking, and he was accompanied by singers. The drummer spoke the sacred text language to invoke. I became more familiar with the text pattern.

After Asubonten arrived, the women sang welcome songs and praises. The *ɔbosom* on Nana Dɔnkɔ slapped the pan to signify his arrival. After a while, the *ɔbosom* left, and the *ɔkyeame* poured libation again, only this time more fervently, and mentioned that the old man (an affectionate name for Nana Dɔnkɔ) was sick; he mentioned Ɔbookyerewa, Amoa Kwame, and others. When he finished, the drummer started up again to invoke Asubonten to return. This time, the drumming was hot, and Asubonten was not disappointing.

Asubonten spoke to me, saying sometimes I am happy then sad, but I should not give up hope; they can help me. I have all of this on tape, so I will not go into details. He did instruct me to go and see Ɔbookyerewa tomorrow, but told me first I should take three eggs and put them on my pillow and sleep, and in the morning give them to him. I should ask my ɔbosom to tell me everything. Asubonten said everything would be all right. I should be strong and stand firm and do not listen to others, and they will help me when I get back home to get money so that I can keep coming back.

Kofi told me that the elder drummer knew a lot of secrets and folktales, and one day I asked the elder if he would share some of the traditional lore with me, but the elder declined. I know I am a stranger and he does not know my intent; am I coming here to contribute to the world of akɔm or just to take what I want like others and leave?

Asubonten later possessed on Nana Asantewaa, and the drumming, singing, and dancing ensued. The akɔm drumming was intense, and you got a sense that this was the old akɔm tradition. Asubonten would periodically call me out to come and dance with him. He encouraged me as I danced and told me not to worry about them laughing at me. He told me when I got back home, I should listen to my recording of the music and dance. The trainee Abena possessed her ɔbosom, but it did not stay long on her. The drummers took an interlude, and this allowed the women singers to display their magnificent singing skills along with Asubonten. The songs sung by the younger generation were punctuated by the distinct voices of Nana Akumsa and the elders. One can only imagine what Nana Akumsa was like in her youth. This elder is incredible, and I am so blessed to have her as one of my teachers. The drummers came back after their break refreshed and invigorated. Nana Asantewaa, later on, possessed another ɔbosom Ɔbookyerewaa, the very same one I have been trying to see. He also called me out to dance and gave me one of his clubs to dance with, and that is when I possessed my ɔbosom again.

I possessed my ɔbosom like I did last night. After the possession, I did not see any evidence of falling and rolling all over the ground; however, I felt sore with more bruises on my body, so I guess I must have fallen again. I was told that Nana Effa during my possession tried to control the ɔbosom, but the ɔbosom stopped him. The ɔbosom must have possessed on me for a while, because after it left, I noticed I was wearing a *doso*. Still, it took a while to recuperate from my possession, and the *akɔm* was still strong in attendance. After some time Asubonten possessed again and stayed a little while and then left.

Last night Nana Akumsa gave me *aduro* to wash my eyes and face. I used it three times during the night, but this morning I noticed the *aduro* had spoiled.

When I visited Nana Effa, he displayed Kofi Asante, one of his *mmoatia*. He is of all the spirits Nana possesses the one who comes most frequently. Akosua, Nana's wife, was leading the song calling Kofi Asante. In between you can hear Maame's voice bringing up the rear, taking the lead occasionally. Kofi Asante is an intense spirit who stutters, loves to sing, and sings most beautifully, as I have captured on tape. He loves to drink and smoke but do not underestimate him. He is packed with knowledge, wisdom, and proverbs. From what little I understand, he seems to speak Asante Twi and the dialect from the Ivory Coast, which they call Gyama. When Nana possesses this *boatia* he never wants to leave. He will keep you busy and involved. He can be impatient and, at times, harsh. His repertoire of songs is vast and pulsating, hypnotic and deep, and if you do not sing them correctly, he would insult you or stop you and correctly sing the song as it should. If you must play with Asante, you had better come prepared with a profound anthology of songs. If you listen to his songs, you will learn a lot about human nature, life, and the world of spirits.

Kofi Asante brought forth an issue I had with people and asked me to say my point. I said that I was disturbed by the people talking behind my back. I know I am someone they have never seen before, and some people wondered if I came to steal their powers and go. He looked at his mirror, laughed, and said *me wie* (I am finished).

Kofi Asante told me I would need to feed the drummers who would drum for me when he was catching my ɔbosom. He also informed me that when my ɔbosom came to me I was not even born yet. It came to me before I was born. I want to see something, but I come with only my naked eyes, not my spiritual eyes. Kofi Asante, slapping his chest, reaffirmed that I have nothing, only my eyes. One of Nana Effa's assistants said to Asante, when you talk, why don't you be patient? Asante said to him, I am Asante, and this is how I talk, and insulted him. Next, Asante said he wanted to show me something, and after I have seen it, I would have seen everything. He said he will give me something, and when I depart for home, I should take good care of it, otherwise it will kill me. If I do not take proper care of it and it kills me, it is I who has killed myself. So, I must take proper care of it.

On Monday, Nana Akumsa gave me herbal *aduro* to wash my eyes and face, along with herbs to make *mpesempese*. Yesterday, Nana Akumsa, Kofi, and I traveled to Traa to consult Ɔbookyerewa, and on the way, we heard rumors about an incident involving the ɔhene of that town. It concerned something about him being in a fight. As we arrived, we found out there was some truth to the rumor that the ɔhene of Traa had been beaten. We were informed that Ɔboɔkyerewa would not work until the case was settled. The story was that one of the ɔhene's children was playing and something happened, and as a result was beaten by another child. The ɔhene went to this child's house to make a complaint. As a result, he got into an argument with the other parent who faulted the ɔhene for coming to his house. The man told the ɔhene he should have stayed at his house and sent for the parties involved to settle the case. The argument became so heated, and the man hit the ɔhene with a stick and the ɔhene had to be taken to the hospital. In trying to make peace, a sacrifice was done, and the meat was eaten. But somehow the case was still not settled, so they sent the case to one particular ɔhene in Takyiman for help.

This ɔhene in Takyiman is the one who installed the Traa ɔhene. The protocol was breached, and the senior ɔhene asked why he had not been consulted before anything was done. As a result, the sacrifice that was done, and the meat eaten, should have been given to the Takyiman ɔhene to solve the case. He therefore told them to go and solve their own problem. So now as we arrived there was an impasse. So many people who have been coming here were fed up with the people of Traa. Knowing this would get nowhere, others went and begged the Takyiman ɔhene to come and solve the case, and he agreed to it and came. Each party had its own version of what happened. The parent did not want to speak because their witness was not available. Ɔboɔkyerewa became fed up and left, and nothing could be done, so we left the shrine area. Kofi informed me that they would try to solve it and finish everything on Friday, and we should try again on Saturday. Back at Ɔboɔkyerewa's shrine house on the main road, we deliberated on what had taken place by the river.

A thief caught by Ɔboɔkyerewa came by to give a chicken, sheep, and drink to be released from the power of the ɔbosom. The ɔbosomfooɔ Nana Kofi Asamadu had to attend to this matter. After he finished, he continued with his conversation between himself and Nana Akumsa. The ɔbosomfoɔ told Nana Akumsa that this problem could have been solved easily. In fact, he is the one who gave us the version of what took place, which I documented earlier, but not the events at the trial. The ɔbosomfoɔ said that the people want his downfall, by causing confusion and delays so that the problems are not readily solved. If Ɔboɔkyerewa does not work, the ɔbosomfoɔ cannot make money to service the ɔbosom. In fact, he is the one who is supposed to be the ɔhene of Traa, but because of his youth, the others are acting in proxy until he matures.

After we arrived back home, I went to Nana Effa with the hope he could shed some light on things for me. He attempted to call Bɔmmɔ, but she sent Kofi Asante on her behalf since she was busy. Asante asked what was worrying me. I told him about my sense of people talking behind my back. He agreed that they were, which was confirmed by suspicion. He went on to say some people thought I was crazy and that I came here to take their things (power) and go, but Asante said he knows the truth. My ɔbosom was coming, he said, but he needs good drummers to call him, otherwise, he will not come. He is very powerful and will speak Twi when he comes and I should not worry about the money that was being spent, but he did caution that after my ɔbosom arrives, I would spend more money than I have so far. Asante indicated he wanted to give me something and I should take very good care of it and not to lose it. He brought forth batteries for me. He also brought cigarettes; all this I had on tape.

*My pen is dying. I had two dreams two nights ago. The first happened after I returned from Ɔboɔkyerewa. I dreamed that Ɔboɔkyerewa was disappointed about the people around him, because of them bringing confusion and not always doing what is right. Ɔbookyerewa gave me a part of the inside of a black chicken. I am not certain of the chicken part he gave to me, but somehow the intestines come to mind.*

*The next dream was about* Nana Dɔnkɔ. *He was sitting on a bench. When I saw him, he was facing 45 degrees looking toward his right, far off into the distance with his head held high. He was well dressed in what appeared to be dark brown pattern stripes. Nana had aduro wrapped in paper, which I felt innately was for me.*

Today is Apisha's birthday and I can't even wish her a happy birthday. I wonder how is she doing? I still have not heard from her and I feel at times abandoned by her and somewhat distant from her. Why has she not written; it is not so difficult she could surely find the time. I have mailed her three letters all not responded to and here it is 7th July.

I told Nana Dɔnkɔ about the dreams I had yesterday, but he did not say much. He only nodded about the dream about Ɔbookyerewa, and when I interpreted my second dream as perhaps at times, he was waiting for me, he said yes! He has waited for me at times. I realized this and told Nana that my problem is that I have difficulty balancing my time between him and Nana Effa. Nana Effa always wants me to be at his house, but never notifying him or arranging the time he may need me to be with him. Nana Effa does not realize that he may have things for me to do. I said I was caught in the middle and did not want to offend either one. I felt if Nana Effa were to talk to him and arrange a schedule, there would be less of a time conflict. Nana said he would talk to his son because he is young and does not understand the protocol. This is what Kofi interpreted for me. I began to use the eyewash *aduro* again.

Nana Dɔnkɔ made the string for my head that will be worn during the possession of the *ɔbosom*. Three *sedeɛ* (cowrie shells), *nkrawo* (a red olden weave cloth), all tied with raffia, a plant whose name I will try to find out, and *bese* (kola nut). This same plant may be the one that was used during my initiation.

Kofi, Nana Effa, and I plan to go to Nkoransa and visit Nana Akumsa's son Nana Yaw Manu. I had the opportunity to speak with Nana Effa about his drinking, and all this was initiated by my concerns and conversations with Nana Dɔnkɔ about his drinking problem yesterday. Kofi, who acted as interpreter, relayed my concerns to Nana Dɔnkɔ. I told Nana I would like to speak to Nana Effa about this problem. Nana Dɔnkɔ said he never spoke to him about his problem, but everyone, from what I gathered, had tried to speak to him about what concerned him, but to no avail. Nana Dɔnkɔ recommended that I go about it this way, by saying that I had a dream that my *ɔbosom* said he should stop and that I would do everything I can when I get back home to help him. Nana Dɔnkɔ said since I am his son, that makes Nana Effa my brother, so I can talk to him. I did talk to Nana Effa, but I wondered if it did any good. Nana did say since he does work for so many people, they all bring alcohol to pour libation, and since he must taste it, he may become intoxicated. Of course, I do not accept that reasoning, but I was not willing to get into a lengthy debate over this practice with him.

In the evening, on July 9th, Kofi and I left for Nkoransa, Akumsa Dumase, which is where Nana Yaw Manu lives. In fact, it is where Nana Dɔnkɔ and their family come from. Earlier that morning, Nana Effa and I went to the market to buy a duck, and on the way home, I stubbed my left big toe terribly on a rock that must have weighed 20 or 30 pounds. Through the pain, I pondered if it was a good or bad sign. I asked Nana Effa what it meant. He said if he stubs his left toe, it is good. I guess I will have big good luck, since it was such a large stone.

On the way to Nkoransa, Kofi and I had some difficulty with transportation, but we managed to hitch a ride on a city vehicle that cost me 220 cedis. We arrived in the middle of them celebrating the *Adapa* the same as in Takyiman. Nana Manu on *dawuro* was leading the occasion, with his senior wife supporting him with *ntwerewa*. They started off with a greeting song, *madwo, madwo ye me ma woadwo ee; ye ee eye me madwo ee, ye me ma woadwo, ee...* Most of the songs are centered around *ɔbrafoɔ dwom/* executioners' songs. At one point, we inquired as to the meaning of some of the songs, and his wives explained to Kofi and me their meanings. The songs were familiar, even though some were much more up-tempo than back at Asubonten's shrine in Takyiman. I was enraptured by Nana and his wives' singing. I loved the way they strung their songs like beads one after another without breaks. Nana Manu, at one point, revealed to the wives that I was recording them. That was all he needed to say, and they performed like they were performing at a concert. When they were finished, one of the women did us a favor by singing specific songs without any accompaniment and explaining their meanings to us. We laughed, sung along, and had fun. I recorded this happy occasion, and lots of songs were sung by Nana Manu and his wives.

The next day I went and greeted the owners and the *ɔbosomfoɔ* for the *ɔbosom* Akumsa, whose town I was now visiting. When we got back, Nana Yaw Manu wasted no time preparing my *suman*, which I will not go into details about. After he was finished, we went to his shrines. The youngest of his *nsuman* possessed on him and inquired about our purpose. After the *suman* was finished, it called its father, who possessed on Nana. The *suman* told me I would be rich. My ɔbosom is to help our people rise up and get land. When I asked about my wife, the *suman* said I will get the ticket, it's on the way. He said my wife's family is rich. I will have lots of possessions, and people will come to me because of my ɔbosom, and people will fear and respect me; no one will dare bother me at home. The *suman* wanted to know if I had any dreams about any animals since I have been here. I told him about the dream of the big black cat, to which he replied that cat is my ɔbrafoɔ, so my ɔbosom showed him to me. The *suman* went on to say that I should ask Nana Dɔnkɔ to give my soul a chicken to purify and feed it since I am his son so that I will always return to help him. The *suman* indicated since he Nana Dɔnkɔ knows my mind, he should do this. He said my ɔbosom would help me to unify my whole family as one so that they may all work together. He said in so many words, I shall be a most powerful ɔkɔmfoɔ. I replied that I would like only to be remembered for helping people. Finally, the *suman* said, just as Asubonten did, they would all help me to get money so that I may go and come many times. I am so blessed everyone wishes that Nyame will help me and that I get lots of money. I informed the *suman* that I wish for Kofi to accompany me so that we may work together.

Nana finished the work making the *suman* for me, and the name of it is Mmere Hurudwo. I will try to get the correct spelling of the name. This *suman* can bring down difficult things. When feeding it with a chicken, it will kill it by itself. All I have to do is lay the chicken on its back, blow a whistle and tell it to eat and the chicken will eventually die. It will drink all the blood. Nana made a padlock to accompany the *suman*. After the feeding of the *suman* was finished, Nana made a circle with powder on the ground, placed a cup with alcohol and *mɔtɔ* in the center of it, and lit the alcohol. He then demonstrated how I should put each hand over the flame and raise it three times up gradually. After demonstrating he made incisions on parts of my body at the joints. When the flame was extinguished, I drank some of the *mɔtɔ,* and the rest was placed on these incisions. When the meat was cooked, Nana put some on top of the *suman* and he said if it wanted the meat, it should push it off. The meat fell off the *suman*, and I had to eat this meat alone. This *suman* is powerful; it communicates with you directly. Mmere Hurudwo cools or brings down difficult things that boil over; sits upon the problems like weight; and protects against enemies.

We left for Takyiman the next morning and arrived between 8 and 9 a.m. Nana Dɔnkɔ was given a brief account as to all that had taken place, and later on he presented my soul with a chicken and said if anything was bothering me I should put it aside. I put the *suman* in Nana Dɔnkɔ's *suman* room. By then, Kofi had left to go to school, and later when he arrived, he had two letters for me from my wife. I was so happy to see her handwriting after reading the card and letter. She had sent two beautiful pictures of her and Etosha. How happy were my eyes to gaze upon them! I showed everyone here the pictures, and they all showed love to my wife and daughter, saying my daughter looks like me. I read my letter to Nana Dɔnkɔ, and he said now that Apisha is his daughter-in-law, he will send her something. They were all so happy, and so was I. In fact, I read the letter and card again before I retired to bed. I can't wait to hold her.

Amoako and Nana Effa came by, and we had a very warm conversation. Amoako inquired as to how things were coming along, and if there were any problems. I told him everything was moving fast and I could not ask them to work any faster. I said I had to go to Accra to call my wife; the cost would be 7,000 cedis, and I would have no more money after this trip. He said he would help if I needed it. I informed him that I wanted to help Nana Dɔnkɔ and Nana Effa build their houses, and when I first wrote to them, I did not know they were related. He went on to reveal something that had been hidden from me by saying there are people here who were very jealous, which I had heard before, and if they had gotten hold of my original letter, they would have wanted things from me and also made it difficult for me to get close to Nana Dɔnkɔ. This is why they decided to go through Nana Effa. They could have told me all this earlier, but I had to see things for myself. The people here are extremely jealous of what the others have and will pull you down if you attempt to succeed.

Now more of the dirt. Nana Dɔnkɔ has been trying to build his house for the longest time, and every time he gets money, he gets ill. Nana Dɔnkɔ's sister Nana Akumsa said she tried to warn his uncle or older brother (I am not certain which one) not to go to his farm or expand it, but he did not listen to her and he died. Nana Akumsa warned Nana Dɔnkɔ not to build his house, because if he does, he, too, will die. Nana Dɔnkɔ said if he completes his house and dies, people will remember him because he had accomplished something. Nana Dɔnkɔ has been having serious stomach problems for over forty years. It first came about at the time of his first son. He had three operations, and every time he got money, he fell ill.

I inquired if his accident (referring to when he fell and injured his hip) was no accident. Amoako looked at me and said it was no accident. Amoako went on to say he traveled to get one operation while Maame was pregnant with Kofi. After the surgery, Kofi was born. Amoako said the house where Nana Dɔnkɔ lives, Nana Akumsa owns, the house where I stayed when I visited Nana Yaw Manu in Nkoransa belongs to his sister Nana Asubonten, and Nana Dɔnkɔ would like to have his own.

Nana Dɔnkɔ is powerful, which I personally have observed. This man moves with a natural Tai Chi spirit. I have seen him at work, always relaxed, single-minded, slow, precise, orderly, and on time. I have often said Nana Dɔnkɔ is not for just one person, but for everyone. Amoako reminded Kofi to write Mike Warren and introduce me to him, so when I go back home, he can help me, I guess since he has compiled so much on Takyiman and its customs. Nana Effa said he will give me the addresses of the Takyiman people living in the United States. Nana Dɔnkɔ and Nana Akumsa assured me not to worry about what people say. I realize I cannot trust everyone. Last night, I almost possessed my *ɔbosom*, but he did not come fully, even though they sang songs to encourage him, but Asubonten came on Nana Akua Asantewaa.

Yesterday, Ɔboɔkyerewa *ɔbosomfoɔ* came by. I inquired as to when would be a good time to come and consult the *ɔbosom*, and he said Wednesday between 3 and 4 a.m. I do not know what it is, but there is something about the *ɔbosomfoɔ* that has not been revealed to me. He seems like a good person.

Nana Dɔnkɔ worked some more on the pad that I will use when carrying my *ɔbosom*. Unfortunately, I did not see what he was doing from the beginning. I did observe him putting different plants that were grounded into balls. These plants were divided so that total was seven, then *sika futuo* (gold dust) was added to each, and each one was covered with a leaf, then a white cloth was placed on top of them. About this time, police officers came to arrest and take Kwabena to the station because of the death of a certain Atta Kofi who pillaged Kofi Sarpon's sister's farm. This man was caught and beaten by Kwabena, and then he took the man to the police station and filed a complaint. The family of Atta Kofi informed the police that Atta Kofi died from the beating he received from Kwabena. This is why Kwabena was arrested. Amoako was called and sent to the hospital where the body was and found out the real cause of the man's death. The man had taken poison and killed himself. Due to the fact that the family tried to conceal the real cause of death, Kwabena was released. Later that evening, Kwabena would not eat or talk; he just cried like a baby. He said the police had beaten him. Kofi and I discussed in some depth the problems Kwabena always gets himself into. I told Kofi he had bad luck and should seek spiritual assistance from Asubonten.

Kofi, Nana Effa, Maame, Kwasi *ɔkɔmfoɔ*, and I were supposed to travel to Akumsa Dumase to do spiritual work for Nana Effa's drinking problem, but the trip, for some reason or another, was postponed.

Around 4 a.m, we left for Traa to consult Ɔboɔkyerewa. He never came, and the people here I found very strange indeed. For example, an elder went and called the *ɔkyeame* and told him we were there and he should bring his things for the *ɔbosomfoɔ* to possess the *ɔbosom*. The *ɔkyeame* told the elder he would return after he went to the toilet. When the *ɔkyeame* arrived, he was empty-handed, and it was discovered he never went to the toilet. The *ɔkyeame* then went to the *ɔbosomfoɔ* and told him he wanted to show him something. When the *ɔbosomfoɔ* returned, the elder asked what the *ɔkyeame* showed him. Where is the gold? The *ɔbosomfoɔ* said nothing. There are more interesting things that the Ɔboɔkyerewa elder said, but I wish not to open it.

Eventually, the time came when they tried to call the *ɔbosom*. After the *ɔbosomfoɔ* prepared himself, the *ɔkyeame* began the appellation.

Ɔbookyerewa is unique; he has two *akyeame,* and at times they both would synchronize in calling him. But no matter how much they tried this time, he did not come. One can hear Nana Akumsa pleading for the *obosom* to appear, but it all was to no avail. After about fifteen minutes, Maame and others joined in singing to call the *obosom,* while in the background this beautiful singing accompanied the *okyeame* appellations. The singer took a brief pause to dig deep into the arsenal of songs to pull one out, but even that did not persuade Ɔbookyerewa to come. We left the riverside and went to the shrine near the road, and the rituals continued. Nana Akumsa offered a drink to Ɔbookyerewa, praying for Nana Dɔnkɔ, and the *okyeame* poured libation for her. A chicken was sacrificed, after which libation was poured. As observed before, it is not unusual for the *obosomfoɔ* not to be involved in these proceedings, except where sacrifice is needed. I had been thinking a lot about Apisha since I had received her letter. I missed her very much.

On Thursday July 15th, Kofi and I left for Nkran (Accra). I stayed at one of our brother Kwame Amponsa's house. Friday, I went to Swiss Air to check in and to the P & T to call my wife. It was so wonderful to hear her voice but, at first, I could not believe it was her. She, too, seemed surprised to hear from me. I can still recall hearing her say with surprise in her words, Sadiki, you call me! Oh! How I love my wife! It was pure joy in hearing her voice, knowing I was talking to her, my wife, my life. I asked her to help me with the ticket for Kofi. Her silence explained her difficulties with money at this moment. She said she does not know if she will make it to Nigeria. She mentioned that Nana Oparebea was in New York. She has been having a challenging time keeping money. She said Nana Nsiah called her but strangely did not say anything about Nana Oparebea being in New York.

I forgot to mention a ritual that took place last Tuesday the 11th. I had to feed the children with rice, and after they had finished eating, they washed their hands in a bucket of water with a small creature that looked like a tadpole and that can walk up the sides of the bucket. They can swim very fast and are nicknamed "water cleaners" in English. If I try to write the Twi name, I will mess it up, but I will try anyway. It is called *gyegyensune*, I think. After the children had washed their hands, I had to carry the water to a road and say prayers and throw it away. This ritual was given to me by Asubonten so that I will always attract children and have them around me.

Early in the morning July 16th, we went to Nana Effa, who carried his *ɔbosom* Asuotipa. Nana Dɔnkɔ acted as *ɔkyeame*. First Nana Dɔnkɔ presented Nana Effa with a new pad he had made for him using some of the same kente I'd bought for making my pad. When Asuo came and after all the formalities, he addressed me and said my *ɔbosom* is not small; he is big and he is not alone. He confirmed that he was from the Tanɔ River, and Ɔbookyerewa wanted to talk with him, but because of the people at Traa, I have not been able to see him. Asuo encouraged me to be patient and not to waver and stand firm. He said at times I have hope and at times none. I must believe that Nana and the *abosom* can help me and I should follow what they say. He said I must obey my *ɔbosom* taboos and tomorrow they will open the mouth of the *ɔbosom*. I should buy lots of eggs, drink, and a gun to shoot and call my *ɔbosom*. I should get everything so that when my *ɔbosom* asks for them, I have them there; he said that Nana Dɔnkɔ should feed my soul, and that he will take all responsibilities for my training needs. He kept reiterating I should be brave because my *ɔbosom* is big, so I should be strong, and if they could not help me Nana Dɔnkɔ would have told me so a long time ago. Finally, he said they will call my *ɔbosom* and I should not worry about money being spent. On Tuesday I will go to Traa to see Ɔbookyerewa, and I have heard that they have a new chief or ɔhene.

Tonight, they tried to open the mouth of the ɔbosom at Nana Effa's place. First Nana Dɔnkɔ gave me herbs to chew and swallow, then he poured libation. Next, I smeared the *aduro* on my face and joints as we did in preparation for carrying the *ɔbosom,* and I licked the rest of the stone. Again, more *aduro* was put on my face and on top of my head. Nana Dɔnkɔ then put some on my ears, joints, and on the soles of my feet. We left for a path where there was no one the *ɔbosom* would encounter. Later on, they told me the *ɔbosom* came on me a little and took off down the path, but he left as suddenly as he had come.

The *ɔbosom* did not stay on me, and here I am, feeling alone and impotent, unable to perform. They were back there waiting on the *ɔbosom* with the expectation that he would talk. I stayed in the bush for a while feeling ashamed, then I mustered up the nerve and said I had to go back, so I did. They were finishing up the pouring of libation, and Nana Effa's *ɔkyeame* Kwabena Kranka came over and gave me an egg, then put a twig or stem into my mouth, took it out, and threw it away. This was repeated two more times. He took an egg and rubbed it against my front and back and smashed it on the ground. All joined in unison prayers, ringing of bells, and invocation beckoning my *ɔbosom* to possess on me, but the *ɔbosom* did not show. Clay was thrown in the air and on the ground. Nana Akumsa prayed and smashed eggs on the ground. Nana Effa came over and pleaded with the *ɔbosom* to make his presence known, asking him to speak English or any language. Mute was the *ɔbosom*. After some time, Nana Dɔnkɔ decided to call it quits and my feelings and hope of being a *ɔkɔmfoɔ* seem to end. I felt like going home. I felt too ashamed to stay there, but then I recalled what Asuotipa fortuitously said to me: "My *ɔbosom* is big, so I must be strong." And Kofi Asante's words: "Be bold." Now, what to do? Tomorrow will come.

I am reminded of the advice Asuotipa gave me: be single-minded. If I do not die, I will take something back with me. That's all. Asuotipa said if you find the money you will not think twice about spending it, but if you work hard for it, you will ponder long and try to save it.

In the morning, Nana Yaw Manu arrived from Akumsa Dumase. He was ill. The events that led to his illness involved a dispute between him and his junior wife. She told him to bring it to his *nsuman* to settle the case, and he did not. As a result, his *suman* made him ill, and now he has come here for help. I recall that last night on the way to Nana Effa's house I stubbed my toe again, and it was the same toe and on the same spot I had stubbed on the way to Nkoransa. Now I wondered if this would always mean difficulties when it happens. I would have to wait and see.

I was told by Nana Effa, Nana Dɔnkɔ, and Asuotipa that my *ɔbosom* is not a small thing and acts like Ɔboɔkyerewa, and that he will make me suffer before I get him. I felt like I was suffering now, but I guess not enough, because he hadn't come.

It just dawned on me how short my time was here. In fact, I felt a little disoriented. Perhaps it was from carrying the *ɔbosom*. Kofi yesterday tricked me into believing that Nana Dɔnkɔ was going to carry Asubonten this morning. I was taken by surprise when Nana Dɔnkɔ told me to wear a white *ntoma*. My mind began to ask a million questions. What's going on? Finally, I realized that I was the one. I did all the usual rituals of preparations, and the *ɔbosom* Twumpuro was selected for me to carry. They put the pan on my head, and it began to move. I originally thought it was him that they were calling, until I realized it was my *ɔbosom* they were invoking into his cage. I could not control what was happening to me. My head was moving all over the place, out of control. The pan almost fell off my head. If it was not for the assistant who caught it, I would have been a disgrace. Now I know why these helpers are there when the *ɔbosom* is carried. I felt the power of my *ɔbosom,* even though he did not possess fully on me.

The pan was placed upon my head two more times, allowing the *ɔbosom* to possess me, then it was removed. Each time after the pan was taken off my head, the pad was allowed to fall on the floor, and whether it fell facing up or down determined if the *ɔbosom* was ready to go or not. I cannot relate all my experiences, since I was not fully conscious of everything that happened. I felt I was not here all the time; what a ride it was. After I carried the pan three times, drummers started to play, and I was told to dance and spin. The *ɔbosom* came, and after he left, I felt him all inside and over my body, especially my head. This sensation stayed with me for a while, which was replaced with a stranger sensation in my solar plexus.

While I was coming back to reality, Nana Yaw Manu went and consulted Asubonten to intercede on the matter between him and his *nsuman*. Three chickens were offered to the *ɔbosom,* but he would not accept them. After some begging, the first one presented was sacrificed. I was not clear on all the details, but somehow the fee for pacification was not appropriate. Eventually, Asuo said that his *suman* would not accept the chickens. He wanted a ram for his abuse. After all the events were over, I went with Kofi to post letters to my wife and mother and decided to use this private time together to inquire further into Nana Yaw Manu's illness. Kofi said

Yaw Manu and his second wife had an argument. One of his *nsuman* taboo women and he invoked this *suman*, threatening his wife, which led to the whole problem. The spirits will not permit anyone to abuse their powers like this. Nana should have known better, but he challenged it. His heart was not pure. According to what Kofi said, this was not the first time he was punished by his *suman*. The last time this happened, he gave a cow to beg for forgiveness. Now his *suman* is punishing him again for the second abuse of power. Nana Effa said the *suman* would kill Nana Yaw Manu if he does not beg for forgiveness. Here is proof that what we do is for the good of things, and the position and power we have should not be used to abuse or threaten others, but to help. There is a price to pay if we fail to remember this.

Nana Effa said he would carry Asuotipa outside the shrine house on Sunday for the first time in over fourteen years. In the past Asuo had said no, but he said yes this time because of me. Normally the *ɔbosom* is carried out once a year at its festival, provided Taa Mensa, the father of all *Atanɔ abosom* in Takyiman, first goes out of his shrine house. If he does not, no one else will think of doing so. They had a plan again to open my *ɔbosom's* mouth but postponed it due to the rain.

On Wednesday they were supposed to try but postponed it again due to the rain. They said they would try again on Thursday. Finally, on Thursday, the *ɔbosom's* mouth was opened, and he spoke. Thanks to Kofi, I have it on tape. Friday, there was drumming, and Nana Kwasi Appia possessed his *ɔbosom* Akumsa, the same *ɔbosom* Nana Akumsa has, and Nana Effa possessed Asuotipa. Asuo stayed for a while, then Kofi Asante came on him. By then, the drummers were tired and complaining, but Asante would not leave. It took Asante some time before he decided to leave, and the other *abosom*, too, left shortly. Akumsa did not take as long to go, but did he perform before he left.

Later that afternoon we went to Nana Effa's house, and I had to offer Asuotipa a chicken. Kwaku Mossi came on Nana Effa and instructed them to take me to a certain river called Aworowa and sacrifice to him three different types of palm wine, a chicken, and an egg. This is to beg the *ɔbosom* Aworowa to assist in catching my *ɔbosom*. Mossi said I would see something at the river as a sign. He also instructed us to get gunpowder to shoot while drumming to help catch my *ɔbosom*.

Late last night Nana Dɔnkɔ, Nana Akumsa, and Nana Yaw Manu spoke to me about the *abosom* and *nsamanfoɔ* and my relationship with them. They made me aware that the *abosom* can never just take someone to be their *ɔkɔmfoɔ* without the consent of the *nsamanfoɔ*; they work hand in hand. Even though the *ɔbosom* is part of the family, it still asks for permission. This is even more so if it is a new *ɔbosom* who wants to take someone as their *ɔkɔmfoɔ* for the first time. We also conversed about the position of Nyame and Asase Yaa and, to my surprise, Nana Dɔnkɔ said they were the same. I do not know why I did not follow up on such an important topic. So much happens here that it easy for me to forget important things like this topic.

If God permits, we plan to go to Traa and consult Ɔboɔkyerewa. I have two weeks left before I leave, and everything must be in place so that all that is needed to be done is to catch my *ɔbosom* and inquire what needs to be done and where I go from here until I return.

I am still the talk of the town. I hear people speaking behind me, thinking I will not understand them. If you are somewhere long enough, you will pick up something in their language.

On July 22nd, Maame and I visited Nana Effa. She, along with his wife and others, sang songs, which I would call a classic representation of *akɔm* singing at its best. Nana Effa's drumming and singing also were at their best, along with others accompanying him. This is one of the finest recordings you can imagine. I am so fortunate to have this documented.

Just two more weeks remain before my departure. I spent the night at Nana Effa's and the plan was to carry Asuotipa and catch my *ɔbosom* later on that day, but it had to be postponed because a chief *ɔbosomfoɔ* had left for the ancestral world; this chief was the previous *Taa Mensa ɔbosomfoɔ* who was destooled.

In the afternoon, we visited the Tanɔ River site where the *ɔbosom* Awowuro lives. I was told that this *ɔbosom* stammers like my *ɔbosom,* and the plan was to see if there is any relationship between the two. I presented a chicken, three different types of palm wine, and an egg. I petition the *ɔbosom* and asked for his help in catching my *ɔbosom*. I informed him that I was sent here by Kwaku Mossi and was told I will see a sign. When the chicken was sacrificed, it did not land on its back as it was supposed to. It just laid there, then in a little while it flipped onto its back. Its kidneys and intestines were inspected and had no blemishes. It began to rain slightly after we were finished, and I thought this was the sign I was to look for, but I was not certain and will be patient.

The festival for Asuotipa took place, and I did possess my *ɔbosom*, but he did not come fully and therefore did not stay long. As I was writing my notes, the children had gathered around me, perhaps out of curiosity, and after a while, one of them started to sing a song about *boroni* and I paused and corrected this child by saying I am not a *boroni* but a *bibini*, informing them I am not a white man but a black man.

During the *akɔm*, guns were fired by those who were there and the *ɔbosom* themselves. Later on, I decided to go to the store and buy biscuits and bread, and on my way, I stubbed my left big toe again badly, the same foot and the same toe. The pain was so excruciating I had to curse out loud. If that was not enough to compound it all, just before I crossed the path I stepped into a puddle of mud; maybe this was my sign.

Lately, I' had been feeling sad and alone, not having electricity and consuming only rainwater or river water. Even though with river water you can taste fishes, this did not bother me. I had gotten used to it.

I felt just downright depressed, so depressed that my mother here, who could not speak a word of English, came by to keep me company. She worries a lot about me, especially when I got that feeling of wanting to go home. She had developed a symbiotic relationship with me; it was her mother's instinct. I knew that this feeling of unhappiness was not good for my *akɔm*, and that I must learn to be patient and not give in to these feelings. If it was the will of God, I would achieve something out of this venture. My time was short; this training takes three years, and I will have to go and come until I have completed it all. I realized that I have become too self-indulgent and distracted by these foolish thoughts. I must center myself.

*I awoke this morning after a dream of being back home in my shrine room.*

*I was in my shrine room just after I arrived from Ghana. I went to the old shrine given to me by Nana Oparebea and took the lid off, and to my surprise, all the usual herbs were there but spoiled. The roots appalled me and set me back somewhat. In fact, I was a little shaken and thought that the shrine was no longer useful for me, and I should stop using it and give it back to the makers or person who did damage to it.*

*The next scene was me still in the shrine room. I was pouring libation at my new shrine for my ɔbosom. I saw a man and woman observing me as I was pouring libation. I tilted the Yawa on its side and continued pouring libation, perhaps to prevent them from seeing. When I was finished, I gathered clothes to go on a trip to New York and visit Nana Nsiah. My clothing consisted of sweatpants. These pants were unusually decorated with designs. I planned to drive myself and was considering the time factor. I saw a former martial arts teacher, Mfundishi Maasi, who has a revolutionary warrior personality from the 60s in my dream as well, and maybe I planned to visit him, but it was not clear.*

The next day I was in a much better frame of mind. My problem was that I felt lonely and did not have people with whom I could converse. My inability to speak Twi made me feel isolated and disconnected, and when I did try to speak, I think too much, like I was solving a difficult math problem. I had a dream, which Kofi related to Nana Akumsa, and she interpreted the dream to mean my *ɔbosom* was coming, but I would have to suffer much. Kofi inquired about a certain ritual called *Kunkuma*, and Nana Akumsa said this ritual is done before the *ɔkɔmfoɔ* leaves to go back to normal life. It is to release him/her from certain taboos. For example, I cannot sleep with my wife while I am in this state of training, because if I did it would bring a serious problem to me from my *ɔbosom*.

This ritual includes other *akɔmfoɔ* bringing their most powerful *aduro* herbs and contributing it to the making of *motɔ*/black powder for me. These plants may be specific plants that can cure snake bites or ones that protect you from *bayi*/witchcraft or other evil. This ritual also protects me in case I break a food taboo. It would not damage or change the power in my body, and my taboos will be classified into serious and not so serious. At this ritual, I will be permitted to eat the not-so-serious ones, but I will have to adhere to the serious food taboos. Then I will be granted permission to sleep with my wife so that the act will not disturb and bring me problems. They will cut my hair, allow me to shave, and so forth; I will be required to wear sandals and not go around barefoot any longer and stub my toes and dress like an *ɔkɔmfoɔ*.

Nana Dɔnkɔ said even if they are not able to catch my *ɔbosom* they will still prepare and give me something to take back home, so when he comes, I can catch him myself.

This day, July 25th, is a holy day, and I am supposed to carry the *ɔbosom*. Meanwhile, I was reflecting on the dream that I mentioned to Nana Akumsa. She interpreted it by saying if I had turned over the *yawa*/pan completely, this would have been a serious problem, but since I turned it only onto the side, it is not so serious, but nonetheless serious enough.

The man who was hired to make the *dosoʼ*/raffia skirt finished it, and his daughter brought it to me last Sunday. I must say, it looks very beautiful and powerful. Today we will adorn it with shells. I am so troubled with the prospect of my *ɔbosom* not coming on me since I communicated my concerns to Nana Akumsa. She said the *ɔbosom* is here, but he is not happy.

The *Takyimanhene* had died, and no one has replaced him, so the *nsamanfoɔ* and *abosom* are not fed and they are hungry and unhappy. Seeing this state of affairs, my *ɔbosom* was unhappy too. The other *abosom* and *nsamanfoɔ* also do not have food to welcome him properly and this too makes him unhappy. I asked Nana to tell me what should I do, and she told Kofi to go and pick a certain plant for me. With this plant, I should get a *Nyame akuma*, "The axe of Nyame."

Last night I went to add water to my bath, and I felt a strange power pulling me back after I was finished with my bath. I tried to leave but felt compelled to stay. I would have to muster up a great resistance to leave, so realizing this may be something spiritual and the *ɔbosom* was here, I did not resist. I wanted to know what he wanted and searched for an answer. Then it dawned on me that he may want me to bathe more. I took the bath and felt the *ɔbosom* coming. I then proceeded to where Nana Dɔnkɔ was and the *ɔbosom* shook me for a while, and then left.

In the morning, an elder graduate female *ɔkɔmfoɔ* of Nana Dɔnkɔ visited him with her two trainees, who were in full possession. Later on, Kofi informed me that she was at an impasse and could not take them any further. This, Kofi communicated, is a problem with so many *akɔmfoɔɔ* who do not complete their course or who were too busy at the time when they should have been paying attention to Nana Dɔnkɔ's instructions.

That night I carried the *ɔbosom* Puroo. They called the *ɔbosom*, but he did not come even when Nana Akumsa pleaded with him, saying that someone was dying and he should come, but all was to no avail. In the morning, we picked up where we left off. I again carried Puroo, and all he did, like last night, was shake me but not possess me. I attributed this shaking to nervousness, which soon dissipated as time wore on. I was told they would try again in the evening. Doubts sometimes crept in whether it was the *ɔbosom* or me, for I wondered if Nana Effa or Nana Dɔnkɔ had this problem when they first started. But I was not giving up hope, even though if I gave into it, it could be discouraging.

People began to chatter, saying perhaps it was not the *ɔbosom* holy day, and that was why he was not coming, but Kofi stated if someone was sick, the *ɔbosom* should come to help whether it was his holy day or not. I could not figure this out and wondered if Nana Dɔnkɔ couldn't either. According to Kofi, Nana Dɔnkɔ said when the *ɔbosom* possesses me, he wants to do something but does not know how to. He went on to clarify that with a new *ɔbosom* that does not have experience living around people, they have to be trained. To me, my *ɔbosom* showed no signs of fully possessing on me with only nine days left.

Kwabena Kranka, Nana Effa's *ɔkyeame*, said something very important. He said this was not what they normally do before they catch *abosom*. You see, the *ɔbosom* has to tell them everything to do so that they can catch him. Hence, if he does not speak and inform them on what to do, how can they do anything for him? I needed help badly.

As I was finishing my writing, Nana Effa appeared. He seemed to sense my disappointment, and he consoled me by saying not to worry; he knew the reason behind everything, but he wanted to see something first. I mentioned to him I only had ten days left; he stopped me abruptly and said, don't worry, you may have ten days, but you can see something in five days. Nana Effa was very serious about helping me. Feeling tired, I came home and took a nap, and had a dream which I recorded.

*Someone I knew told a man whom I did not know about all the medicine and nsuman I had. This person and the man continued talking for a while. I did not hear all the conversation, but I did hear him mention Bɔa me (help me, and the name of a suman). After the man left, I questioned this person and asked him why did he tell that man these things about me. He did not answer but just stared far off into the distance. I saw this very same man in the distance. He had one arm or a broken arm. He was wearing a light-colored ntoma. I told* Nana Effa *what this person had done.*

*The next dream was about me taking an examination, which I failed. I saw the examiner give me a score of either 26 or 36 out of 100. I had answered a few questions, and they were correct, but the unanswered questions were the ones that worked against me.*

*In the third dream I was in a supermarket or some store. The cashier or salesperson wore glasses that were tinted brown. I inquired about buying mɔtɔ and something else that was in two white blocks wrapped in plastic. The mɔtɔ was wrapped inside a banana leaf. Either the man or I tried to put the blocks and mɔtɔ into the banana leaf, which was too small, and it did not fit properly. I then asked for a brown bag I saw in front of me to put them in, but the man would not give it to me. He proceeded to ask me why they would not fit in the leaf. I explained, but he still ignored my request. He then left, and I followed him and asked him his name so I could lodge a complaint to his supervisor. I asked other employees who were around. I called his name to ask as he was going through a door.*

Nana Dɔnkɔ, Kofi, and I went to see Nana Effa, and he was consulting Bɔmmɔ and ended up possessing Mossi and, as you would you have it, this was the time I should have brought my tape recorder. Mossi said my ɔbosom is three: one is a stammerer, one cannot hear, and the other ɔbosommerafoɔ. Mossi did not say which was the main ɔbosom, but he is not small, he is big and will not come as yet. He will come only when he wants to and has lots of children and we should try to catch one, then the others will follow. The rest will follow if the child is treated well. Mossi said we should play big drums for three days, get a stool for the ɔbosom and ten thousand cedis for drummers to play and eat. We should get a tree called *Nyame dua*/tree from Nyame and put a brass pan on it. We should get gunpowder and guns, and on the third day we will see something and it will rain. He said my ɔbosom feels sad, and the rain comes after we do anything for him, he cries. Mossi cautioned that people would come to see what I have and I should not show them all, just a little. He reiterated that Nana Oparebea was trying to make me fail and not succeed when I go here and there so that when I go back home, I will beg her forgiveness. Mossi said he is not sure if the big one will come or not, but we will wait and see.

Mossi told me he wants to go back with me, but he will come and see me first in my room, and then I will know he is going with me. He inquired about drinks, and I told him that there is Guinness stout. He said he would have to taste it to see. He mentioned that one of the *mmoatia* would travel with me and I should give Bɔmmɔ a biscuit, toffee, and candy and ask her for three things I need. He indicated he knows my ɔbosom but will not say anything. He spoke of the dream I had about pouring libation and used that opportunity to talk about Nana Oparebea. He asked me if I needed money to give to Nana Oparebea, and since I did not have it, I sold things for money and told her if I could not pay it all, I would give my possessions. I raised the question of whether I should give back my old shrine to her. Mossi stated, you paid for it, so do not. He said to wait until I had something to see. Mossi looked at me and said that I think a lot about home, my wife, and how all the money I spent was gone. He added that I wanted to help my family. He advised me to think of one problem at a time, and I should move around as if Takyiman is my home. He counseled me about not feeling sad and suggested to Nana Dɔnkɔ I should be given something to take back home because others will come to see what I have attained. They should catch a young *ɔbosom* for me so I can do work. Mossi cautioned if I was given too much to take back home some may say I had stolen it. Maybe he was referring to my stay here, since it is a short time. He surprisingly said one of my *ɔbosom* is female, some like alcohol, some like *pito*, beer, and such things, and some do not like either. Maybe by this, he meant just plain water. Mossi gave Nana Dɔnkɔ some advice that they should not worry too much about the language because eventually, the *ɔbosom* would communicate. Finally, he reiterated that my *ɔbosom* is from a river (*asuo*).

Nana Effa had planned to carry his *ɔbosom* outside on Sunday past but did not. Asuotipa came and informed them that since his father Taa Mensa's wife, the former *ɔbosomfoɔ* had passed, how can he celebrate? His father is mourning and would blame him for not observing the mourning rites. Asuo plans to send one of his children to pay respects. Kofi Asante will go, and they will have to purify them after.

That same day, I had the opportunity to observe Nana Effa bathing his *ɔbosom*. This purification had nothing to do with the funeral. This was in preparation for carrying him outside. He did not allow anyone but me in the shrine room but kept a small crack open in the doorway. He commented that when you are bathing, you do not allow others to stare. The *yawa* was polished clean, and the clay markings were painted back on the *yawa*. The design I have drawn. My brother is an exceptional human being and ɔkɔmfoɔ. If only he would control his drinking.

My eyes have been itching terribly for some time now these past few weeks. It could be a combination of the *aduro* herbal baths, the smoke, and dust. I notice my sexual desire has been so much under control that I am amazed at how much I forgot about it. I had no nocturnal dreams or unusual erections, no thoughts of sex and the like, even though I do think of my wife a lot. Nyame and nature are wonderful.

As I reflect back on a reading I had from Nana Akumsa, she also read one *ɔkɔmfoɔ baa* (female *ɔkɔmfoɔ*) who Nana Dɔnkɔ trained. This *ɔkɔmfoɔ* complained that when her *ɔbosom* predicts or does good work helping her clients, some people degrade her by saying it is from the devil. I personally witnessed one day a man with a Bible in his hand insulting Nana Effa's *ɔbosom* by saying they are sons of Satan.

These Christians are the very same ones who come under the cloak of darkness to the very same *abosom* they insult in the daylight for help to get *nsuman* and spiritual *aduro* to put in their churches to heal patients, proclaiming their healings are from Jesus Christ and their Christian God alone.

In time, the *ɔbosom* catches these hypocrites, making them accountable. I will relate one incident Nana Effa shared with me concerning a certain pastor his *ɔbosom* helped. This pastor sent the *aseda*/thank-you through a mediator, which the *ɔbosom* refused to accept and instructed the mediator to tell this pastor that he should come in person to give the *aseda*. It is these very same charlatans who come in the dark of night so that no one will see their hypocrisy. They wish to maintain their pure Christian images.

My eyes were still bothering me a lot, especially this morning. They were irritated by something. I had eight days left; it is countdown time. People still call me *boroni*, which I disliked very much. I tried to correct them and say "*Dabi boroni.*" When I do this, they just looked at me dumbfounded, especially the children, perhaps wondering why I was denying who I was in their eyes. I could not blame them; after all, the children learn this from the adults.

Living in America had taught me that things were either black or white, and this had warped my sensibility. The people here do not look at things in such a simplistic way; to them, the only people who travel on airplanes, wear suits and ties, carry strange money, do not know their culture, and speak a non-African language are these *boroni*. And to them, I am like those people. I do not think their perception of me is racially motivated as if I look white. Even though at times I have asked them if you stand me next to a white man, you will see the true difference, and if you say *boroni*, which one of us would you expect to respond first? I have also realized that some of these people have never seen a white man and are just repeating or imitating each other when they see a stranger from another part of the world. I often wonder if they refer to all foreigners, no matter where they are from, as such. Even though I state that some have never seen a white man, I find it very problematic. Since my time here, I have seen white people working and driving around town, confirming my belief this is not solely about racial issues.

People are people everywhere you go. You see the same drama played out everywhere. For example, I heard of the horrible killing of a woman's son. This woman came by to see Nana Dɔnkɔ last week to narrate to him how her son died. He won the best drummer competition in all of Ghana and came to his home in Wankye to prepare to travel abroad. His brother from the same father, not the same mother, took him to a bar to celebrate and put poison in his drink and he fell dead. The mother went to consult Obookyerewa, and the brother was caught by the *obosom* and went insane as part of the punishment. It was said that after he goes to the toilet, he smears feces all over his face and body and walks about town. I do not know if the *obosom* eventually killed him or not. There are many stories of jealousy, envy, and hatred driving one person to kill another. People do not like to see others progress more than themselves. Another example I heard was of someone who would not help his children to go to school because he did not go. People all over the world have serious problems. This again reminds me of what Abena (Rose) told me about *bayi*; people do not want others to prosper more than they do.

These writings are very therapeutic and give me the opportunity to recall and reflect on all my experiences and acquired knowledge. I recall another thing Mossi said to Nana Donko, that if I do not have something to take back with me, people will question where I came, and I may feel that I have wasted my time and money here and may not return.

This morning I visited Nana Effa's shrine and saw Bommo, who repeated a lot of what Mossi had said. Bommo indicated she will send two of her children to help catch my *obosom* so that I can send it back with me. She also noted that she would like to give me two of her children to take back but does not know if my main *obosom* would like it even if I wanted it. She informed me that when I come back, she would come and get me and take me to the bush and no one will know for how long.

Bɔmmɔ inquired about the dream I had about the big cat and said this is my *ɔbosommerafoɔ*. Kofi also related to her the dream I had about pouring libation and she said it is my *abrafoɔ*, which shows me things in my dream. Bɔmmɔ used this opportunity to thank me for the sweets and said I should bring her a drink and she will give me something to burn in my *kunkuma*. I should not give this to anyone, or else they will get the power. She informed me that when my *ɔbosom's* mouth was open, the bad people tried to keep him from speaking and that she will give me *aduro* with egg so that he will speak. She said I think a lot about helping my wife and family back home, and I should give a ram to my *ɔbosom* after he is caught. I should pray a lot for him to come so that they may catch him. She said one will come, but the drumming has to be very hot.

Amoako brought me the Father's Day card my beloved wife Apisha sent me. I was so happy it arrived today, because I checked yesterday and it had not yet come.

Everyone began the preparation for the *kunkuma*. People brought herbs, and Kofi contributed the herbs that he was told to collect. I went to Bɔmmɔ to get the *aduro*. She said she would contribute to my *kunkuma*. It was *motɔ* inside a red cloth called *nkrawo*, and I was told to give it to no or else the power would go to them. Bɔmmɔ again advised me to pray hard.

Back at Nana Dɔnkɔ's, where the *kunkuma* was about to be prepared, I was given an egg to speak to and then it was sacrificed. Next, a chicken was slaughtered, and it, too, was accepted. I purchased *ntoma*, towels, clothes, razor blades, and Vaseline all for the event. I was deeply moved by Amoako giving me a *Gye Nyame* stool. My mother sat me up and down on it three times. I was so deeply touched by the gesture and experience.

We were now waiting for Nana Effa before we proceeded with the rituals. I had an eye-opening experience watching the blacksmith make a bracelet called *Nkamere* for me. Yesterday I bought a *sankɔfa* bird ring for myself and a ring for my wife with two serpents, which represent our two energies always together. I now had seven days before I left.

Yesterday when I had finished bathing, I reached for my glasses, which I had placed on the bath cover, and the bath pot fell. I was a little puzzled by this but decided to pick up the roots, wash them off, and put them back into the pot and add more water. This morning when I went to bathe, the pot fell again, spilling its contents. Again, I was befuddled; I thought something or someone was trying to tell me something. I thought of changing it. I immediately went to notify Nana Dɔnkɔ as to what had happened, and he told me the bath was finished and had to be replaced with another; it was over. This experience taught me that spiritual forces are communicating with me.

The preparations were finally finished, and I presented a new cloth, towel, soap, *mpaboa*/traditional sandals, Vaseline, and razors, all before I bathed in water for the first time since I had begun my training.

I had purchased two black chickens to be sacrificed before the *kunkuma* ritual. Nana *ɔkyeame* Kofi Boɔ performed the rituals. I do not recall if Nana Dɔnkɔ cut and gave the chicken to him. I have photos of him alone doing the rituals and Nana Dɔnkɔ sitting back. One chicken was offered to Nyame, and the other to Asase Yaa to accept my *kunkuma* ritual. It was said that my teacher was not always there when I may have moved up and down. Perhaps I moved in secret without their knowledge of doing things, meeting with people or women they may not have seen. Nyame sees everything and Asase Yaa, the earth, also sees everything. If I did not break any rules or taboos, they should come and accept the sacrifices. The chickens were slaughtered, the first to Nyame and the second to Asase Yaa, and both were accepted.

My hair was cut, first by Nana Kofi Boɔ, Asubonten ɔkyeame, and then I shaved my face and cut the hair under my armpits and my pubic hair. They removed all the *nsuman* from my wrists and legs. I was sent to bathe, accompanied by Nana Akumsa, who first washed me, prayed, and left me to finish my bath. After I was finished, she greased my body with Vaseline and I finished the rest. I put on my white *ntoma* and *mpaboa*, and the drumming began; I took a seat. The drumming made three *akɔmfoɔ* possess their *abosom*. Nana Effa's son, who was one of the *ɔkɔmfoɔ* who was possessed, came and greeted me three times. Each time I was greeted by the *ɔbosom,* I began to shake. It was not until after the third time that I was greeted and embraced that I began to possess.

My *ɔbosom* did not stay too long, I was told, because the drumming was not hot enough. Later on, I was almost possessed when Nana Yaw Manu was possessing, and a photo was taken of me beside him. The *ɔkɔmfoɔ* who greeted me was named Kofi. He impressed me a lot with the display of his *ɔbosom* dancing and never seemed to tire. In all, he had possessed four *abosom*, two I know: Kofi Asante and Ɔbooƙyerewa. The first and second, I did not know them. His *abosom* was the best dancer so far as I can say since I have been here.

All the while, the preparations continued, and the *mɔtɔ* was finished. The breaking of food taboos commenced; some of the *mɔtɔ* was added to eggs and the chickens that were sacrificed. Nana Akumsa fed me my food taboos.

She placed on my tongue different kinds of food that I was forbidden to eat. I had to bite a small piece and spit it out three times. After the third time, I was permitted to eat a little of that particular food. This went on with all the food I tabooed and did not eat.

I recall my *nkamere*/bracelet and *kawa*/rings were added to the *mɔtɔ* and chickens when they were cooking. Maame also fed me later on, I recall. As I write, I do not remember all the events in perfect order, and I now recall that when *ɔkɔmfoɔ* Kofi possessed his *ɔbosom* Ɔboɔkyerewa, he got into a dispute with Nana Manu's *ɔbosom* because he was monopolizing the stage too long, so to speak. His *ɔbosom* left soon after the incident. Now I will rest until tomorrow.

It was now three days before I had to leave and so much had happened since Friday.

I will finish later. Yesterday, I carried the *ɔbosom*, but he did not come. Asubonten said we should offer him food and drink, and then he would come, but the rain prevented us from doing so. An *akɔm* took place later on, and Ɔboɔkyerewa came and inquired how many times I had been to see him. I told him, and he said the reason why he never came is the fault of the *ɔkyeame*. He instructed me to sleep with seven different foods, such as sugar, atadwɛ/tiger nuts, kenkey, bread, *mansa*, banana, and pawpaw. I should have all this on tape. And Nana Dɔnkɔ should carry Asubonten today and he will tell everything.

Nana did indeed carry Asubonten for the last time for me. Asubonten said my *ɔbosom* feels shy and will not speak, and we offered Asuo a drink to beg him to speak for me. Asuo said my main day is Tuesday, and I also have Wednesday and Friday. I should not touch the *yawa* on Thursday and

Sunday. Asubonten said before I touch the ɔbosom I should bathe first, and they should tell me the *adae*/holy days and the normal days for the ɔbosom. I must not touch my wife on the night of the ɔbosom's working days. He will eat chicken and sheep and will not eat duck, goat, or guinea fowl.

When I arrive home, I should not touch my wife for 21 days, and I should bathe with *aduro* four times a day, which they will give to me. He said when I arrive in the United States, I should eat seven eggs. Yet still, the ɔbosom will not tell his name, he will only bow his head, but the father smiles. Asubonten said he is bigger than him, and he is an ancient ɔbosom from Takyiman, not America. If I take good care of him, the father will follow. He said the ɔbosom is powerful, so I should take care of how I use him. Still, the ɔbosom will not state his name, and after some cajoling, he finally said his name is Kwabena Bena. I was so happy and elated to hear this; I was beside myself. Asubonten instructed them to give me *aduro* to take with me so that I will see the ɔbosom and know how to use him back home. Asuo told me to get a pot, *sedeɛ*, and sand from a river and a plant from that river and plant it. He said to get a pad to place on the stool for the ɔbosom to sit upon. He said he will speak at home, but here he feels shy and the reason why the ɔbosom does not come fully is because of the old *aduro* from Nana Oparebea, which he does not like. So, after it is all gone from my body, he will come fully.

The next day Nana Dɔnkɔ called me to the shrine room and made some incision at my ankles on both feet and took a black pasty substance—perhaps it was *mɔtɔ* in shea butter out of one of the horns sitting on the clubs—and put some on my cuts. He looked satisfied.

Not too long after, Nana Akumsa possessed her ɔbosom Akumsa. This is the first time I had the privilege of seeing her possess. In the manner of these *ɔbosom*, Akumsa sang a song in between her dialogue. The songs are like part of the conversation going on.

Before I left, Nana Kofi Boɔ and I went drinking *Kunkuma pito* and I got a little drunk. I felt so silly, laughing at everything and anything. I also became sad and depressed with the realization that the next day I would leave my family here and go home. Later, they presented me with a *Gye Nyame* stool and *fugu* as a departing gift and things for my wife. I did not know how to fully thank everyone, but I tried. I will miss them all very much.

I am at the market station with Nana Effa on my way to Accra, but unable to get transportation. Finally, Nana Effa said I am taking a son of Taa Mensa and have not notified him, so he went to bid goodbye. After that we were able to get transportation. On the bus Nana advised me to ring a bell so that my *ɔbosom* will follow me on my way home. The bus was crowded, and it was a long ride. At one point the bus ran over a four-legged animal and Nana said my *ɔbosom* took something.

Nana Effa, Kofi, and Kwame Amponsa, who is another brother that lives in Accra, accompanied me to Accra. Kwame was very helpful to me while I stayed at his house. I am very grateful to him. As I reflect, I was given a lot of *aduro* and *nsuman*, and I recall Kofi Asante telling me that the *ɔbosom* will do many wonderful things, but I should not boast about it. He also said my *ɔbosom* is an *ɔbosommerafoɔ* and is very severe with those who offend him and I should be careful with him. The *ɔbosom* will speak back at home and do more things than in Takyiman. Kofi Asante said he will follow me home, but his wife Nana Effa could not go as far. He also gave me powder to use when I wished to call him, but he did not instruct me on how to use it when I wanted to call him. I will talk to him about this in dreams.

Finally, I was in Madina, Accra. I left yesterday, thinking I had to be at the airport at six in the morning, but it was six in the evening, and this led to problems of where to stay for twelve hours. I said goodbye to a lot of people on Wednesday and Thursday, which was very difficult. Tears flowed like water, naturally on my part. I was given so much *aduro, bodua suman,* my ɔ*bosom* Kwabena Bena, his pad, and all the other things I needed. I have the *kunkuma* they prepared for me, the *doso,* and much more. I will write more when I am on the plane.

*Saturday morning, I had a peculiar dream that I was arrested by a police officer and taken to the station. I knew the officer was wrong, but I could not get him to listen to me, so I went to his superiors and informed them about his injustice, and when I was explaining myself, I went from speaking to hand gestures or signing with my hands while I was sitting at a desk opposite him. I was never taken to a cell or anything as such (This was the night after my flight was overbooked and since I was on standby, I could not leave).*

I missed my flight on the 4[th,] and this caused quite a bit of anxiety. I arranged to leave on the next flight, which was on the 6th, the day my visa expires. I have no idea if this will bring me problems returning on an expired visa. I sent a text home telling Apisha not to meet me in New York. I am now on the plane to Geneva, and tomorrow I will be in New York.

In Geneva I experienced a very challenging time by their local security. These officers carried semiautomatic guns and would on several occasions asked me for my passport and where I was going. People around would look at me as if I'd done something illegally; that's why I was being questioned. This made me recall my experience leaving Accra on SwissAir; the plane was held up because my resident card came into question. I had to stay on the stairs while they confirmed if my card was authentic or not. Everyone was seated except me. Eventually I was permitted to board.

I arrived safely in New York. My wife picked me up and followed the previous instructions I'd given to her for when I arrived. She had the seven eggs for me to eat and other things. My ankles were bothering me and itching. They were also oozing from the incisions. Eventually, my ankles began to swell up, but in a few days, they were back to normal.

After I settled and took my bath and became acclimated, I decided to pay respect to the local *akɔmfoɔ*. Most important to me was to greet Nana Yaw Opare Dinizulu. I made some calls to one of his branches and got his contact number. I called and introduced myself to Nana Dinizulu and explained my intent, and he invited me to his home in New York. My wife and I drove to New York with our daughter. I presented Nana with a drink and gave them my background information, which he accepted. I do not recall if he poured libation. I believed his mother was there in the house, along with family members. I told him I was trained to a Tanɔ *ɔbosom* in Takyiman and asked him if he had ever trained one. He said no. It was the first he ever met one. We stayed a little while chatting, then I left and returned to D.C.

*M'anansesem a metooye yi, se eye de o, se ennye de o, momfa bi nkɔ momfa bi mmera.*

My first day in Takyiman with Mr. Gyimah and Nana Effa to my left.

Nana Bekoe in front of shrine house.

Nana Manu feeding a suman he gave me, at Akumsa Dumase.

Nana Manu, at Akumsa Dumase.

Cooking my fugu.

Preparing to cut hair for graduation.

Asuotipa shrine

Dancing at initiation ceremony.

Women cooking yam at Kwabena.

On the way to Bookyerewa shrine.

Nana Mamu about to possess at my graduation.

Calling the ɔbosom at my initiation.

Possessed at initiation.

Obosom greeting at initiation.

Obosom left at initiation.

Kofi cooking fugu.

Nana Dɔnkɔ and Yaw drumming at Asuotipa corn festival.

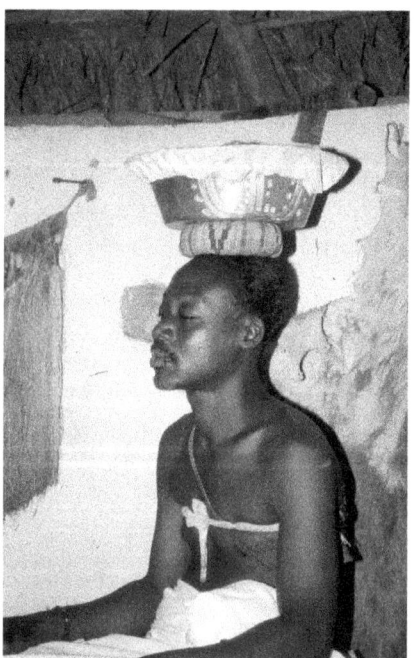
Nana Effa carrying Asuotipa at corn festival.

Nana Effa possessed his sumanbrafoɔ Mossi imitating how Akan dress.

Nana Kwaku Boadu at Asuotipa corn festival.

Nana Bekoe greeting a woman.

Young men at Bɔɔ Yaw shrine.

Tano river at Traa, site of Boɔkyerewa.

Kunkuma ceremony at graduation.

Young men at Asuotipa corn festival with future Asubonten ɔbosomfoɔ Yaw Badu back row first left.

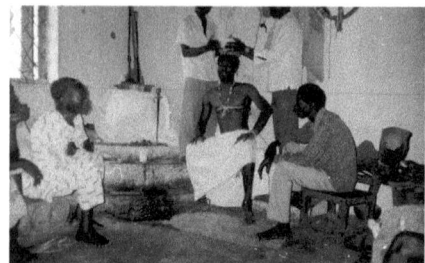
Carrying ɔbosom.

Graduation celebration.

Cooking graduation moto.

Possessing Kwabena Bena at graduation.

Nana Effa possessed and myself at Asuotipa corn festival.

Me and my teachers, Nana Effa, Nana Akumsa, and Nana Dɔnkɔ, with unknown person.

Nana Boadu assisting me while possessed at Asuotipa corn festival.

Herbs boiling to cook fugu.

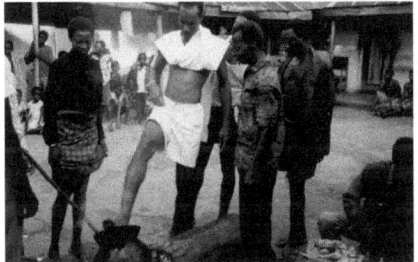
Cooking moto for graduation.

Nana Akumsa feeding me foods no longer taboo at graduation.

Nana Yaw Manu possessing one of his suman.

Final moment surrounded by everyone that assisted me in my graduation.

After my hair is cut.

My obosom displaying.

Graduation shaving.

Nana Akumsa putting gold on my wrist to go and thank members in the neighborhood for supporting my training.

Visiting ɔkɔmfoɔ trained by Nana Effa paying respect.

Visiting ɔkɔmfoɔ displaying.

Nana Akumsa and family member.

Asubonten leaving at initiation.

Asuotipa corn festival. Nana Effa possessed by one on his mmoatia, Kofi Asante who has materializes something.

Adding power to my doso at graduation.

Graduation: I am about to put my foot in smoke.

Akumsa Dumase, Nana Manu feeding his nsuman.

Asuotipa on Nana Effa, dancing at his corn festival.

Nana Boadu dancing at corn festival.

Kofi Asante giving Nana Dɔnkɔ a drink of what he materialized.

Dancing at Nana Effa corn festival.

Kwaku Mossi imitating Akan people.

After corn festival surrounded by children and adults.

Possessed and dancing at Asuotipa corn festival.

# INTERLUDE

## 1991, THE RETURN

At the end of October in 1991, I left Miami, bound for Ghana. I arrived in Accra, Ghana, at the Akotoka airport and was met by Kofi, whom I was truly happy to see. He said he had received my telegram on Saturday, and I told him I had sent it two weeks earlier. He informed me that someone took possession of it and did not give it to him until Saturday. From Accra we traveled by bus to Kumase. We had a few hours layover before we continued on to Takyiman.

We arrived in Takyiman on the start of the *Asubonten Afahye Yam* festival. Immediately we went to the shrine room to greet and pay respect to all present. I saw many familiar faces; it had been two years since I had last seen everyone, but I proceeded from where I left off two years ago. Nana Dɔnkɔ was carrying Asubonten, whom we first greeted, and after much introduction and recognition of familiar faces, I, through Kofi, communicated the purpose of my visit. I presented Asubonten with a bottle of gin from Holland, a sheep, cloth and 10,000 cedis. Asubonten thanked me and offered me a cock as a welcome saying, "You always feed someone before you ask their purpose."

That evening I had a dream.

Nana Dɔnkɔ *gave me three guns, and I put two of them behind my back in my pants and carried the other in my hand. I was shooting at people and realized that I had used up half of my bullets and wanted more.* Nana Dɔnkɔ *said he gave me the guns, so I have to get the bullets. I asked someone for some bullets and he said I have to be like the police to get some and showed me packets of bullets and I took some.*

Nana Dɔnkɔ said this dream is showing me that my *ɔbosom* is fighting my enemies back home. He will shoot them, and I will see something when I go back home. Everyone, even the elders, said that this is a good dream. Nana also said he would give me *aduro* for this dream.

I traveled to Nkoransa Akumsa Dumase to visit Nana Akumsa, who was celebrating her Yam festival and her son Nana Yaw Manu, who precipitated me having a dream.

*I dreamed that I went back home, and some of the akɔmfoɔ trained by Nana Oparebea were having a celebration. I went down some steps in what seems like a basement and saw shrines there. They belonged to Nana Kwabena Brown. Nana Brown did not look like himself in the face; his face had changed. People were sad and crying. I saw his daughters crying as well. One of them took me to the steps and we sat down, and she put her head on my shoulder crying.*

I told this dream to Nana Akumsa, who interpreted it to mean I was seeing death in Takyiman, which has nothing to do with back home. Today I heard news of an elder who had died; I had the dream about four or five days ago.

On October 28 or 29th I had a dream about an ɔkɔmfoɔ from Bonkwae.

*I dreamed that he came here to my town to visit me. He went into the bathroom, and while sitting on the toilet he asked me to listen to the music I (or he) had taped.*

Nana Dɔnkɔ interpreted this dream to mean his ɔbosom is going to my town to help me. Nana said there is an *aduro* he will give me. Nana Kwabena Kranka and Nana Dɔnkɔ both said that this also means money when you sit or go to the toilet.

I visited Nana Effa and his ɔbosom Asuotipa, who gave me a cock to sacrifice to my ɔbosom. It was as with Asubonten; Asuotipa said you do not ask of someone's purpose until you feed and welcome them. During the consultation with the ɔbosom, he reminded me of what he had told me, that I would suffer. He inquired if I had fed my ɔbosom before I traveled to Miami to let him know that Miami would be his new town, as I had done when I took him to Washington, D.C. I said I had no one to assist or help me. Asuotipa said I should have given him a ram anyway and said to him, "I do not have anyone to help me, but this is for you and you can do with it as you wish." He informed me that my ɔbosom would have killed the ram. Asuotipa said after I had done this, my ɔbosom would be able to catch and kill my enemies and I would have seen something. Concerning the accident that almost took my wife and children's lives, Asuotipa said it was because of them my wife's life was saved.

Asuo went on to say that the spirit of my children along with my ɔbosom saved my wife's life. I was also told because the ɔbosom was not fed he allowed those around me to suffer, letting me know what I needed to have done. In other words, the ɔbosom could withdraw his protection and blessings from me. He also said I have three abosom around me, Kwabena Bena, one that likes to visit my wife, and Taa Kora. He stated that Kwabena Bena is the youngest of all my ɔbosom, and that is why he was sent first. The father or elder always sends the youngest to see how thing are first before he follows. I have heard this is what happens before Taa Mensa eats yam. He sends his younger son Yentim to eat the yam first and reports back to him how it is and if it is good to be eaten. After Taa Mensa eats his yam, the Yam festival begins. He mentioned that a powerful ɔbosommerafoɔ would come soon. I would say that this ɔbosommerafoɔ has already come. I possessed him when Nana Dɔnkɔ was feeding his nsuman.

Asuotipa said Nana Effa and I should sacrifice a black chicken to him, and he will put something inside it for me; we should use this to make aduro that only the two of us would eat. If anyone else did eat it, they will die. Asuo asked me if I know my wife has abosom. I told him yes.

Asuo said my wife's family has problems with her. I should thank her mother (her aunt Janet who raised her) because she has helped a lot. He also said people are afraid of me even though they do not act like it. He added Nana Oparebea, too, is afraid of me, but I, too, am afraid of her. I give her too much respect, (maybe for me that is a kind of fear too). Asuo made me aware that it was my ɔbosom who made the way for me to come here, that if I had not come my family's life would be in jeopardy. He inquired if anyone gave me money to come here. I told him no; I got the money from the insurance we received from my wife's car accident. He wanted to know if I owned the car. I said no. He said that is what he meant.

The money did not come out of my own pocket. Asuo said my wife sees, but I do not. I told him yes, she sees better than I do.

I will attempt to note down things I neglected to write for the past two weeks. I recall Asuotipa saying someone close to me has tried to surpass me but cannot. Nana Effa supported this by telling me today that this person is afraid of me (that is, my ɔbosom). I will now try to recall the conversation with Asubonten, when he told me to sacrifice a cock that has three different colored feathers and tie black, red, and white yarn around its feet and a drink. This work is for my wife's case back home, the car loan, and the accident that happened. Asuotipa added I would go to Bonkwae and make a sacrifice by giving a double-edged knife, a guinea fowl, and a drink to Buruma, and he would remove Nana Oparebea from me. I did the ritual at Bonkwae, and the ɔkɔmfoɔ gave me mɔtɔ to eat and instructed me to eat some before I go to sleep and after I awake, but not to speak before I do the rituals.

Asubonten said he and Ɔboɔkyerewa were there to protect my wife. He also revealed since I am his child, and I came here for help, they could not allow anything like this to happen. I told him about my concern about the welfare of my mother. She has heart problems. Asubonten said this is something she was born with and I should not worry. Nana Kwabena Kranka, the eldest son of Nana Akumsa, and Nana Dɔnkɔ's nephew will make a heart *aduro*, or tonic, for my mother. Asubonten gave me a ritual that involved getting white cloth, three *sedeɛ*, money and I am not certain of what else. When I find out I will note it down and offer it to a blind person. I should also say to my ɔbosom while giving these items to the blind man that I need his help, for I cannot see, hear, or anything else that concerns me, so that he can help me do these things.

Nana Asantewaa possessed Ɔbookyerewa after Kofi and I traveled unsuccessfully to Traa to consult him. He said he did not or would not come because of one Aworowa *ɔbosomfoɔɔ* whom he had to punish. This priest's family brought him here to see Nana Dɔnkɔ. He was carried in on a makeshift stretcher, unconscious as they took him into one of the rooms. He had long *mpesempese* and looked advanced in years, maybe seventyish. Ɔbookyerewa told me to go and take a good look at him in the room. I had never seen anyone in such a state before. He told me this *ɔbosomfoɔ* drank too much and would abuse his clients and throw away the *ɔbosom* profits in drinking. He had been warned four times before to stop and would not stop, so that is why he was being punished. He also said if anyone stole from me I should take an egg, call the name of the one who had stolen from me if I knew it, and throw the egg on the ground, and he would catch the thief. He also cautioned me that if this thief returned the items stolen from me I could not use them until a sacrifice was offered to him to notify him that my property had been returned. I guess this was to let me know because his power would still be active and affect anyone with the stolen goods until the thank-you ritual had been done. This includes me; he also said if I steal he would act the same way toward me and kill me.

The Aworowa *ɔbosomfoɔɔ*'s family came over to me and pleaded with me to go and talk to Ɔbookyerewa to spare his life. When I approached Ɔbookyerewa, he would turn his back toward me. This is very reminiscent of how he was when I saw him in my dream. After I pleaded a couple more times, Ɔbookyerewa reluctantly turned to face me and said if they bring to me the sacrifice, drink, and money before three days he might spare his life. Unfortunately, the family never came back. Sad to tell, later on I heard this ɔbosomfoɔ died.

I was constantly in Asubonten shrine room whenever anything was going on, even if it was just conversations taking place. This allowed me to witness and carefully pay attention to all that I have observed and raised a lot of questions in my mind. I witnessed one work being done for someone that piqued my curiosity. I saw a chicken brought in with three cowrie shells tied around its neck. I inquired as to what it was used for. I was told this is so that people will not laugh at you. Another time it was stinging nettles tied around a chicken's feet, and around the neck of a bottle of gin. I was also told this is to bring back one who has traveled far. The nettles will itch them and pull them back home. The nettle is then removed from the chicken's feet, and the drink and put between the opening of the ɔbosom's stool. I have seen a plant called "get something," but I do not recall the Twi name or its usage.

In retrospect, I remembered Kwaku Mossi telling me to make a sacrifice facing my town with a bunch of palm nut and drive a nail into it, saying what I want done with regard to my wife's case. Then I should place gunpowder on the nail head, light it, and after it ignites blow bluing powder over it.

On Sunday I went and consulted Asuotipa, who mentioned that he would give me a *suman* that is a *suman*mmerafoɔ that will catch bad people for me, and I should take good care of it. Asuo also said if I want to know more about its function I should inquire with Mossi, since it is very much like him. Sometime later on we consulted Akua Bɔmmɔ, where Nana Effa brought forth the *suman*merafoɔ out of the shrine and it appeared to burn him, and he tossed it into the air, and it fell near my feet. I picked it up and handed it back to him. It had a somewhat intimidating appearance, with the foot of a hawk, scorpion claws, fishhooks, a small bell, and what looked like a big seed covered with skin and a string of lead beads attached to hold it.

I recalled what Mossi had said about this *suman*; he said it is powerful and I should take very good care of it. Mossi told me not to reveal its name to others, nor tell them its taboos or sacrifices. He emphasized that it catches bad people. Mossi also advised me that I should come back and consult to get more clarity about the *suman*. We then proceeded to perform the sacrifice with the black chicken. In dissecting the chicken, we found a small shell in its intestines. Only Nana Effa and I ate the meat.

The *suman*merafoɔ that was brought forth by Bɔmmɔ needed to be fed. First, a circle was drawn with white clay, but I could also have used ash or powder. The *suman* was put in the center of the circle. Nana Effa then took my left wrist and cut three knicks and smeared my blood on the *suman* to let the *suman* know that I am the one it should protect and fight for. It should also protect my family, wife, and children. It will catch *abayifoɔ* and thieves. After that, Nana Effa took some *mɔtɔ* and rubbed it into the incisions. I sacrificed a chicken to the *suman*, telling it all my concerns and needs; no one else was present except the two of us. I threw the chicken, and it flipped about four times, once on my foot, on the *suman* itself, and finally it landed on its stomach face forward with its wings spread afar. We were a little concerned, and I pleaded for the *suman* to eat properly. We dissected the chicken to look inside at the intestines, kidneys, and heart. Everything appeared okay. This was contrary to the black chicken, which landed on its back when it was sacrificed earlier.

I came back the next day and presented a drink and egg to Bɔmmɔ for consultation about the *sumanmerafoɔ*. Akua Bɔmmɔ and another spirit name Attia instructed me on the *suman*. People were present at the shrine room as well. I was told the name, which I was advised not to mention. All I can say is that it does not like to be challenged. I poured libation with gin, but never directly onto it, only near its claws. If I poured directly onto it, it would get drunk and misbehave and do bad things. It likes perfume oils or what they call lavender here, and this I can pour directly on it. I also cannot reveal its taboos. I purify it with *ɔkomfentikoro*, *Atanagya*, and *Ntum*. It has a bell attached to it, and when it rings, this will inform me that *abayifoɔ*, thieves, or any bad thing are coming my way. The *suman* will eat only yam roasted on fire, not boiled. If a client comes for help, I must first offer the *suman* a baby chick, and when the work is a success they should thank with a regular chicken, drink, money, or even a ram. If by chance the *suman* has helped and the client refuses to pay, I can send the *suman* to collect its fee. The *suman* was born on Kwasiada and therefore is called Kwasi, but its working day is Friday's *Fofie*.

Today is my birthday, November 13th. Peter Ventevogel, a researcher from Holland about twenty-four years old, has taken up residency in the compound for about six months now. He came here on an introduction from Mike Warren. Nana Asubonten, Nana Dɔnkɔ's sister, would always call him Bediakɔ. We somehow manage to get into a disagreement over money. He traveled with Kofi and I to Accra. I did not have enough money for both Kofi and me to travel to Accra, and so he gave Kofi gave 5,000 cedis. Kofi, unbeknown to me, gave him my film to develop. I thought Kofi was giving him his own film for development, since he and I both use Kofi for taking our photos. All this took place in Accra, and after we arrived back in Takyiman, Peter came to me, wanting his money for the film and saying I could buy them now or later if I wanted. Nonetheless he wanted his money now. All the while I was trying to understand what was going on, because I thought it was his own film Kofi had put in the shop for development. He informed me the photos cost him 5,000 cedis. I gave to him the cedis and from there on we did not have much to say to each other after that misunderstanding. I wish not to continue with this topic, since I am here to learn *akɔm* and I am documenting my spiritual journey as an *ɔbosomfoɔ/ɔkɔmfoɔ*.

I consulted Asubonten, and during this occasion he likened me to a child who comes running fast to his father, and thus the father (Asuo) cannot push me away. Asuo went on to add, I am now sitting on his lap. He informed me that my *ɔbosom* wanted to talk but was not able since my mind did not understand their language. He said as I come and go, I would learn the language. He thanks me very much since I have returned, and beckons everyone to come and thank me. He told me that my mother almost died and her spirit is very sad about me; he said I should give her five eggs and tell her not to worry about me, and that she should support what I am doing, that what has come to me is from Nyame, and she should eat these eggs to pacify her *okra*. He said after I do this, I will see the change in her. Asuo said he would visit me, and my *ɔbosom* would communicate with me in dreams.

I told Asubonten a dream. Asubonten said his *ɔbosomfoɔ* Nana Dɔnkɔ will give me *aduro* to wash my face after I narrated a dream I had.

Nana Effa *and I were at Traa at the Ɔboɔkyerewa shrine, and I had a plant in my hand. Nana took the top and gave it to Ɔboɔkyerewa and said he should protect and help me.*

Asubonten interpreted this to mean the family of Ɔbookyerewa are upsetting him and soon he will kill. Asuo said I should buy a white cock and get sand from a road that forks ("Y"). I should smear the sand on an egg and give it to him so that he will always help me to return, and protect me, my wife, and children and would help me with what else was on my mind. He said I should get three white and three red kola nuts, and three *pesawa* (old coins not in use), put them in a white piece of cloth and give it to a blind person.

This evening I was eating with Nana Dɔnkɔ as I usually do, and my *ɔbosom* came. They said he told them he is from Takyiman and does not want to leave. Nana Dɔnkɔ begged him to go, because if I stay here my family will suffer back home. Nana encouraged him that I should go and come and that will be okay. Later on, after Kwabena Bena left, Nana said Kwabena Bena is a serious *ɔbosommerafoɔ* like Ɔbookyerewa and people should be careful of him. Nana Dɔnkɔ told me to offer two knives and I should call all whom I wish to protect and sacrifice a cock and ask him to protect them all. Nana reinforced that I could offer any type of chicken, even hens, except any white chickens, unless the *ɔbosom* ask for one.

Nana Dɔnkɔ loves telling stories, and one in particular was about how *aduro* came among people. One day a farmer went to farm and got possessed by a *ɔbosom*. People thought he was ill because he would come in and out of possession. The farmer went into the bush and the *mmoatia* took hold of him. They opened his mouth so the *ɔbosom* could speak. At this time there were many illnesses and diseases among the people, and the *ɔbosom* taught the farmer how to identify and treat the diseases with plants. As the people began to multiply, they brought all sorts of problems to the *ɔbosom*. The *ɔbosom* indicated that he could not handle all their problems and therefore instituted the ɔhene to hear their cases and solve their problems.

*M'anansesem a metooye yi, se eye de o, se ennye de o, momfa bi nkɔ momfa bi mmera.*

**BONO AKOM PANIN MISSION**

Registration Number: AB 2074

This is to certify that Mr. Blackman Keth Anthony (Kwaku Sakyi)

has successfully been trained and initiated as "KUMKUMA" Bono-Priest for the period of 18 months at Techiman, Brong Ahafo Region of Ghana.

This Certificate is therefore issued under the Authority, and is also permitted to set up his / her Mission to practise wherever service may be required.

This certificate is given on this 4th day of Sept 1990.

_____  
Akomfohene (Bono)

_____  
Asubonteng Priest

Graduation certificate.

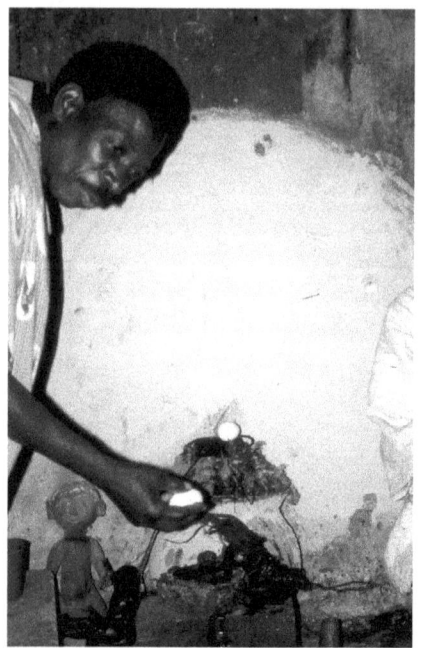

Nana Kofi Boɔ at nsuman room.

Bɔɔkyerewa Ɔbosomfoɔ Nana Asamadu and me.

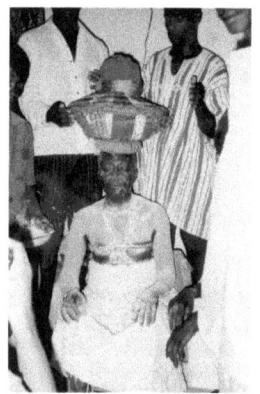

Nana Dɔnkɔ carrying Asubonten during yam festival.

Asubonten Afahye.

Ɔhene pouring libation at Ateokɔsa Tanoboase.

Ɔkɔmfoɔhene and senior akɔmfoɔ.

Nana Dɔnkɔ and other akɔmfoɔ at festival.

Nana Dɔnkɔ with Ɔkɔmfoɔhene and Nana Kwaku Boadu chatting.

# CHAPTER THREE

## 1994, CONTINUING PROGRESS

Spiritual independence is what we practice, and it refers to believing that if you ask the *ɔbosom* to help you, the *ɔbosom* will help you. Your mind must never show doubt or indecision (ambivalence); it must be pure and free of distracting thoughts.

When a ram cannot be sacrificed at a given time, the hair under the neck, on top of the head, and end of the tail is cut and placed on top of the pan as a promise to make the sacrifice at a later, convenient time. The meaning behind these hairs, I will explain: The hair under the throat is to say that this ram is for the *ɔbosom*, and I will sacrifice, cut, and give to him. The hair on top of the head is to say the *ɔbosom* is the head, the leader. The tail hair represents that the *ɔbosom* will have the sweet parts; that is everything.

In the case of a chicken, when you cannot sacrifice at that time, you pluck the feathers from under the neck/throat and top of the head, but never the tail, as a promise to sacrifice later. The meaning is the same as above.

The ɔbosom does not like the heat of the day and therefore does not come out, nor is sacrifice given to him at that time. Asuotipa said he is a water ɔbosom, like the fish that does not come on the surface of the water when the sun is hot for fear that it may die. So, does this mean Asuo fears the heat? Of course not, and should not be taken literally. It only means that he will not function when it is too hot. Most of the time, the heat is greater at noon. Noon is a when the sun is straight above our heads and pushes our shadow down. It is a time of uncertainty and ambiguity, will it stay that way. Is the sun going to proceed onward or retreat back.

The ɔbosom when it first possesses throws *hyire*/clay up to the sky and sprinkles some on the ground to signify that it offers respect and thanks to the father, Nyame, and mother earth, Asase Yaa, and that some should stay with them. The clay also represents purity.

When chickens are being sacrificed, only the liver is given to the ɔbosom, and it is placed on the *yawa*/pan. I have seen Nana Effa give the heart as well. The feet and head are set or thrown at the clubs for the Amoa, that is, the children or *mmoatia* of the Tanɔ. The saying is that the children do not eat at the same table as the father. They get theirs when any falls on the ground or floor. Interestingly enough, these same parts are given to the children. I have also observed them just walking up and taking it off the clubs. I have come to realize that this is a ritual to attract children like the *mmoatia* and keep them close to the shrine.

The reason why ɔkɔmfoɔ tastes the drink first and spits it out, is to make sure that the drink is acceptable before he offers it to the ɔbosom. There are specific drinks the ɔbosom likes and some it taboos, and this process is a precaution. After tasting the drink and making sure it is acceptable, the *ɔkɔmfoɔ* says "We," stating it is good. If it is not so, the *ɔkɔmfoɔ* says nothing and simply removes it. When company visits the *ɔkɔmfoɔ* or the elders, the *ɔkyeame* consumes some of the drinks first if it is already opened (to demonstrate it is approved, not harmful) before it is offered to the guests. This ritual is called *nom suro,* taking away the fear. In case of unopen drink, the *ɔkyeame* does not have to drink the fear.

The *Tanɔ ɔbosom* can go to the funeral and pay respect to the departed. The circumstance in which the *ɔbosom* may go is if the death of someone is mentioned in the shrine room or if the *ɔbosomfoɔ* notifies the *ɔbosom* that he intends to go, as in the case of a relative or another *ɔbosomfoɔ/ɔkɔmfoɔ.* At the funeral, the *ɔbosom* may give advice to all in attendance or perform rites at the corpse. When this happens, both the *ɔbosom* and *ɔbosomfoɔ* have to be purified with a ram, but in case only the *ɔbosomfoɔ/ɔkɔmfoɔ* goes and does not mention to the *ɔbosom* his or her intent to go, then only he or she has to be purified.

In the case of the death of *Atanɔ ɔbosomfoɔ/ɔkɔmfoɔ,* when this happens, the *ɔbosom* is placed on a *kakyire* of *nyinya* (pad on the ground of the shrine room). Libation is poured, and the *ɔbosom* is notified of what has happened and asks to change and choose a new *ɔbosomfoɔ* before the old one is buried. The family members would gather and *aduro* is sprinkled or sprayed into the air so that many young candidates may become possessed. Eventually, they become possessed and the one who shows he has the most power and carries the *ɔbosom* properly is the one chosen to be the new *ɔbosomfoɔ.* In case family members are disagreeing and jockeying their candidate to be the new *ɔbosomfoɔ,* the *ɔbosom* will not claim his own until the family is of one mind. If this ritual is not done before the old *ɔbosomfoɔ* is buried, then the family members will have to bring their candidates to carry the ɔbosom and see which one he will take. The concern is always that if the rituals are not properly adhered to, the ɔbosom may go with the departed ɔbosomfoɔ.

In May 1994, I saw Taa Kora for the first time. He resides at Tanɔboase, and I had never seen a Tanɔ like this before. Why not? He is the first and eldest of all Tanɔ. I witness him in all his majestic splendor and radiance of a truly high ɔbosom. He evoked such an emotion in me. The ritual that preceded his possession is far too complex and sacred to describe. You will just have to believe me when I say it is. I was told by him that someone challenged me not to be successful here, and by doing so, this someone challenges the Atanɔ abosom of Takyiman. However, my ɔbosom has caught this person, and I will see this when I get back home. He said if we doubt his words, we should bet with him. No one did.

I learned from the ɔhene of Tanɔboase and owner of Taa Kora that atadwɛ/ tiger nuts are important, and on special days I should chew some and spray it on the yawa three times. But first, I should say what I need, and after spitting, I must polish the yawa with it. Kofi advised me to polish the yawa with egg yolk, then atadwɛ. The ɔhene gave me mɔto so that what I say comes to fruition. First, I put some on my left hand and touch my tongue to it and say what I need before eating the rest. What I say will come true.

I was curious about why they put only the egg yolk and not the whole egg on the yawa. I asked Nana Dɔnkɔ, and he said the yolk and not the surrounding part of the egg are used because it (the white) protects the most important part, the yolk. When I am feeding the ɔbosom eggs, I should use fertilized eggs, for this is most important, since it has both male and female essence.

Nana also instructed me that I can sacrifice either male or female chickens, but never a white one. I can also give a male or female sheep to the *Tanɔ*, but never the kind that has four eyes (a sheep with black concave circles under or around the eyes). These are considered the eyes of *abayifoɔ*, and they utilize them to see. And most of all, never offer deformed animals. He instructed me to sleep with my *ɔbosom* on sacred days and to keep the *nsuman* in a separate room from *Tanɔ*.

While at Tanɔboase, I presented a chicken for sacrifice, a bottle of gin, and 5,000 cedis, along with *atadwɛ* (tiger nuts) and *akpeteshie* for Amoa. I was told to say what I wanted to Amoa, chew the *atadwɛ* and spit it three times on Amoa.

Mossi warned me about worrying too much, saying when I do this, it will affect the *ɔbosom*. Kofi added that the *ɔbosom* uses my soul/spirit, and if something bothers me, it will affect the *ɔbosom* and he will not be happy, especially if I am sad. Mossi went on to say that part of *akɔm* is being patient (*to oboase*), and in this manner, a lot of things can be accomplished.

If someone has a personal problem that is difficult for them to solve, they will look for anyone on whom they can rest this burden. That is why when someone gives you a gift and you do not know why they have presented you with these gifts (especially food), if you accept or eat the food, you will inherit their troubles and have serious problems breaking free of them. A woman with a problem gave me a loaf of bread and said she was walking with a problem, and it wants her to stay (referring to her husband). She wanted me to be her emancipator and release her from this burden. She presented me with a loaf of bread. After she left, I gave the bread to the children to eat, since no harm would come to them, as she was not looking to them to solve her issues.

If you break taboos that you are ignorant of, the *ɔbosom* will not hold you accountable. The same with a woman on her menses; *akɔmfoɔ/abosomfoɔ* are not supposed to speak directly at them, even in the case of your wife. The exception may be due to circumstances that dictate that you speak to her. You can go to the *ɔbosom* and make the necessary sacrifice, explaining why it was necessary for you to communicate at this time, and the *ɔbosom* will overlook the taboo.

It appears that rituals are the doorway by which interaction between the two worlds takes place. It is through rituals that the *abosom* and the *nsamanfoɔ* know what is on our minds. Even if the *ɔbosom* knows what is on our minds or what is happening to us, we must still do the rituals. This is because the *ɔbosom* wants us to speak and unburden ourselves about what is worrying us. By doing so, we are saying to the *ɔbosom* that we are aware of our problems; we are getting it off our chest and we want it to solve our problems.

Kofi and I were instructed by Nana Dɔnkɔ to go to the forest and collect a plant called *Bra kesɛ*. This was for me to bathe. This plant is used for protection against bad *aduto*. That is what we call bad power that is sent to harm someone. The spirit of the plant will deflect and return anything bad sent my way to anyone competing with me. This is a very powerful plant that reverses bad *aduto*.

Kofi, on the behalf of Nana Dɔnkɔ, informed me that if my wife and I had a quarrel and I decided not to eat her cooking, the *ɔbosom* may become annoyed with me and punish me. The reasoning behind this is if I refuse her food only because I am upset with her, then I, too, am refusing to allow the *ɔbosom* the opportunity to eat. The *ɔbosom* eats with the *ɔbosomfoɔ/ɔkɔmfoɔ*, and by saying no to my wife, I am also saying no to him eating. The *ɔbosom* considers my wife as one who can prepare his food and bring it to him to eat, and since he has no problems with her, why should he be denied her food? If I have a problem with her and am upset, I should not refuse her cooking, I should solve the matter or seek help to get a solution.

When the food for the *ɔbosom* is being cooked on a fire, the cook has to make sure that nothing else shares the same fire. If that should happen, the cook is sharing the power of what solely should be used for the *ɔbosom* is tabooed. The same for the sharing of *aduro* with something else while being cooked on fire is taboo.

Anything taken from a tree that has been struck by lightning can be used as *aduro*; it is the same for two trees touching or crossing (X) and rubbing up against each other, and when the winds blow, they make sounds. These types of trees and their *aduro* are what you want to represent in your relationship between you and the *ɔbosom*: as always together, being one, and never apart.

*Aduro* can be represented in many functions. One of my favorites is called "the sun never sets." When one is collecting parts of a tree for a specific purpose, I was told I can collect the bark from both the shaded and sunny sides of that tree. This is done so that the *aduro* will work sunup and sundown. In other words, the *aduro* will never rest working for me.

Yesterday, a *suman* named *Bɔngan* was made for me. I was told it is very powerful, and only three *akɔmfoɔ* have one: Nana Akumsa, Nana Asantewaa, and myself. We poured libation first, then sacrificed a chicken to it. I will now attempt to describe the *suman*. It is made from a horn from a particular animal, and on one side there is a small gourd that contains its *mɔtɔ*, and on the other a *dufa*, all attached by a string of white beads called *ntwerewa* (to pull). Before sacrificing, I must drive the horn into the ground, circle it with clay, and place a mound of clay on top of the horn upon which an egg is placed standing upright. If the egg balances or stands without falling, then he accepts the work. If it falls, he does not. This is important before I do anything, especially in traveling to *akɔm* or somewhere unfamiliar, for if it falls, it indicates I should stop whatever I plan to do. This is also an indication if I should continue with the sacrifice. If all goes well, I should slaughter the chicken or hold it at the nape of the neck, asking Bɔngan to kill it himself. First, I walk seven paces, crossing one foot over the other until I take seven steps, then hold it until it dies. The egg can be used to polish the *suman* or given to a favorite child to cook and eat. I will feed *Bɔngan* the heart, and the meat can be cooked any way you please and anyone can eat its meat, except menstruating women. Yaw Mensa, the son of Nana Akumsa, made *Bɔngan* for me on her behalf. He said that it can do anything, and there is no limit to its function. It is to be worn over the neck, hanging on the left side of my chest with my left arm through it. I can take it anywhere I travel, to *akɔm*, and so forth, but must ask permission first by giving an egg. The *suman* can assist in possessing my *ɔbosom* and worn, especially when carrying the *yawa*. I should make sure to eat some of its *mɔtɔ* before I carry it. In general, I can do anything with this *suman*, but I must eat some *mɔtɔ* first, then ask. *Bɔngan* will talk to me in a dream, and he does not like to be ignored. He taboos menstruating women very seriously.

I can help a client with this *suman* by doing the same rituals and giving them some of the *mɔtɔ* to eat, but I should eat some first. How I came by being given this *suman* is very interesting. Nana Akumsa, while I was in her company with Nana Dɔnkɔ, told me that she has observed my character over the years and considers it good, and because of this she would like to give me something, a *suman* called *Bɔngan*. She also said that I would be one of three individuals in Ghana to have this *suman*. She gave me a list of items to get to make the *suman*. The one I found most interesting was getting the blind man's stick. I had to buy him a new one and convince him that it was a better walking stick.

Nana Dɔnkɔ's second wife has an uncle, Nana Kofi Nimo, who visits her frequently and spends a lot of time conversing with Nana Dɔnkɔ about healing. He took a special liking to me and decided to give me a *suman* called *Asabre*. This *suman* is used mainly for court cases or if someone bothers me. If you have a problem communicating your thoughts in court, it is good for that. It taboos nothing but *abe kwan* (palm nut soup) on Fridays. If I get it contaminated, I have to give 1,000 cedis, a fowl, and a full bottle of gin to purify. Before I use the *suman*, the one wanting help has to provide the gunpowder. If they do not have any, I can sell some to them. You put some gunpowder on it and mention the name of the opposing person and light it to smoke. When this happens, it will take on the case. If the powder does not ignite or smoke, Asabre will not take on the case. I can cut or hold the sacrifice by the nape of the neck. I will also walk seven paces and cross my feet when holding its neck. I must break the left leg and wing of the chicken if the sacrificed is accepted. When the chicken is dead, I pull its tongue out and perform a ritual licking it three times and put it on the *suman*. Then I feed the *suman* the neck bone with both legs.

After that has been eaten, I should eat the legs, or if not, I should chew some and spit it three times on the *suman*. I will use the rope for tying the name of the person who needs help or the adversary with three pieces of a part of a sweeping broom, a finger of pepper, and animal hair (make sure the hair is pointing away from me). Take seven seeds of *famwisa*, chew them, and spit them on the *suman* three times after it is tied. Take some of the *mɔtɔ,* place it in my palm, and blow it away three times, then eat some before I give it to the client. Put a stone on top to weigh the case. I can use the *suman* any day I wish. Nana Nimo also gave me a gourd with the *mɔtɔ* for it, which can be given to anyone to counteract *bayi*. I will taste it three times before I give it to anyone. To purify the *suman* and rope, use *ɔkomfentikorɔ*, *pia*, and *nunum*. If I cannot get all three, I should just use any two. I can sacrifice with other *nsuman*. I can charge clients any amount to do the *suman*'s work. When the case is won for *aseda*, I can charge a chicken, drink, and any amount of money. If someone wishes to rent the *suman*, they must offer a chicken and drink; if he accepts, then they can rent it for any fee I desire. When they are finished with the *suman*, I can charge the same for the return. It should be polished with egg.

Playing with marbles is a favorite pastime for children, especially boys. I recall the fun I used to have playing with my collection of glass marbles back in Trinidad. But the marbles I am about to refer to are a seed from a tree, which it is called *Ate*. The usage of marbles is an essential part not only to spiritual work but in divination as well. Sometimes the *ɔbosom* will ask for marbles as a sacrifice, and when the *ɔbosom* does so, it means that people are not taking you seriously and are pulling you here and therefore it will serve as a reminder to the *ɔbosom* that people should not play with you as if you are a marble, a toy. It can also relate to the *ɔbosom* to represent that he can use your body and play with it (as in possession) day or night, like Ate. In this way, the ɔbosom uses the ɔbosomfoɔ/ɔkɔmfoɔ for useful purposes. Anything that is used as marbles in any culture can be substituted.

A *suman* named Ibrahim was made for me by Nana Yaw Manu. This *suman* is to be buried in my yard to call all people from the four cardinal points on earth to come to me for work. He gave me *mɔtɔ* in a plastic wrapping for counteracting any *adubɔne* thrown at me or anyone. It should be used to put into the skin of clients with an incision and to eat.

The way to set up Ibrahim is to show the *suman* to the sky three times, touch it to the pot, then put the *suman* into a small pot and cover it with a metal lid. Put burning coals on top of the lid and add some gunpowder to the coal to make it smoke. Sacrifice chicken on the fire. Take four *sedeɛ* (cowrie shells), show them in four directions and ask for people to come from the east, west, north, and south. While placing a shell in four directions, ask for support for my *ɔbosom*, all my work, and family in everything and, most of all, good health. Take the feet and wings and put the right foot east, the left foot west, the right wing north, and the left wing south. Cover the *suman* with dirt to form a mound, and plaster it with cement. I may make any design I desire on the cement. I should pour libation every Friday and eat the rest of the chicken with the family.

Today, I offered a drink, chicken, and marbles called *Ate* strung with red, black, and white thread as a sacrifice to Asuotipa.

There is always a tree no matter where you live that children abuse, swinging on it, carving their names into it, climbing it, chopping or breaking off branches for no useful purpose. They will ignore all other trees except this unfortunate one. You will see prospering trees that are never abused surrounding it. This kind of tree is called *Anisandua* (the tree that the eyes return to).

Spiritually, this tree can represent the *ɔbosom* and the *ɔbosomfoɔ/ɔkɔmfoɔ*. Like Ate, you will use him anytime when he is asleep, has traveled, or is working. You will call and disturb him. This *aduro* is an important *aduro*. On the flip side, it can function for the condition of someone desperate and in need of help.

I was introduced to a special chicken called *ɔkoko dwan*, or is it called *ɔdwan ɔkoko*, which is translated as ram chicken. It is more commonly called *Asense*. This chicken looks very strange, somewhat ruffled with straight feathers. It is given to the *ɔbosom* in lieu of a ram until you can afford one.

I came here without knowing how to feed my *ɔbosom* properly, and this came up in the shrine when I was consulting Asubonten, who informed me that I should have given my *ɔbosom* a ram before I traveled here. A chicken is too small to feed all my *ɔbosom*. When I was sacrificing the ram, I should have asked him to travel with me wherever I go, possess me, and to protect my family at home while I am away. I was also told not to eat cows, and when I sacrifice anything to Kwabena Bena, whether chicken, ram, or drink, never to share the meat with women.

I sacrificed a chicken at Nana Effa's shrine and presented a drink. He gave me *aduro* in the form of *mɔtɔ* incisions instead of a *suman*, which he thinks would be difficult to get through immigration. This *aduro* is to help my *ɔbosom* to come and see all and say everything and aid me any time at my work when I call him.

Kofi and I have been looking for a vine called *Homakyebere* (snake vine), and finally we found it. This plant has many colors (white, green, orange, yellow, and gold), while the root is somewhat salmon in color and is said to look much like a particular snake that supposedly has the same color. Nana Dɔnkɔ says this plant is a powerful *aduro*, and when you bathe, it will penetrate the skin and give you a long life. When someone wishes for your death, they will die before you do. He suggested that I use some first and get as much into my body as I am able before I recommended it to anyone. It will counteract *bayi* and make my enemies change into something. I will have to verify exactly what he means by changing into something. After it is dried, the root essence will last up to three years. It is a very powerful *aduro,* not to be taken casually, and very few *ɔkɔmfoɔ*, according to Nana, know about this plant. I am so fortunate to have been able to meet with remarkable men like Nana Dɔnkɔ and to be one of the very few to ever use it. I pray to Nyame and Tanɔ to bless Nana Dɔnkɔ.

We went through the trouble of getting this plant so it could be used to make a *suman* for me by a *Ntoa ɔkɔmfoɔ*. I was told that this *ɔkɔmfoɔ* is older than Nana Dɔnkɔ. Nana and I traveled to his town, Bonsu, to see him and offer him drink and sacrifice so that he would help me get something. I was told that Nana told the *ɔkɔmfoɔ* he needed help for his son (that being me). The items this *ɔkɔmfoɔ* required to do the work have been the most difficult for me to get so far. I will name a few: skins from *Aboa* keseɛ, *sisire, akokɔ kɔkɔɔ* (cock with red feather), and plants such as *Ode ase* and *Homabire ase ne hahare*. Other materials included *biribire* (black) *kɔkɔɔ* (red), *fitaa* (white) strings, and a strong string called *Bɔfo*, and *Ako pa/ Awedie* (parrot tail) to name a few.

For divination, I needed fifty *sedeɛ*, *asɔsɔ ba* (small hoe for falling palm tree), *twerebɔɔ* (pebble from stone for lighting fire), *adonnoma* (small bell), and a cock. Some of these items I have no idea of what they are, but I was told that the work that this *ɔkɔmfoɔ* is going to do is very rare, and it will improve my divination. I also needed plants called *benkum ne nifa hahare*, *asuo mu oteɛ*, *tafamere*, and *asɔsɔbia*, whereas divination required kola nut (*brafoɔ*), red bead (represent woman), and green bead (represent *ɔbosom*).

The items needed to make the things are always given first. After they are acquired, then the *suman* or whatever it will be is made. Kwam Froɔ, as he is called, with the assistance of Kofi Nimo, a nephew of Nana Dɔnkɔ, and Nana himself all participated in making the *suman*.

The first *suman* is called *Kofi Fofie Akorɔma*; it is male and covered with a red felt cloth (*nkrawo*). The second is female and is called *Brɛnsɛmase*, and it is covered with a white cloth. Their appellation I am not allowed to reveal. I was also informed that these *nsuman* can catch *abosom* for me. *Bɔfo* is for government cases. Red, black, and white strings are for tying court cases. White is only for family matters. When tying, you should use one finger of pepper, three months of a sweeping broom, pull some of the tail hair, and tie them all together along with the written name of the adversary, then place a stone on top of the *suman* to weigh it down. I can work with them on any day, but *Fofie* is a special day. I need to make sure to always bathe first before touching them.

I witnessed before the sacrifice is offered *Taafamerɛ*, *Piaa*, and *ɔkomfentikorɔ* rubbed into the palms and used for pouring libation on the *suman* and into the mouth of the chicken to be a sacrifice. There are two options that I can use for sacrificing, one holding the chicken by the nape of the neck or cutting the throat with a knife. Squat and rub the blood on the *suman* between my left knee. Offer the heart, the neck, the feet, and the wings. I have seen the feet inserted into the neck. Never share its food with women, and sacrifice to it alone.

A few days ago, Nana Effa informed me that when I am going to funerals, I should carry *Nyinya* leaves in my pocket so that the *ɔbosom* will not follow me there. I can also chew crabgrass with kola nuts before I go to the funeral. He said the *ɔbosom* do not like funerals, which is in far contrast to what Nana Dɔnkɔ told me, saying that Tanɔ will go to the funeral to pay respects to the dead and do something to send the dead off. So, I am a little confused, and somehow, I will try to reconcile and verify this with Nana Dɔnkɔ. I have seen during the *Apoɔ* festival Taa Mensa go to where his old *ɔbosomfoɔ* is buried (he died in 1989 while I was training) and give respects to him by sprinkling *hyire*/clay on the burial site. I was told that the whole celebration of the *Apoɔ* is to celebrate the death of his mother, who was the first to possess him, that is, give birth to him and die. Perhaps the rituals I described for the *ɔbosomfoɔ* were really meant for his mother, the first ancestress who possessed Taa Mensa and created the lineage for future *ɔbosomfoɔ*.

Kofi and I were conversing, and the topic about stealing came up. He told me that if someone stole something from me and I suspected who the culprit was and went to the *ɔbosom* to ask him to do something he would not do anything. He said the reasoning is that I already suspect someone, so why should the *ɔbosom* do anything? I would have to follow through with what is on my mind. Now if, on the other hand, I keep my mind and heart clear and hand it over to the *ɔbosom*, then he will do the work for me. In the former circumstances, if the *ɔbosom* catches the thief, I might say, "Yes! I suspected this person." In this way I will take the credit away from the *ɔbosom*. The work of the *ɔbosom* depends heavily upon an uncontaminated mind. If I have seen something, the *ɔbosom* will not come and say he too sees something. If I have a problem with my wife, the *ɔbosom* will not possess and say to her you have a problem with your husband. The *ɔbosom* functions properly when there is no credibility issue. It brings liability to me when I know something and use my *ɔbosom* to inform others of that thing. It is best to send them elsewhere to get advice from another *ɔbosomfoɔ/ɔkɔmfoɔ*.

If something about me is worrying me about my *ɔbosom*, perhaps I offended him or broke a taboo, the *ɔbosom* will not use my body to say to me that I have offended him. When I am suspicious that maybe I have done something wrong, my mind is no longer clear and the *ɔbosom* cannot act freely. That is why it is always suggested that *ɔbosomfoɔ/ɔkɔmfoɔ* should try to preserve and keep an open mind free of unnecessary thoughts that may cloud the clarity of the *ɔbosom*. Whatever I think, the *ɔbosom* thinks, and if I possess the thoughts of the *ɔbosom*, they are not his thoughts, but my thoughts. This is a problem.

Chickens are sacrificed plentifully at the shrines, and I had the opportunity to witness their reaction in many distinctive ways, which only made me very curious about their interpretations. A few examples should suffice: when a chicken is sacrificed and thrown and lands on its feet, and if it runs or walks, I was told that the *ɔbosom* or *suman* will go with me. If it lands on its chest and spreads its wings outwards, I will be covered and protected. Nana Effa personally told me when the chicken rubs both feet together back and forth this means that I and the person (client) will work together or cooperate, which I also interpreted to mean the ɔbosom and I, or client will have a symbiotic relationship in solving their issues.

I was told that if I should take up with or show interest in another woman, the ɔbosom will not approve of this sort of behavior. He will think like a husband, that his wife has taken up with someone else to replace him. This will cause difficulties when I try to possess him. The ɔbosom does not want my thoughts or mind clouded and preoccupied with someone else instead of him. The same goes for if something is worrying my mind, say perhaps family issues that have not been addressed, and if I possess, the ɔbosom should not reveal such a problem, for this will damage his credibility as well as my own. The ɔbosom strives to foster respect and credibility by being a seer of hidden things, and when the ɔbosomfoɔ/ɔkɔmfoɔ compromises this when possessed and speaks on those topics that are already embedded in the mind, it becomes an issue of honesty. When someone is divining, the divination functions best when the diviner has not been told what the problem is by the inquirer or by anyone seeking help. If by chance the ɔbosomfoɔ/ɔkɔmfoɔ is notified of the client's situation before the ɔbosom is possessed, the work will be spoiled because a seed was planted that will take root in the mind of the ɔbosomfoɔ/ɔkɔmfoɔ and word will get around that the ɔbosom has no ability to see hidden things.

Kofi, Nana Dɔnkɔ, and I went to Tanɔboase to consult Taa Kora, who reaffirmed again that my ɔbosom had caught someone, and I would see this when I got back home. This, too, was reiterated yesterday by Asubonten, who also said my ɔbosom has caught someone and I would see who it was when I got back home. Asuo also echoed that I should place the knife he had given to me in front of the shrine, and every time I pour libation or make sacrifices, I should feed it and ask Ɔboɔkyerewa to work for me and assist my ɔbosom. If I had done this, the ɔbosom would have caught them by now.

I consulted with the divination system, which Nana Dɔnkɔ taught me and which was affirmed by Kwam Froɔ. I wanted to get more details about the information I received from Taa Kora and Asubonten about my ɔbosom catching someone. I also recalled Mossi and Asuotipa mentioning the same thing about my ɔbosom and, naturally, I wanted to test out the new divination system. Interestingly enough, it spoke about one particular person challenging me because of what happened during their ɔbosom festival. Not too long ago in Miami, I tried to intervene to spare this particular priest from punishment from their ɔbosom and I was injured accidentally by something their ɔbosom did to punish the ɔkɔmfoɔ. I told this individual they should give me a chicken to purify since I spared them from the wrath of their ɔbosom. I also saw that this ɔkɔmfoɔ had stomach problems, and his ɔbosom does not want to kill him but rather just teach him a lesson. The ɔkɔmfoɔ's wife and ancestors want the ɔkɔmfoɔ to have a pure heart and mind and is pleading with my ɔbosom for the ɔkɔmfoɔ's life. Reflecting back, it was not only Mossi or Asuotipa who had first mentioned my ɔbosom catching someone, but Taa Kora and then the old ɔkɔmfoɔ Nana Kwam Froɔ in Bonsu, who also gave me a divination system, which I added to the one given to me by Nana Dɔnkɔ.

I am continuing to practice my divinatory skills and am feeling more comfortable with them. When I consulted, I saw that my ɔbosom was angry at someone here in Takyiman. It is a man, and I will see him before I leave Ghana. I was also shown that my ɔbosom Kwabena Bena is working and has someone assisting him.

Today I consulted about a particular *aduro,* and the *ɔkɔmfoɔ* in Miami, who showed up in my divination previously, appeared again. It indicated that this *ɔkɔmfoɔ* is jealous of me and is using their *ɔbosom* to counteract or stop my *ɔbosom,* but this will cause more serious problems for that person. I saw that by doing this it will put their life in more danger. Back then I had pleaded for the *ɔkɔmfoɔ*'s well-being, but now, since the divination has revealed the *ɔkɔmfoɔ*'s true intentions and that he is competing against my *ɔbosom,* I will no longer beg for their well-being. I will let the will of my *ɔbosom* be done.

Nana Effa gave me a *suman,* which I shall wear around my waist. It consists of three different spirits. Each is differentiated by its associated colors and has its own cowrie shell. I will start with the middle one first, which is called Asre. I call upon Asre for assistance by speaking into its cowrie shell.

The one next to it is called Boa me. It is covered with *nkrawo* (a red cloth) and will catch all evil directed toward me. The third is called Ntwerema, to pull or get things, and it is covered in black. Nana also showed me the plants used for purification (*abamaha, bɔmaguwakye, pia,* and *ɔkɔmfentikoro*) and pouring libation. I feed it with six flower essences, and when feeding with a chicken I use ash, *hyire*/clay, or powder to make a circle around it and drip the blood on the circle, not on the *suman*. It will make me a leader or first among many, and when I travel somewhere, I tell it to make me their leader or when competing always first.

Time is going fast. I have only three more weeks before I leave Ghana again, and there is so much more to accomplish. I learned that the *ɔkɔmfoɔ* are not only highly respected here, but feared as well, all due to him or her having a *ɔbosom*. When people get to know and see the working of the ɔbosom, they respect the ɔbosomfoɔ/ɔkɔmfoɔ for fear that if they offend, they might get punished by the ɔbosom.

It is common practice that if a family has a problem with their daughter conceiving children, they will marry her off to an ɔbosomfoɔ/ɔkɔmfoɔ so that the ɔbosom will help her to conceive. It is through the ɔbosomfoɔ/ɔkɔmfoɔ that the ɔbosom changes the bad destiny of a person to a good one. The ritual to do this was given to me by Kofi. What is required is millet, palm kernel, and other items to sacrifice by begging the ɔbosom to see if the destiny can be changed. The ɔbosom will then go to Nyame to inquire and then come back to inform.

People often swear by Ɔboɔkyerewa to harm another, and if the curse is not turned in three days, the ɔbosom will act accordingly. To turn a Ɔboɔkyerewa curse, offer seven eggs, gin, ram, and money. Libation is first poured with water to call Ɔboɔkyerewa. The one who made the curse will beg Ɔboɔkyerewa to return to the river and lean against its wall or sit three times, in other words do not act. He or she then states why he or she made the curse and throws the egg on the ground. If the egg is accepted, it will land with part of it up facing Nyame. If down, it signals that the egg was not accepted and the one who has cursed will be notified that they are not saying the whole truth. Nothing must be hidden. If all still does not go well, perhaps the council of elders found the wrong person guilty, and the judgment should be corrected. Once it is corrected, the egg will be accepted. All Ɔboɔkyerewa curses can be changed in three days. The reasoning is that if you sleep three nights without changing what you swear by, Ɔboɔkyerewa will take it that you are serious; he will then act accordingly and will insert his special knife into the ribs of the one who is cursed and leave it there. It takes a little while for Ɔboɔkyerewa's power to make the victim fall ill. If the curse is not rejected by the owner soon, the area where the knife is inserted will rot and nothing can be done to heal the area, even if Ɔbookyerewa removes his knife. Once it has rotted, even if you use persuasion to change the *ɔbosom's* mind by offering him a chicken, nothing can save this person. You will see Ɔbookyerewa's mind. The chicken will peck the knives on the ground three times as a sure sign that the person is doomed. The officiating *ɔbosomfoɔ* may not say anything directly, but those familiar with the shrine protocols know what it means to see the chicken peck on the knives, not on the clubs.

To say thanks for the work, the person gives what is called *Aseda*, which includes a combination of chicken, money, or gin.

At the foot of the shrine on the floor, there are items such as horns and war clubs sitting on three large knives. Eggs are sacrificed on the horns and clubs. Before a chicken is sacrificed to the *ɔbosom*, the chicken must peck three times at the eggs that were sacrificed on the horns or clubs. This indicates that the *ɔbosom* has agreed with what is said and will do the work proposed. If instead the chicken pecks the knives, it means he will kill. If the chicken does not eat at all, it indicates the *ɔbosom* will not act or agrees with what is said.

These horns have a powerful *aduro* inside them. It is a place where *aduro* can ward off evil. At major festivals, especially the Yam Festival called *Afahye*, the *ɔbosomfoɔ/ɔkɔmfoɔ* will take the horns to perform rituals around the shrine house, dance, and fix them it to the ground. This is to guarantee that rain will not fall and spoil the *Afahye*. There is sometimes cloth inside these horns. I recall back in 1989 before I left for home Nana Dɔnkɔ had *aduro* from the small club at the Asubonten shrine put into incisions on my feet. It had a waxy or oily substance, like shea butter with a nail in the center.

I took time to take notice of what was kept on a Tanɔ shrine. Normally there would be an elephant tail. This not only has reference to the grandeur of an elephant as being superior to all others but is also used for summoning offenders to the shrine. When the *ɔbosom* summons someone and they fail to appear, the *ɔkyeame* will be given the elephant tail by the *ɔbosom* to take and summon this person. If they still refuse to come, the *ɔkyeame* will leave the tail at their house. This elephant tail should not sleep overnight in that town or else something bad will happen to that individual. For fear of something terrible, the one summoned will obey. He will be handed the tail and have to carry it against his chest, cradling it in the left elbow as if it were a baby. All that I have described is done publicly. Whether that person is a chief or commoner, they will walk with the elephant tail to the *ɔbosom*'s shrine house.

Kofi and I continued our conversation about the importance of the elephant tail, which is called *Mene*. The tail represents a chief, and when you are summoned, it is as if a chief summons you. If by chance you do not have the capacity to understand this and insult or beat the messenger, it is like insulting or beating a chief. If you refuse to accept the summons and accompany him, then the messenger will leave the tail on the spot where you have refused to take it, which is most likely at your home. The chief of the town will be notified of all that has transpired, and he himself will have to tend to the matter at hand and try to persuade you to change your mind and obey.

In the olden days, this refusal was grounds for the chief of the town asking you to leave his town if the case was too egregious. The ritual performed is called *ɔtware nsuo*, that is, to cut or cross the water, which means leaving the town behind. I am not sure if this practice is still in effect. If with consideration you come to your right mind and decide to accept it and leave with the messenger, you will have to present a bottle of gin, and libation is poured before it is picked up. Whether you are innocent or guilty, if you are summoned, you have to appear.

I was cautioned to use the *nsuman* and *ɔbosom* wisely and never against the family, only to assist them with their needs. The same goes for when you are curious about the character or nature of someone; divination is one thing, but to send these forces to investigate is something else. For example, if you want to know the character of someone, perhaps you are interested in that person in a romantic way and you have sent your *suman* to investigate. If the *suman* has found out that this individual has some intention not too good in their heart toward you, the *suman* or *ɔbosom* will want to pursue it further. If they concluded it is not good, then they will act in your defense and catch and punish that person. This is a problem, even though this person may not have acted unfavorably towards you. Either way, this would lead to litigation between you and that person's family. Everyone will want to know how such a thing could be done, and the family of the person will not look favorably upon the *ɔbosomfoɔ/ɔkɔmfoɔ* and fault him or her for not using the *ɔbosom* properly.

Nana Dɔnkɔ clarified something I have always wondered about as far as *ɔkɔmfoɔ* marrying each other. He advised me against such a thing, stating that such a thing is forbidden. Two *akɔmfoɔ* married to each other will pull the *ɔbosom* and this will create a power struggle one way or another. The *ɔbosom* will always go to the one who treats it best or the more powerful ɔkɔmfoɔ and because of this, the ɔbosom may kill one of them. I recalled being warned not to refuse my wife's food if I am angry at her. The ɔbosom will not take this lightly since she is the one who cooks my food and he eats when I do.

When an ɔbosomfoɔ/ɔkɔmfoɔ has sex with someone, the ɔbosom acts unfavorably toward that person and, most of the time, something unfortunate may happen to them. This is why we never go before the ɔbosom after having sexual relations because something else is pulling your power. It is as if a person has two lovers, and one does not like the other. This can cause serious problems in the relationship between the ɔbosom and the ɔkɔmfoɔ. Nana continued with an example of one female ɔkɔmfoɔ who slept with a male ɔkɔmfoɔ who died shortly after. The female ɔkɔmfoɔ could not work with her ɔbosom again after the sexual liaison. He cautioned that such unions never last. Personally, I know of a few back in the United States who are married, and maybe their ɔbosom tolerates this, but not *Bono abosom*. I guess it is like mixing too much power together; something unpredictable is bound to happen.

Another concern was acquiring too many *abosom*. It is a dangerous practice with too many mouths to feed, too many taboos to observe, which one might forget. There is always the risk of serious contamination of one ɔbosom by another due to different taboos. This can be a major hurdle for any ɔbosomfoɔ/ɔkɔmfoɔ to leap over. No two ɔbosomfoɔ/ɔkɔmfoɔ have the same amount of power, and the ɔbosom is always attracted to the stronger; such is in the case of marriage. I was informed that it is not necessarily the ability to possess that is important, but the ability to attract or draw power and utilize it properly. Take, for example, the differences between a ɔkɔmfoɔ/ɔbosomfoɔ, and the *abusua panyin*, owner of the ɔbosom. The owner always has the bigger say.

The training of an *ɔbosomfoɔ/ɔkɔmfoɔ* is a very demanding process, with taboos and expected behavior. One such restriction is that when you have any visitor, whether family or friend, and it is time for them to leave, you are limited to how far you can accompany them on the road. When you are seeing someone off, it is customary to travel with them as long as you like, but for *ɔbosomfoɔ/ɔkɔmfoɔ* you do not have such privilege; you cannot follow them across the road, which is your limit.

The eating of specific foods is forbidden, and the eating of certain acceptable food has its taboos, like corn. Certain foods such as eggs must be eaten whole. In their totality, they are never shared. Every social gathering requires some form of offering alcoholic drinks to the guests. This is especially seen in the shrine rooms. The *ɔbosomfoɔ/ɔkɔmfoɔ* taboos drinking any alcoholic drink that has not been open in front of him/her, especially if he or she is in a not-too-familiar location. The rational thing is that we live in an environment of uncertainty and fear of someone or something spoiling our *akɔm*, so if you have not seen the drink opened in front of you, you do not know if it contains poison or something that may compromise you. The only exception is if the one offering the drink, drinks the fear (*nom suro*), that is to drink some first to take away the fear and uncertainty. As a side note, I have witnessed too many people and *ɔbosomfoɔ/ɔkɔmfoɔ* inebriated regularly.

Some *ɔbosomfoɔ/ɔkɔmfoɔ* have gotten into serious trouble with their elders and *ɔbosom* because of this very detrimental addiction. The local alcoholic beverages—*nsa fufuo*, which is palm wine, *pito*, a millet beer—can get you drunk, but they are not as strong as gin and other European alcoholic beverages. These drinks are only a recent phenomenon, and many have acquired a taste due to the importation of these foreign substances. *akɔm* has been around for centuries and has never had to come face to face with such social crises confronting the shrines and society.

The culture has to change. I feel that part of the problem has to do with the bottle itself, which must be returned empty to retrieve the deposit. The client will wait until the bottle is empty, and no *ɔbosomfoɔ/ɔkɔmfoɔ* wants to give back a half-full bottle. I surmise that one solution to this problem can be if the *ɔbosomfoɔ/ɔkɔmfoɔ* keeps extra empty containers just to pour the surplus alcohol into so they can return the bottle and use the alcohol for libation later for themselves.

I had the opportunity to observe Kofi giving the *Akwamuhene* money on two occasions, and each time he placed the money under something concealing it. I inquired as to why he did this. Kofi said it is not proper to go directly and give a chief, *ɔkɔmfoɔ/ɔbosomfoɔ* or anyone important anything directly. Normally you would go through an *ɔkyeame,* who would in turn give it to the *Akwamuhene.* If there is no *ɔkyeame* available, you can also give it to a child to present it.

Again, this can relate to the offering of open drinks to *ɔbosomfoɔ/ɔkɔmfoɔ* and, I might add, chiefs. There is always the fear or concern of someone using *aduro bone* to spoil or contaminate a person of importance. If this is the case, the one accepting the item, such as the child or *ɔkyeame,* will not be harmed by it since it was not intended to do them harm directly. They will be immune to its power and not be harmed. Again, this is not widely practiced. The influence of Christianity and Western education is spoiling these ancient practices.

Kofi and I have been conversing, and he is giving me advice about convincing my wife to stop her pursuit of becoming an ɔkɔmfoɔ and support my akɔm. Since my ɔbosom came first, he is for her and will sit to her left. One cannot serve two elders, you can only have one head of the family; since she is my wife, she has an important role as the cook, lead singer, the one who mobilizes and leads the other women. She will help others to understand the culture, which she, too, must learn. Most important, besides the elders of the shrine, she is the one the ɔbosom expects to see whenever he comes. I have not detailed all the responsibilities of the wife of the ɔbosomfoɔ/ɔkɔmfoɔ, but she is the one who I will always look to for support. If she is not fully able to support my role as ɔbosomfoɔ/ɔkɔmfoɔ, this can interfere with the proper functioning of the ɔbosom. She has to know that the ɔbosom is there to support her, the children, and the family. My mother is the mother of the ɔbosom. My father and my abusua have to be made aware and be educated on their roles. They need to be aware of the seriousness of their duty in supporting the ɔbosom and my akɔm. I know that the ɔbosom sees what is going on, but I pray to him anyway to be patient and understand that they have not been brought up and educated to think this way and therefore do not realize their function as an akɔm family.

Today I purified my soul.

Inspector Aduma, a close friend of Nana Effa and of mine, visits him quite frequently. He is married to an ɔkɔmfoɔ, and she, too, accompanies him on his visits to Nana Effa. We were chatting and joking, and this is a very common topic that ɔkɔmfoɔ will make jokes about marrying each other. She joked about marrying me and I, with my knee-jerk reaction, said no. I was too serious, but she was joking. Later on, Inspector said it is strictly forbidden for ɔkɔmfoɔ to marry each other, for the ɔbosom might go to the other to make them more powerful, and if both *ɔkɔmfoɔ* pull for the power of the *ɔbosom*, it will kill one. In other words, the stronger will pull the power and the weaker one will die. This confirms my earlier conversation with Kofi on this topic concerning why we do not marry each other.

Kofi, who has been around *akɔm*, has heard and seen a lot. He told me it is taboo to see leftover fufu the next day. If I happened to see it, I would have to fast until the evening to purify myself of this. I will confirm this with Nana Dɔnkɔ. Why is this so? It is also taboo to mention a spider before a *ɔkɔmfoɔ* eats food. If such a thing were mentioned, I would have to fast until the evening. This taboo does not apply if it is mentioned while eating. If this happens, I only will have to spit it out and then continue eating. It is also not taboo if it is mentioned after I am finished eating.

I had the pleasure of following up our conversation on taboos and not eating the leftover food with Nana Dɔnkɔ. Nana said *ɔkɔmfoɔ* do not look at or eat leftover food in which soup is poured over it as in fufu. The reason for this is that the *nsuman* consider it taboo, and if you see this, you have to fast until you see the moon. This is to say to the spirit that you respect its taboo and will purify yourself since the spirit too will not eat. To eat such food takes away the power from the *nsuman* and the *ɔbosomfoɔ/ɔkɔmfoɔ*. By not eating this type of food, you are saying you will never leave anything leftover or unfinished, and your *suman* should continue the work the next day to its full completion. This is how you want your spirits to behave.

Nana also confirmed that some animals and spiders are forbidden to be mentioned if *ɔbosomfoɔ/ɔkɔmfoɔ* is eating. The mention of their names take power away from the *nsuman*, who will not eat, and when *ɔbosomfoɔ/ɔkɔmfoɔ* hears their names, he should also fast to show respect to the *nsuman* and not eat when the taboo is mentioned. One way to look at taboos is that they are there to help us maintain and show respect to our helping powers. To divulge a taboo reminds the *nsuman* or *abosom* of something they should not hear, and fasting is part of the ritual of sharing the sorrow with the spirits. This is how fasting has become a part of *ɔbosomfoɔ/ɔkɔmfoɔ* life. If you hear your taboo such as a lion while you are eating, you should not swallow, but spit that food in your mouth out and then you can continue eating. To hear it and swallow causes your powers to become ineffective. In addition, the lion is a symbol for Tanɔ such as Ɔboɔkyerewa, Taa Kora, and my *ɔbosom* Kwabena Bena. This is not to say they are considered as one, but more so act like one, so one should be careful.

When the *yawa* is carried and the *ɔbosom* possesses the *ɔbosomfoɔ*, the *ɔbosom* looks to the right where his parents are and may listen to any suggestions they may have to offer before he speaks. Again, it is considered improper for the *ɔbosom* to speak directly. He always speaks through an *ɔkyeame*.

Some *ɔbosom* such as Taa Kora are never carried and only speak through their *ɔkyeame,* Ateokɔsaa, whose *yawa* is carried when you wish to consult Taa Kora. It is the same with Ɔboɔkyerewa; his *yawa* is not carried, and he never speaks directly to anyone. He looks into the Tanɔ River when he is possessed and sees images rolling by in the water. He moves his head at times, quickly left and right, and he sees the passing images and listens for suggestions of what needs to be said before he speaks.

All Tanɔ see images before they speak or give advice. Many times, when I was first training some five years ago, I needed to see Ɔboɔkyerewa so that he and Asubonten could work together in supporting my *akɔm*. One time on the way we could not get to Traa, his town, because the pathway was flooded due to the heavy rain. As a result, his banks and mirror were contaminated, since sediment had clouded the water so he could not see his images, and I had to return back.

I often pondered as to why we consider dogs to be taboo, and it was revealed that it has to do with the role the dog played in bringing fire to the *abusua*/clan. As the story goes, lightning struck a tree, which caught fire, and a dog grabbed ahold of a branch or stick and brought it to the *abusua* to maintain the fire. So, the dog is not killed and eaten by the *abusua* out of respect, since it did something that was beneficial to the family. In the case of the goat, it assisted Tanɔ, and we also did not eat them.

The *nsuman* I wear every day. I can bathe with them on. They do not taboo water and therefore cannot be spoiled by it. That's how they are.

I was told never to allow anyone to walk behind me while I am eating because *ɔbosomfoɔ/ɔkɔmfoɔ* want to see everything in front of them. What takes place behind your back can harm you if it is with ill intent, and since we cannot see what is taking place behind our back, we must safeguard ourselves. The *ɔbosom* can protect our back, which is why we say "*wo gyina makyi akyi gyina pa*" (stand behind me on good standing), but we must not act too foolishly.

To summarize, Bono *ɔbosomfoɔ/ɔkɔmfoɔ* take all other *akɔmfoɔ* as their brothers and sisters and therefore do not have sex or marry them. This is not widely practiced among other groups as among the Bono. I am certain that this is due to cultural differences and standards about taboos. But I am certain that if someone eats your taboo and you sleep with that person, this could lead to serious setbacks. Since the other ɔkɔmfoɔ are obligated to obey their taboos, they cannot change them as easily as common people. When ɔkɔmfoɔ marry ɔkɔmfoɔ, the power would go to the stronger of the two, leaving the other one in a compromised position.

Nana Dɔnkɔ gave me smoke *aduro* to burn early in the morning on *da bɔne* before I do any work at the shrine. I will add this to the incense pot I bought in the market. The plant is called *nsɛ dua nsɛ homa* (it is not a tree nor a vine/rope); it is a tree but can be bent and used as a rope. I must make sure it is properly dried first and add *famwisa* three times and smoke to the shrine room.

I was taught *aduro* to change a person's mind. Get up early in the morning, do not speak to anyone, wash face, mouth, and armpits with water fetched by children who have not dreamed (a metaphor for sexual dream) the day before. Grind the *aduro* (not mentioned) to a paste by adding the water washed within a grinding pot or stone. This is to be put into the food of the one you wish to call back. Use half of the *nkateɛ* shell (peanut) and scoop the mixture three separate times to place it for the food. Each time when putting into the food, say all that is desired and what you want that person to do. Give food to the person to eat, and make sure you never eat any; also, make sure no one else eats the food.

When the yam introduction *Adapa* comes around, get up early before anyone else, pour water outside the shrine room, go to the shrine room, and pour libation to *ɔbosom* informing *ɔbosom* that you will do yam introduction on that day and tie the yam outside for all to see.

On *Kwabena*, place three tubers of yams in a basket or *yawa* and cover them with a white cloth so the ɔbosom does not see them. Inform him of all that will be done in forty days on his *Afahye*, that you will give him a ram, and he will eat eggs and new yam. After finishing, polish the *yawa* with egg and *atadwɛ* (tiger nut). Take dirt from the yams and place it on the *yawa* and on my head and family members who will also taboo the yam. Tie the yam and attach it to the shrine outside. Do not cook yam on that day to feed ɔbosom. *Afahye* will last eight days, and I will sleep in the shrine room for the whole duration. Do all this before anything else is done. From now till the *Afahye* I will taboo all yam products.

When someone keeps losing things like money or other possessions and feels like their life is being swept away, this is a sign of *bayi*. Give a chicken to the ɔbosom, then place this individual on a sweeping broom, give a bath and *mɔtɔ* incision, and some to eat. That is all.

Nana Dɔnkɔ is very busy making *sɛbe* for my *batakari* (smock), and Nana Kofi Nimo gave me a few *sɛbe* to attach to my *batakari*. Nana Effa added his as well, and I will sew them all on. I spent considerable time laying them out. Nana Dɔnkɔ recommended one for the back. When we had some leisure time from all the work, he informed me that he will make a *suman* for me. He told me his uncle gave him this *suman*, and he has never given it to anyone. The *suman* is a war *suman* called *Brɔkruma*. I will check the spelling later. This *suman* is to be worn on the on the back of the *batakari*. It will protect me from knife and gun attacks in battle, and any circumstance that may evoke fear and flight. In essence, it will make me brave in the face of death. The *suman* receives blood and *bɛsɛ* (kola) for sacrifice. To feed it, I will place the *suman* on a sweeping broom, purify it with *pia*, *mae*, and *nunum*, squeeze the juice on it and in the chicken's mouth and pray, walk and count seven paces (crossing legs while walking) and finish with a left leg over right with right hand on hip. Hold bird with the left hand until the *suman* eats. Break the chicken's left foot and wing under my knee. Pull the tongue out and place it on the *suman* and drain blood on it. After it died, I recall Nana holding the chicken and hitting it left and right on the ground three times. Take care when opening the chest and look for the heart to see if it is torn away from the inside or if blood is gathered in the chest cavity. All this means it has accepted the sacrifice. Feed the *suman* with the feet, head, and liver. If I do not eat this meat, throw it away. Use *mɔtɔ* to cook the meat and eat with men only. It is mostly for personal use, and I was cautioned never to hit anyone while wearing the *batakari* or get into fights. But if my life is threatened, I should call on *Brɔkuma* or extend my left hand and recite an incantation out loud; this will cause the person to fall and hit the left side, injuring themselves. If the threat is great, they may break the left leg or arm. If I do have to fight with the *batakari* on, it must be a life-or-death situation. Polish with a whole egg. Women do not eat its meat.

The *suman* can also help clients. I plan to talk to Nana to get more information on this *suman*. As far as I understood, he has never given it to anyone, and I am the first. He told me some history about this *suman* in which a war almost broke out and his uncle had to use it during that time. Nana did not give any details, but this was a long time ago. Women, he said, do not touch the *suman*. I can greet them while wearing the *batakari*, but never to hug them because if they do come into contact with the *suman*, they have to present it with a chicken and *bεsε* (kola nut) to purify. The main taboo is women. He reiterated this *suman* is for the *batakari*.

I was taught to change the *nkrabea* (destiny) of a person. Present the *ɔbosom* with a chicken, drink, and the items listed below to inquire if he will change your *nkrabea*. If ɔbosom agrees, then perform this ritual. Boiled eggs with a little salt added, and get a specific nut kernel and a chicken. The client eats the eggs and chews a piece of the kernel, asking the soul to change and exchange the old *nkrabea* for a better one. Say you want it to be hard, like the kernel, so that nothing bothers it. Sacrifice a chicken. Then, put a bottle of gin, a specific grain (handful or cupful), white cloth, some kola nuts, and money (coins and dollars) in a calabash, and let the person talk to the ɔbosom and tell the ɔbosom why they want to change their *nkrabea*. Ask him to change the *nkrabea*. Lay the cloth on the shrine floor and turn items over on the cloth, making sure none spill out. Pour libation and leave it there for eight days.

According to Nana Dɔnkɔ, there are three methods of divining, other than through possession. They are sand, *sedeɛ*, and *Asuo Yaa*. I have also heard of fire as another method, but it not very popular. I have witnessed the *bodua* and the *kahyire* as methods. They are all called ɔkyeame, and they serve as the voice of the ɔbosom. Nana always emphasizes that they must always be challenged to get the right answer before I speak, or else I could possibly fail in what I hear or see. I think when he says challenge, he may mean verify.

When someone comes for help and I want to know how serious their case might be, I will grab a handful of shells, put them aside, and count by three. If three remain after I have counted, all this means that their problem will never finish or be solved easily. I should do the ritual all over again and ask if I can solve one or two of their problems. If one remains after counting by three, then I shall handle that one problem.

The shells can say a lot, and it is important to know how to decipher their proverbial wisdom, especially when they speak in combinations such as *bese, ɔbosom asɛm*, or *sekan*. When one or two more shells or symbols are caught between the fingers, this is called biting, which could mean conflicts between two or more individuals, or something going on between two persons. Two or more symbols remaining in the hand tell a story, but I must always challenge their meanings. I have used some of these symbols for divination. One is *Nyame akuma*, known as a thunder stone, and used to represent laws and functions of the *abosom*. Another is *Akommerɛ*, a red bead used to symbolize worry and overthinking. *Sika asɛm* means debt, financial obligation, or losing one's money. Yes or no answers can be derived from speaking to two shells and asking *sedeɛ ɔkyeame* to choose by touching one. If they fall at both, there is no choice. If they fall in between both, ask them to choose. I should not touch the *sedeɛ* on *Kwasiada* (Sunday) and *Yawoda* (Thursday), the same as the *ɔbosom*.

Along the way, I learned the origins and meaning behind the days of the week:
*Benada*/Tuesday: Appellation and greeting, *Abena* (from *ben*, to be cook)
*Wukuda*/Wednesday: Appellation and greeting, *Ku* (to shave, remove)
*Yawda*/Thursday: Appellation is *Awo* or *Prɛko* (from Yaw, to feel pain)
*Fieda*/Friday: Appellation and greeting is *Fi* (to come out, leave)
*Memeneda*/Saturday: Appellation is *Mene* (to swallow)
*Kwasiada*/Sunday: Appellation is *Si* (to purify, to clean)
*Dwoada*/Monday: Appellation and greeting is *Dwo* (to be cool)

*domankoma* created Kuntu, who assisted in everything, and one day Kuntu got beside himself and got into a disagreement over the creations with Ɔdomankoma. Ɔdomankoma told Kuntu that he had heard about Ɔdomankoma Oboɔdeɛ, not of Kuntu Oboɔdeɛ, and he killed Kuntu.

Ɔdomankoma had another faithful servant named Fo, and he asked Fo to cook Kuntu in a big pot. When Kuntu was cooked, Fo reported to Ɔdomankoma. Kuntu was well done and Ɔdomankoma was called that day *Abenada* from *Aben*, which means cook. Ɔdomankoma instructed Fo to let the meat cook some more and report back on any changes.

Ɔdomankoma asked Fo to check on the meat, and Fo returned, informing Ɔdomankoma that the hair on the body came off or was removed and called that day *Wukuda* from *Ku* (to shave off). Meanwhile, Fo overheard some people mumbling about what happened between Ɔdomankoma and Kuntu and why he was killed.

Some said it was because they got into a disagreement about who created things and Ɔdomankoma killed Kuntu, and people became fearful and blamed Ɔdomankoma for killing his servant and retired to their domicile. Fo reported back everything he heard and Ɔdomankoma named this day *Yaoda*.

Again, Fo was called upon to further inquire as to what people were up to, and observing, he saw that they were beginning to come out of their homes and returning to where they were before, which he immediately reported to Ɔdomankoma. This day was called by Ɔdomankoma *Fieda*, from *Firi* (the day people came out of their homes from *Firi* to leave or come from). Fo was asked to find out more information on what the people were doing. Fo saw them eating and drinking and told Ɔdomankoma, who called this day *Memeneda* (from *memene*, to swallow).

Fo continues to observe and report back to Ɔdomankoma that the people were seen washing their clothes due to them staying in their homes eating and drinking. Ɔdomankoma called this day *Kwasiada*, from *Si*, to wash. Fo noticed a calm and coolness about the people, and all seemed to be normal and reported this to Ɔdomankoma, who called this very day *Dwoada*, from *Dwo*, to be cool. Ɔdomankoman, grateful and appreciative of the help and service Fo performed, informed him that he will do something that people will remember and what Fo did and never forget his name.

Therefore, Ɔdomankoma added the name of Fo as a suffix to all things relating to people and the service they perform, and we have the name like *Abibifo*/Black person, *ɔkɔmfoɔ*/traditional priest, *Akuafo*/farmer, and so forth. And so, the days of the *Bono/Akan* week came to be.

Nana Akumsa gave me three eggs to give to Kwabena Bena when I return home.

*M'anansesem a metope yi, se eye de o, se nnye de o, momfa bi nkɔ momfa bi mmera*

1996 Ateokɔsa, ɔkyeame for Ta Kora.

The old 'red' priest leaning forward towards the god. Photograph by Robert Sutherland Rattray, Ghana, c. 1923. © Royal Anthropological Institute

Me at Apo festival.

Yaw Mensa feeding Bɔngan.

Clients at Traa, for Bookyerewa.

Maame cooking.

Maame and me.

Me during akɔm, Apo festival.

Nana Asamadu and me.

Nana Asamadu and me.

Nana Bekoe.

Ta Mensa at Apo festival.

Drumming at Apo festival.

Apo festival.

Me dancing at akɔm during Apo festival.

Nana Kofi Asamadu, Nana Akumsa, myself, Nana Dɔnkɔ, and Nana Kwasi Owusu.

Libation poured at Apo festival.

Aduro: Humatre.

Aduro.

Nana Dɔnkɔ, Kofi Nimo and I visiting Ntoa ɔkɔmfoɔ Nana Kwam Froɔ in red shirt.

Ɔbosomfoɔ feeding ɔbosom.

Nana Dɔnkɔ and onlookers watching for a sign.

# CHAPTER FOUR

## 1995, FUNERAL AND TRAVELS TO THE DREAM WORLD

The death of Nana Dɔnkɔ affected me greatly. Back in the United States on *Kwabena*, I was carrying Kwabena Bena, and the pan almost fell off my head onto the floor. This disturbed me for some reason. Not too soon after that happened, a call came in from Kofi in Takyiman. My wife had answered the phone and, according to her, Kofi instructed her on how to prepare me for the bad news. All I remembered was that she said Nana Dɔnkɔ kicked salt, and the *ɔbosom* came immediately.

When a *ɔbosomfoɔ* dies, the funeral and the burial have to be special. The *ɔbosomfoɔ* in the lifetime bathed many spiritual plants, and therefore the body of the *ɔbosomfoɔ* cannot touch the earth so as not to contaminate or spoil his spiritual powers. A special *suman* will be buried with the *ɔbosomfoɔ* that will be protective of his spirit and will continue to do so in the next life. The grave is dug out in a particular shape. I will try to get a diagram to compare it to the burials and rites of ancient Egyptian kings. Some bracelets such as *nkamere* and a ring called *ka* or *kawa* will be buried with the ɔbosomfoɔ, and some will remain behind for the next ɔbosomfoɔ, who will inherit his stool. The ɔbosomfoɔ must never be buried with all his spiritual protection, for fear that the ɔbosom will follow him into the next world and this will prove to be a serious problem for the ɔbosomfoɔ who follows.

I took some time to visit the old man Nana Dɔnkɔ introduced to me last year. He wanted to make a *suman* for me. Kofi and I had to go to a place where they slaughtered livestock. At this place we will find *ɔpete*/vulture. They would cast aside unwanted meat parts, and this would attract the vultures. Kofi had a gun, and our plan was to kill one for a *suman* to be made for me by Kwam Froɔ. All we needed was its head, legs, wings, and heart. I had to prepare a bath of a small palm tree in a pot with three eggs to be given to him after seven days. The rest of the work for this task is too comprehensive to reveal.

Nana Kwam Froɔ informed me that when an *ɔbosom* possesses upon a *ɔkɔmfoɔ*, the *ɔbosom* will use the soul of the *ɔkɔmfoɔ* and his/her soul should not run away. When the soul runs away, the *ɔbosom* can never fully possess the *ɔkɔmfoɔ* and, therefore, will not perform properly. That being so, the soul of the *ɔkɔmfoɔ* is the most important thing, and the *ɔkɔmfoɔ* should do all he/she can to take care of it and keep it strong and happy. When the soul is at peace, the *ɔbosom* can come freely and use the *ɔkɔmfoɔ* for good work.

The *suman* called *Akɔmmere* is fire by nature, and you must never use a knife to cut the string or anything put into making the *suman* because the power of the knife will cut the power of the *suman*. When cutting it, you must use a broken glass or bottle. Fire is used to burn the edges of the string used in making this *suman*. Since the nature of *Akɔmmere* is fire, the fire will not harm it.

This is a very powerful *suman* used for protecting the *ɔkɔmfoɔ* and his/her *akɔm* from contamination or bad spiritual power. *Akɔmmere* is the senior to all the *nsuman ɔkɔmfoɔ* will wear, and it serves as a reminder to the *ɔkɔmfoɔ* even if he takes many wives (that is, *abosom*), there is one that was first or senior, which must not be neglected.

If *ɔkɔmfoɔ* does not have this *suman*, the *kawa* can be used as a substitute by biting it; it too can also be used to protect against contaminations, whether they be words, sounds, sight, or food.

Now, back to when *ɔbosomfoɔ* dies. The wife of a dead *ɔbosomfoɔ* must mourn his death for forty days. She must not eat anything but plantain (*fufu*) and not greet anyone whose spouse is still alive. She may greet others whose spouses have departed. The reason for this is that she does not wish her regret or sorrow upon someone else. This is also a sign of respect for the living and her deceased husband. In this manner, she is saying she is not free with just everyone. A string of red beads is worn around her right shoulder and wrist. On her left wrist, she wears *Gyabunu* and the teeth of a certain animal for about one year. If she is going somewhere she should not, the teeth will bite her to stop her journey, and when this happens, she should pour libation for protection and to get permission before continuing. She will wear mourning clothes, put clay marking on her body, and have special attendants. Her head is wrapped with cloth in a style that leaves the top of her head open.

When an *ɔkɔmfoɔ* is traveling to a place he or she has never been before, he/she should pick leaves from both sides of the path leading to this place, crush them up and pour libation with its liquid, saying that these plants know all who traveled this path and therefore you beg them for protection so that nothing bad may happen to you. After the *ɔkɔmfoɔ* is finished, he/she throws the plant left and right behind the back.

Next, the *ɔkɔmfoɔ* picks up a stone and throws it behind the back. The reason why nothing is done to the front of the *ɔkɔmfoɔ* is because the *ɔkɔmfoɔ* sees where he/she is going in the front and can fend for himself/herself, but not what is behind. The *ɔkɔmfoɔ* begs the *ɔbosom* to protect his or her left and right backside.

Kwam Froɔ gave me an unwritten list of plants to be used for making a *nsuman* for me. The first is called *Amaneno*, which means the state or nation's mouth. This *suman* is used for when *ɔkɔmfoɔ* plans to go to an *akɔm*, he/she will take plants from both sides of the path, crush them, and pour a libation on the *suman*, saying that he/she will encounter no challenges, will be first or among the first in everything, will sweep away all competitors. This *suman* can do anything.

When one is celebrating *akɔm* or yam festival and the *ɔbosom* possesses, the *ɔkyeame* will give the *ɔbosom Amaneno* to sweep the air spiritually to remove all obstacles. Then the *ɔkyeame* will fasten it on the ground and ask the *ɔbosom* to step with the left foot three times upon the broom before dancing, so no one can challenge the *ɔbosom* and cause the *ɔbosom* to fall. If *Amaneno* says you will die, you will die; if it says you will live, you will live. When anyone comes for help, it can help them. *Taafamee, akɔmfentikoro, ntum, mae* are all used to pour libation and purify the *suman* and before sacrifices.

The next *suman* is a mirror called *Hwee*, that is to see, to look. This is mainly used for divination. This mirror can be used to see far and near, even in the next town. Whatever it shows and says will come to pass. The *ɔbosom* can use this if so needed. The plant used in the purification and libation of this *suman* is the same as in *Amaneno*. The only plant used in making this *suman* is that found in a cemetery and a small bell. This *suman* can be used for calling the *ɔbosom* when the *ɔkɔmfoɔ* is not able to use the pan. The bell sounds please the *ɔbosom,* and it shakes when the *ɔbosom* comes. The *ɔbosom* can use it to look like it would a *bodua* for seeing things. A *bodua* is made from any animal tail, for example, a sheep, cow, or horse, and bound in leather with spiritual items; it is used to spiritually cleanse or remove annoying or disturbing things from one's environment. It can also be used for seeing things spiritually and as a status symbol.

Soul purification items: *Bayere*/yam; *nkosua nson*/seven eggs; *akoko*/chicken; *nsu*/water*; dwere*/plant.
The eggs and yam are boiled. Spread mashed yam on a plate and crushed eggshells are sprinkled on top. Break an egg into seven pieces (I have seen two eggs used) and place one at each cardinal point and three in the center.

Water is poured to call the ancestors and the soul to announce what is taking place. The plant is dipped into the water and strikes the tongue three times, calling the soul each time by name, saying "*kra* so and so *kuse.*" The participant is asked to repeat, then spray out the mouth after repeating the words spoken. The plant is placed in the center of everything. When the *kra* is pacified with words, the chicken is asked to peck or eat three times. When it does, it is slaughtered, and the blood goes around the plate three times, then a little is allowed to fall on top.

I was told by Kofi that no blood should be allowed to fall on the top, but Yaw Mensa, who will inherit Nana Dɔnkɔ, said to put a little on top. I will verify this later. The chicken is not allowed to flip but is held firmly. After it dies, cross both wings over the neck of the dead chicken. The yam and eggs are eaten by the one purifying the soul first before others do. Family members and children are invited and encouraged to eat with the one whose soul is being purified.

The chicken is pulled apart (rather than cut up like for the *abosom*), and seven feathers are placed under the foodstuff. The back is all in one piece: the wings, liver, and *afode* for fortune, the head for the soul, neck to support the head, legs so that the soul can travel, waist along with the kidneys for productivity is placed down.

The rest of the chicken can be eaten by others. Everything is covered and kept in a corner of the bedroom until the next day, when small pieces of everything are thrown on the roof of the house, then ritual meat parts are eaten.

*I fell asleep and had this dream: Nana Dɔnkɔ had arrived, and he was surprised to see me asleep and wanted to know why. I should wake up, now that he has come. Suddenly I awoke from the dream feeling his presence; he came to eat yam.*

*Another dream: I saw many akɔmfoɔ going to an akɔm and I wanted to go, but* Kofi *was trying to persuade me not to go. I said to him, how come I cannot go, all the akɔmfoɔ are going, I must go. One of the drummers whose father is an* ɔkɔmfoɔ *in Nkoransa was there. I asked* Kofi, *who is it that guides me and what is its role. He could not answer. The drummer said the ɔbosom* Kwabena Bena. *I went and shook his hand and thanked him for the answer. I told* Kofi *his role is to stand behind me as* ɔkyeame *and the ɔbosom will lead.*

An *ɔkɔmfoɔ* from Nkoransa named Kwame Agyeman and I were conversing about a *suman*. Actually it was about the beads for the *suman* earlier that night.

*In the dream, he told me the suman is called Dɔ, and he began to point to other nsuman and name them Frɛ, Gyabunu, and so forth. Sometime later, I met a woman whose head was covered. She told me the suman was not caledl Dɔ, but ɔbosom gye ware. She began to pull and stretch the suman like a rubber band. By this I was not sure if she meant the ɔbosom will give me long life or that the ɔbosom will be long as in the relationship with me.*

*I was somewhere with Nana Kwabena Brown, and he had one of his children with him, but I did not recognize her. She wore light-colored clothes. I was showing Nana Brown one of the books by Rattray, the Ashanti religion and art book my wife had copied for me. I showed him the passage on kunkuma. Next, I was with old man,* Nana Dɔnkɔ, *and there was a woman to my left in between us.* Nana Dɔnkɔ *and I talked about kunkuma. The woman had a broom, and he took it from her. There was filth and feces on the ground, and he started to sweep it all. He told me this before he swept, and he excitedly, in fact almost happily, swept the taboos away. Nana then told me that I must take some pieces of the broom from each end of the broom and put on either side of the suman. I motioned to him my left hand then my right, bringing them together. Next, we started to play, and I rolled on the ground with Nana. We got up and ran fast like children playing. Nana needed something for the suman or medicine you cannot buy or have it given to you; instead you must steal it. Nana went on someone's property and stole what look like a vegetable or fruit. The police came after us, and we both ran into a building with people who sheltered us. We hid under the window to avoid the police. Our clothing changed by themselves. I remember some were wearing white T-shirts before the change.*

*I dreamed that my wife was a police officer, and somehow the department wanted her gun back. On that particular day, she did not hand it in. The next day, I saw her in white pants and a T-shirt. I decided to hand in her gun instead of her doing so. There was a fence we were passing through and that fence separated us from them. I could see them all as we approached the partition. I thought I would have to throw the gun over the fence, but they might not catch it. So I asked if I could walk on the side they were on and hand them the gun. They said yes, and I did. My wife said nothing; she just kept her head down.*

I recalled that last year I asked Nana Dɔnkɔ why he hit a rock against a slab of stone whenever he was pouring libation for the *nsuman*. He said this is done when you are pouring a libation into *nsumanabrafoɔ*. I also noticed that when feeding them yam, it is always roasted on fire instead of the customary boiled yam.

There is a pot of spiritual bath kept in the *nsuman* room that is only renewed once a year during the yam festival. I must find out why it is kept for one year. The stools when cleaned for the yam festival are scrubbed with a plant call *nhyire*.

To be a good *ɔkɔmfoɔ*, one has to thoroughly observe and study the nature of plants and animals so that they can be used properly in a spiritual manner. Kofi informed me that any plant that crosses from one side of a path to another side of that path can be used spiritually for the eyes and ears, the reason being that this plant wants to see and hear everything that is going on, even on the other side of the path. I also think the path represents the place *ɔkɔmfoɔ* wishes to be on, and any plant that travels along a path can benefit the *ɔkɔmfoɔ* spiritually.

The herbs in spiritual bath kept in the *nsuman* room can also be contributed by the help of other *ɔkɔmfoɔ*. The *ɔbosomfoɔ* can ask other *ɔbosomfoɔ* or *ɔkɔmfoɔ* to add their knowledge of plants to the bath because each one knows something the other might not know. This bath can be used for all sorts of spiritual problems like convulsions, fainting, witchcraft, or any bad thing that may plague someone. When the bath is being made, a *nkamere* (bracelet) is placed at the bottom of the pot, and this bath is kept for one year.

*I dreamed that I was somewhere back in the United States. I am not sure where exactly, but I was going someplace with other people, but I do not recall who they were. I was sitting in a car, and somehow there was a coffin or people were bringing a coffin into the car beside me. I got up to move out of the way into the back seat, but when that door was opened, there was a coffin there as well and I backed away. I could not fully see the entire box. I knew there were others helping me, but again I cannot fully recall their faces, only their presence.*

*I had a dream about Asuotipa. I was at* Nana Effa *and I saw Asuo in a pan, but it was a little larger than the one he is currently in. This pan was sitting on a big stool filled with water. I was wearing a muslin top, and standing beside the pan holding a smaller one and placing it inside in the other, just like how it is in reality. The ɔbosom cautioned me that I should be free of contamination, especially my right hand, since that is the hand of the ɔbosom. Most important, I should not sleep or touch a woman the night before I touch the ɔbosom, referring to the woman's vagina (since that is what the left hand is for). The stool was covered with a white cloth, and as I was putting the pan in the larger one, I was bending low, looking at the stool, and I noticed that a piece of medicine (plant) had fallen on the floor. It looked like a root or a piece of stem, dark in the middle, and the bark covering was light.*

*Another dream: I saw* Nana Effa *using medicine consisting of mɔtɔ and shea butter, and he wiped with* mpɛsɛmpɛsɛ *and then rubbed it on the front part of his body, and then back of his kidneys. He then placed his hand on his waist.*

Today I carried Asuotipa, but Kwabena Bena came instead. I wondered if the above dream was telling me that Kwabena Bena would come through him, since they are all water, and I should not touch any woman.

*I dreamed Ɔboɔkyerewa ɔbosomfoɔ came by to visit and then left, but not completely.* Yaw Mensa *had two rams that had escaped, and he could not find them. We went looking for them, and someone told him that they saw* Ɔboɔkyerewa ɔbosomfoɔ *stealing them. In fact, he took them and hid them in his car. He was dressed in white as usual. He sacrificed the rams at Traa and ate the meat.* Yaw Mensa *went looking for him, and we found him later. When he saw us, he attempted to run and hide, but we discovered him. He was attempting to seek refuge in what appeared to be a karaal on a little hill. He kept pacing left and right, and* Yaw Mensa *was either cursing or arguing with him, and eventually threw something at the ɔbosomfoɔ. Next* the ɔbosomfoɔ ran and hid in a bar, but he had no place to run and hide. I saw him trying to hide in a crawling position on the floor in a room. His wife was just sitting in the middle of the room on a chair, saying nothing; she was just looking down. His brother who usually accompanies him was sitting at a table off to the corner in the back of the room near the ɔbosomfoɔ's wife. I asked his brother if he stole the ram, and he said yes! I also got the indication that he was stealing money too. I went to the ɔbosomfoɔ and said to him I was disappointed. He looked like he had mpɛsɛmpɛsɛ. I told him what he did was not right, and I was ashamed, pointing my finger at him. Now he was wearing a black and white fugu top. Yaw had left by this time. I recall looking at his brother to ask him how to say something in Twi and repeated what he told me, and when I was finished, I left.

I had a dream that I was traveling somewhere, but I am not sure where. I was driving either a car or a van, but not certain which. It was nighttime, and for some reason or another I was not aware of a wall ahead of me. I might have fallen asleep at the wheel, but I did not see the wall, and as a result could not stop the car. But for some reason the brakes were applied, and the car stopped before it hit the wall. My ɔbosom Kwabena Bena *intervened and said he stopped the car and saved my life. My destiny was in his hands. It seemed like there may have been others in the car, but not too many. I was not clear if they were people or spirits.*

Kofi Nimo gave me a *suman* called *Kasa bi*. At the time I thought the list for making *Bɔngan* was complicated and the items challenging to find. *Kasa bi* has twenty-six items on its list for making this *suman*, but it was worth it.

All the ingredients were tied with white string, while the matches and *odi* were tied with the black string. This *suman* was supposed to be my last *suman*. K*asa bi* means to say something, anything that you want the *suman* to assist you. Kofi Nimo told me this *suman* should be my last one, and I should not collect any more after this one. This was also confirmed by Asubonten. I regrettably did not adhere to the advice given to me. I must apologize to the *ɔbosom* for that short-sightedness.

This *suman* coincidently reminded me of a dream I had a while ago back in Miami about a *suman* that was kept on shea butter behind my shrine door. K*asa bi suman* is for protection and will also protect me when I am possessed by the *ɔbosom* against all challenges. Anyone who feels threatened or wants help can come to the *suman* for protection. It is kept on shea butter, which is very important when working with this *suman*.

If someone is owed money and has not been paid, first you tell the *suman* this with drink and sacrifice, then give them some of the shea butter. You rub it into the palms, arms, head, and face, then go straight to this person, touch his/her exposed body, whether it be their arms, shoulders, thighs, or whatever, and ask them for what they owe you. If this person still refuses or responds unfavorably, do not worry. Do not argue with this individual; this is what it likes. Eventually, they will listen and not ask you to go away. Even if you left, they would not stop thinking about you and eventually give you what they owe you.

If you desire your wife or husband to do something for you, like not traveling, or taking another, do what is desired as above and sleep with him/her, and even if you do not say what is on your mind, he/she will ask you about what is on your mind, and you will get what you want.

If you desire to call someone's power to yourself, do the same, except you do not have to touch or tell them what you want, but say all to the *suman* and blow the whistle, and that person will bring and give you their power things.

When I am at a *akɔm*, and someone challenges me, I will feel cobwebs around my face. I should wipe it off and throw it away while saying something and invoking the name *Kasa bi*. If by chance the cobweb becomes overwhelming, I blow the whistle, and the one who challenges me will eventually have difficulties breathing or complain of pains in the ribs. If I am accused of catching this person and wish to defend myself, I can say I do not know who or what did this to them, but I have *aduro* (three *nnufa* for *Kasa bi*) to help them. When using the *dufa,* make three incisions on the left and right sides of the ribs, rub the *dufa* on a stone with alcohol, putting the mixture into the cuts and both hands; stand behind this individual with hands on both incisions, pull toward me three times, asking the person to cough after each pull. When finished, give the person some to drink. That is all. For the work I can charge chicken, money, eggs, and drink, and whatever else I desire for payment.

If I am in a car traveling and I see cobwebs or feel them on me, I must stop and not go any farther, for something bad is going to happen. If someone desires another, you must make a sacrifice, blow the whistle, mention the name of one who is desired, and they will come to the one who desires them, but the *ɔbosom* may not like this type of work, so I should be careful. When trying to get a job or promotion, or any matters concerning a job, make a sacrifice, use the shea butter, and go greet the person who has the power; they will give you what you want.

For court cases or any serious matter, I will make a sacrifice, then write their name and tie black or red string. I always should tie away from myself; only the white string is for my usage. I can use *Kasa bi* even if it is working on someone else's case. I can tie the other string for use. The *suman* eats chicken when it is held by the nape of its neck, right foot crossed over left. It will also eat guinea fowls. When the *suman* is laid against the shea butter, it will make the butter very powerful. To purify the *suman*, use *Taafameɛ*, *Atanɔgya*, *ɔkomfentikoro*, *pia*, *mae*, and *ntum*. Pour libation on the *suman* first, then into the chicken's mouth before sacrificing it.

Nana Kofi Kyereme made a *suman* for my wife to wear when she was divining. I was told to collect and buy these two yards calico, *nkrawo*, strong string, and *nsa* (gin).

*In a dream I was home in Miami inside my shrine room. My wife was sitting a little off from the shrine. She looked like she was eating. I was standing to the right of the pan, which was on a stool and tilted on its side, not sitting flat on its base as it should. I noticed that its contents were transparent, and I could see the blood through it. I mentioned this to my wife, and I felt that the ɔbosom had been contaminated by her menstrual blood. I wondered if she was still on her cycle, but somehow, I felt she would not do such a thing, because she knows better. By this time, she was standing up.*

Tonight, my brother Amoako told me that he heard that Ɔboɔkyerewa Ɔbosomfoɔ either took or borrowed money from Yaw Mensa. This may be related to a dream shown to me by the *ɔbosom* which I neglected to write.

*I dreamed that Yaw Mensa went to Traa. But the night before I had the dream, Kofi saw Yaw, Kwasi Komfo, and Ɔboɔkyerewa Ɔbosomfoɔ, in a* bar.

Kwabena Bena, you are powerful—*wa ben* (you are cooked).

When an *ɔbosomfoɔ* pours libation, there are certain elements which are traditionally mentioned. I made a list of them:
- Long life and protection for self and family
- Health, strength, and prosperity in their job and life
- Help people find jobs to progress in life and find a spouse and children
- Freedom from accidents, miscarriages, and other calamities befalling them
- Protection against witchcraft, blindness, deafness, and impotency
- Prosperity for the town and its people
- Prevent anyone from being victimized by bad and evil people or spirits
- Prevention from *aduto* used against them by witches, spiritual people, and *ɔkɔmfoɔ*
- Help others to evolve spiritually on their path

I saw in the newspaper that in the Upper West Region of Ghana, they also celebrate a festival called Kwabena Bena. I wonder if the festival might to be related to my *ɔbosom* Kwabena Bena?

I often wondered what is the purpose of spiritual possession, or *akɔm*? *Akɔm* is when a spirit, essentially an *ɔbosom*, uses your soul and body to make itself present on earth. This *ɔbosom* is a family *ɔbosom* that helps, protects, and provides for a particular family and the community at large. The *ɔbosomfoɔ* is ever ready when needed to serve the *ɔbosom*, allowing the ɔbosom to communicate through him. The ɔbosom has to have the ritual of opening the mouth so the ɔbosom can speak. A bad spirit can possess upon an individual, and when this happens, it is considered as something not good, especially if the spirit misbehaves, or harms the one it possesses. Ancestral possession is when a family member has died, and that spirit possesses upon another member. In rare circumstances, it may possess outside the family if it wants to prove a case. *Suman* possession is when a *suman* possesses upon someone. These spirits are not like the *ɔbosom* and are not family spirits. They do not have to have the mouth ritual done in order to speak. They can be attached to any family for generations and become a part of the family, but they are not inheritable like the *ɔbosom*. The difference is that anyone can procure one for their needs, and if they like you, they can possess upon you, but you can never do that with a family *ɔbosom*.

Today Mr. Gyima took me to visit a *Kramo* (Muslim). He told me that this *Kramo* helped an old man and an old lady by giving them a *suman* which is worn around the neck when possessed. Mr. Gyima also informed me that he would like me to have one. The *Kramo* asked me what I wanted, and I told him to see better. He said he would help me by giving me five things, including a *suman* which will make the *ɔbosom* happy and it will also call people. (He means to see, divine, and to see witches).

*Nsuman* that are worn on holy days include *Yɛntumi kahyire*, a *suman* made of raffia and worn at the back of the head; *Akommere*, a *suman* for the head; *Bɔfoɔ*, which means hunter, is a *suman* made of *krani* beads, which are clear beads with white stripes; *Nimo*; *Sedeɛ nson* (seven cowrie shells) is worn on the ankle. This *suman* has a song that goes like this: *Mo sre no ne ho bɛ ho*. Others include *Akoroma kyere ma ni dadaada*, meaning do not hate other ɔkɔmfoɔ; Tɔtɔ ntɔ, meaning not to be extravagant; and *Nkom moa yɛ bra oo*, which is a song that calls for *akɔm* helpers.

The *Asuo Yaa* is a pot which represents the wife of the ɔbosom and is used for female ɔkɔmfoɔ. Items from the sea, rivers, palm wine, water from a sacred stream, along with divination symbols are put inside this pot. The ɔkɔmfoɔ will also use special plants to bathe the eyes and face and put them in the ears to see and hear.

Use three stems of *nsomme mmu* to stir the pot for three days; when the ɔkɔmfoɔ possesses, it means that the ɔbosom has come to the pot and the ɔkɔmfoɔ is pushed aside immediately.

If someone desires a visa, someone owes them money, or anything else, tell them to bring an egg laid that same day, smeared with salt, and give it to the ɔbosom.

*In a dream Nana Dɔnkɔ appeared and he was sitting on what looked like a bed to the right of the new ɔbosom and Nana Yaw Manu was to the left of the ɔbosom. Nana Dɔnkɔ was saying to Nana Manu adeɛ, waiting on his response. The ɔbosom was looking at Nana Manu for an answer as well, but still, he would not give one. The ɔbosom would look toward Nana Dɔnkɔ as he repeated adeɛ, adeɛ, then to Nana Manu for an answer, but there was none.*

*I had another dream about a new ɔbosom that showed me his kahyire. It was made of white cloth that strung through each dufa. I could not make out what was spaced between the dufa, but the cloth was not thick nor was it flat, and it seemed beaded. I am not sure.*

I visited Nana Kofi Kyereme on October 24th, and he told me that when you see a whirlwind that captures any leaves with its spin and try to catch any of the leaves. You can use them as powerful plants when making *bodua*. This will aid you in seeing things as if you are looking up into a whirlwind.

*In this dream I was somewhere, and a woman came to me for consultation. She was standing before me dressed in a two-piece outfit, a top and bottom. The color was somewhat beige, her hair was out and combed back. I was sitting on a stool; to my left was* Kofi, *and to his left was Kwadwo Owusu.* Kofi *had Bɔngan in his hand. I was putting on my nsuman to possess the ɔbosom. I grabbed a handful of nsuman I did not want to use and gave them to Kwadwo to put away. I put my horn sebe on first but struck it three times against the wall; next, I took Bɔngan from* Kofi *and did the same. I was holding Hweɛ (mirror) in my left hand, and I had a bell in my right hand. I saw myself dressed as when I am about to carry the pan, except I was not wearing ntoma.*

*I dreamed of one ɔkɔmfoɔ whose name I do not care to mention; he and I had some misunderstanding. I am not sure if he challenged me or not, but as he was walking, my ɔbosom Kwabena Bena had caught him. Kwabena Bena was making hand gestures similar to a martial artist, blowing air out his mouth and pushing his hands forward up to the sky. As I looked at the back of the hand near the wrists, it reminded me of elephant hair. Next the ɔbosom caught up with this ɔkɔmfoɔ, and he placed one hand on the top of his head and would slap that hand. He did the same for the ɔkɔmfoɔ eyes, ears, his chest and I am not sure if he did it on his back. While all this was going on the ɔkɔmfoɔ could not do anything, as the ɔbosom moved around him. After he was finished, I saw this ɔkɔmfoɔ lying in bed ill. The ɔbosom had spoiled all those parts of his body he touched except his mouth so that he could speak. Maybe to admit his wrongdoing?*

*I was some place in the United States looking for my wife, who had been kidnapped by a Yoruba ɔkɔmfoɔ whose name I will not mention except I would say I documented dreams of him before. He held her in what looked like a department store building. I did not see where she was being held, but I had a gun and was looking. I saw Afia, the daughter of one of my brothers Amponsa, and I went toward her and placed my left hand behind her head and whispered into her ear, asking if she knew where he was. She whispered back to me that he was in another area other than where I was looking. I continued looking for him, and I heard sounds of him, and I slowly walked up toward him. When I saw him, I fired my gun and shot him in the head, his back, and I can't recall where else. As I carried the body off, I was observing the bullet holes in his body. My wife was taken home or somewhere safe before the encounter.*

Yesterday, November 4th at Bonsu, Nana Kofi Nimo told me that the *ababo* seed for the game *Oware* is used in divination to represent the family. He went on to say that Old Man/Nana Dɔnkɔ forgot about this one. It also means that you want the support and unity of the family, and if someone comes for divination and that seed goes toward him/her, it means they do not have the support of the family. In the game, getting all the seeds on your side represents the family as one, and any that you do not have or leaves you means you do not have the unity or support of the family.

Any tree struck by lightning is a very important source of power. Whether the tree survives the lightning strike or not does not affect its spiritual power, because either way, the spiritual power of the tree was affected by the lightning strike. A tree that survives a lightning strike has the ability to withstand the destructive power of lightning and is therefore immune to it, and when you have bathed this tree, it will transfer its power to you so that a lightning strike will not kill you when hateful people try to use that power to destroy you.

If the tree dies, its power is still within the tree and bathing in it can also transfer its power. In either situation, the power of lightning will be transferred to you and strengthen your spirit and protect it against lightning. This being the case, it is the safest way to get lightening power into the body and spirit without direct contact to its destructive power. I personally feel that the tree that lives is the more potent of the two.

To keep the *ɔbosom* or *suman* busy at work, a pad of poison ivy, stinging nettles, or any plant that itches is placed under the *ɔbosom* or *suman*. This plant prevents the *ɔbosom* or *suman* from resting or sitting. Every time they try to rest, the plant will itch the spirits and they will complete the work so that they may rest.

*Feeling tired I took a nap this afternoon and visited my favorite world, the dream world.*
*I took a bucket and went looking for the Tanɔ River. On my way, I passed by some interesting rivers. I saw a man who looked somewhat Asian and told him in Twi I would like to go to the Tanɔ River. He seemed to laugh at my broken Twi and pointed left. On my way I saw a bridge but did not cross it; instead, I went under it to find the river. Again on my way, I saw more interesting rivers, and somehow I recalled or felt the presence of Nana Dɔnkɔ, at least his spirit. I traveled to one source that I felt was deep enough to put my bucket into, then to another which was a trickle. At this*

source it trickled low enough to put a cup to fetch some water, but I soon realized when I put my cup in there, I was collecting moss and did not want it in the water. I decided to go back to the first source and dip the bucket and fetch some clear Tanɔ water.

Then I had another dream of the Tanɔ River, but this one is not as clear as the first. I was trying to get to another town before a train that was being delayed for a while at a stop before moving on. I saw Nana Antwi, who inherited Nana Dɔnkɔ, Maame, and Kofi. I took what looked like two rims of a bicycle and rode them as a bike. I crossed a big bridge (Tanɔ River?) and went up a hill.

*M'anansese a metooye yi, se eye de o, se nnye de o. momfa bi nkɔ, na momfa bi mmera.*

## Final Funeral Rites

For the Late

### NANA KOFI SAKYI
(Alias Kofi Donkor)
(AGED 75 YRS)

Whose sudden death occured at HOLY FAMIL
HOSPITAL TECHIMAN On 6th August 1965

respectfully invite the company of

M/Mr/Mrs .DISTRIC SECRETARY..........

to mourn with them at TECHIMAN as follows
WAKE-KEEPING:- Friday 18th August 1965
FINAL FUNERAL RITES:- Saturday 19th Aug. 19

All Sympathizers are cordially invited

Toska Press, Techiman

### CHIEF MOURNERS

Nana Kwame Poku (Adontenhene) Nana Kwabena Mensah (Taamensah Bosomfour) Nana Kofi Asumadu (Bookyerewa Bosomfour, Tras) Obaapanin Akua Tema (all of Techiman)

FATHERS: Kojo Ansu, Kwasi Kune, Ata Kojo Kwabena Takyi, Kwabena Saase,
BROTHERS SISTERS:- Okyeame Kofi Bour, Kwabena Afena, Afua Asubonteng, Ama Akoman, Okomfur Akua Anane, Afia Mansah, Yaa Bouh (all of Techiman) Adjoa Nyarko (Akomadan)

NEPHEWS & NIECES: - Abusuapanin T. K Boateng (alias Nana Kwabena Antwi, Abusuapanin Kofi Ankomah, Op Kwasi Badu (alias I. K Badu (Retired Health Inspector) Kwabena Amponsah, Yaw Mensah, Kofi Kontor, Kwame Asamoah, Kwaku Forkuo, Kwasi Obeng, Kwame Yeboah, Kwasi Danso, Nana Diapimhunu, Kwaku Peter, Yaw Dove Yaw Boateng, Akosua Antwiwaa, Akosua Manu Adjoa Dinkyini, Yaa Gyambibi, Abena Foriwaah Adjoa Nyameyedo, Adjoa Sikayena, Afia Kyeremaa Ama Bobia, Afia Akaa, Adjoa Mansa. Adjoa Krsa Ama Bour, Akua Abebrese, Yaa Tawia (all of Tech

Obosomfor Yaw Mann (Akumsa Domasi) Kwabena Krah (Tanoso), Kwabena Afirim (Anyinabrim) Adjoa Donkor (Kenten) Yaayaa (Tanoso), Lydia Forkuo, Joseph Boateng PZ (II of Kumasi))
SONS:- Kofi Nsiah (Blacksmith) Kofi Tawia, Kofi Korpo, Kwaku Dapaa (Blacksmith) Kwasi Mensah Kofi Nimo, Kwasi Amponsah Paul (all Farmers) Kojo Kune, Mr Yaw Anane Amponsa (Contractor Mr Hayford Amponsah (Wartsan Project Techiman Kojo Owusu Kusuprim (Headmaster) Kwaku Adam Donkor), Kingsford Amoakohene (TESS Driver) Yaw Duku (Driver Accra) Kwasi Aduo (Tipper truck Driver Tech) Komfoo Kofi Effah) Kwame Amponsa (Burger) Kwabena Takyi Worker TESS) Kofi Sakyi Daniel (Cultural Research Consultant) Kwasi Owusu (Carpenter Tech) Kwaku Antwi, Kwame Owusu, Kojo Oppong Adelaide (Teacher Ashtown Pri Ksi.) Kofi Asua (Blacksmith) Kwasi Aduo Fitter) Kwasi Effah, Kwaku Sakyi (Miami USA)
DAUGHTERS: Adjoa Amponsaa, Akosua Antowa Yaa Donkor, Adjoa Afera, Adjoa Kune, Yaa Kormaa, Ab.na Donkor, Afia Owusuaa, Ama Komfoo Adjoa Badu, Afia Serwaa, Yaa Badu (all of Tech) Akosua Amponsah (Miami USA)

Abena **WIDOWS**
Afia Munufie (Senior Wife) Adjoa Asamoah

Funerary card announcing the transition of Nana Kofi Donko

Gyambibi shrine at Ampoma.

# CHAPTER FIVE

## 1996: RETURN AGAIN, DREAMS AND WISDOM

At the end of September 1996, I left the United States and arrived in Ghana safely. I greeted everyone who was very surprised to see me, especially Nana Effa, who said that he had had a dream, but doubted I was here.

Kofi and I began our usual conversations about *Bono* culture. I found him to be very informative and gifted. I love Kofi. I inquired about the word ɔ*bosom* and if it meant the worship of stones. He replied that this interpretation is not true. The root of the word comes from *oboɔ* to create, for example, *Odomankoma oboɔadeɛ*, which means, The Creator created things. Odomankoma created the ɔ*bosom* as a form of worship toward himself. In fact, we can say that Odomankoma created the concept of worship. Kofi elaborated that everything else was created by the ɔ*bosom*. If you investigate the origins of the chiefs, you will see that the *abosom* played a significant role in their inception. The whole concept of traditional politics was created by these *abosom*, in fact, everything.

My next serious conversation was about Nana Effa. Nana has the habit of when you are leaving him, he would accompany you a little distance from his house to see you off, then return home. Kofi explains this to be the act or function of what is called *Okwan gya so*. This is a protocol that takes place when you come to visit or consult an *ɔkɔmfoɔ*. Perhaps during the consultation something came up that should remain private, and this custom would provide the *ɔkɔmfoɔ* the opportunity to speak privately to the client and discuss their problems. Another reason for this custom is that when you visit an *ɔkɔmfoɔ*, the *ɔkɔmfoɔ* would not like the visitor to encounter any problems and would walk her/him a quarter of the distance from his house, extending his powers to look over and protect the visitor as he sees her/him off. If anything bad should happen after you leave an *ɔkɔmfoɔ*'s house, people might say, because you visited such and such an *ɔkɔmfoɔ,* something bad happened to you. This same practice is extended to visitors when they visit chiefs. If the chief cannot accompany you, then his *ɔkyeame* would represent him.

I presented Asubonten and Asuotipa with a welcome drink, and I have to do the same for Old Man, Taa Kɛsɛ, Taa Kwasi, and Ɔboɔkyerewa. Nana Effa offered Mossi *pito* on my behalf. I left and returned back to Nana Effa's house after he told me to come back. I gave Kwabena Bena a chicken and a drink. Later on, I possessed one of my *ɔbosom* who advised me not to think too much and to offer Asuotipa a ram and drink, and Mossi a chicken and *pito*. After this I was told what had happened, and as I proceeded home it started to rain. I saw Africania, and we chatted for a little while. At home, they were turning a curse that involved Ɔboɔkyerewa at Asubonten. When they were finished, Yaw Mensa offered Kwabena Bena a drink, three eggs, and a chicken as a welcome offering.

I went back to visit my brother Nana Effa, and sometime later he possessed Kofi Asante, who gave me advice about my problems. He said that is one of the reasons why I came. I discussed some of my issues with him, and he informed me that I have contamination in my shrine house, and I should not eat any food prepared outside. He indicated that the closer I get to my *ɔbosom*, I will find obstacles on the path to trip me up and prevent me from accomplishing this, and if I am going somewhere and I trip or stumble, I should remember the place where this happened.

*I dreamed I was in the Asubonten shrine room or some sorts and saw a man holding a duck ready for sacrifice. I am not sure if this man was me, but I saw myself later on holding what looked like its egg, and it reminded me of a green sea turtle. Later on, I heard* Kwabena Bena *say that I had taken a friend and had not informed him. He went on to say that if I did not give him a chicken, eggs, and drink, he would chase her away.*

*This friend told me she had a dream that she was fighting with two women. I do not recall how soon after she told me, so I had this dream. My mother visited me and informed me about the dream the woman had. Concerning the two women, my mother said one represents her mother and the other me. She said the woman had some problem with her mother and relating to her mother's menses and the other woman is me. She stated that this woman did not like foreigners and that relates to me.*

I learned that when you sacrifice a ram, the cooked meat that is put on the *ɔbosom* is called *Ntrenam*. This meat is for the *ɔbosom* only. The tongue is placed on the first vertebra when the vertebra is offered to the *ɔbosom* and, according to Ɔboɔkyerewa *ɔbosomfoɔ* the vertebra is eaten solely by the *ɔkɔmfoɔ* of the *ɔbosom*. The vertebra is afterward strung with a rope to hang in front of the shrine so that the ɔbosom will come and see or be reminded of how busy he is. If there is not too much and only a few, then the ɔbosom is not busy and is inspired to work harder.

I was informed that on the last day during the yam festival, which is Mono-Bena, the soul of the ɔbosom is purified. I will try to observe this ritual very closely tomorrow and see all that is involved and who are all the participants. It was mentioned that certain individuals had to be present for this to take place, and this ritual was done once a year.

*Kwabena Bena had possessed upon me, and Asubonten was upon Nana Asantewaa, and the elder Kwabena Antwi was there. Kwabena Bena called Nana Antwi and told him that he was upset because he was not here for Asubonten's yam festival, and he fined him a drink. After Nana Antwi brought the drink he told him, now take this drink and give it to Asubonten to apologize for not being here. Asubonten on Nana Asantewaa was to our left while talking to Asubonten. The clothes of the ɔkɔmfoɔ fell to the ground (shame). Asubonten apologized and lifted it back up.*

Nana Effa showed me a plant that is called *Nkasenkase*; it looks very familiar to me as a plant called Amaranth. This plant, according to Nana, is used for what they call *kata* (mucous). You boil the flowers with *abe* (palm kernel), and the leaves are used for boiling. I inquired if there is any spiritual usage of this plant, and he said he knows of no spiritual use. I will try to find out further information about this plant. Another familiar plant is *Nkɔgyame* (don't go and leave me) or *Gyinantwi* (to stand still). It is what I know as Spanish needles. The leaves are used for eye problems, and I have witnessed their use as one of the ingredients for annual purification for the ɔbosom and to attract money.

Kwasi Komfo showed me a praying mantis nest that is used when making a *suman* called *samando kuruwa* for the ancestors. I was also made aware by Nana Kofi Kyereme that the *nsuman* akommɛre and *Atenka*, also called *Awuokuo*, are never worn when one is going to the farm. These two are the most senior and important of all the *nsuman ɔkɔmfoɔ* wears. Nana Akumsa, when she was alive, also brought this to my attention. Nana Kyereme continued by saying that *Gyabunu* is to prevent you from being harmed when you see spirits. They will not disturb or cause you any trouble as long as you wear this *suman*. Now I understand why Maame and the co-wife of Nana Dɔnkɔ will wear this *suman* for one year during his mourning rituals. So, anyone who might be easily disturbed by seeing ghosts or spirits may wear this *suman*. Nana also stated that the *suman* called *ntwerema* is used for pulling anything to you. It was also mentioned that *ɔkɔmfoɔ* do not have to wear all *nsuman* every day, only on special days like *dabɔne*. I wore a number of these *nsuman*: *Akofofuo* are white beads, representing *ɔkɔmfoɔ* should not hate one another; *Nimo nimo* are blue square beads worn around the left knee; *Samando kuruwa* (*Krani kesɛ*, "cat eyes," even though they are called so they do not have the white solid lines) is worn for the ancestors; *Bofo srɛ me* (*krani* beads worn around the left knee); *Nkom moa* (*krani* beads worn around the left wrist) represents *akɔm* helper; and *Yɛntumi* (worn around knee). As far as *nkamere* (iron bracelet) and *kawa* (small rings) are concerned, *ɔkɔmfoɔ* can wear them anytime.

*Boa me* is a *suman* made with *sedeɛ* (cowrie shells), and it has a long string worn around the wrist. Place the *suman* on top of a sweeping broom that is put on top of a pot used for cooking *motɔ*. Get a fertile egg, pour some of the white out and pour libation using the plants *pia, taafameɛ*, and *mae* into the egg, then some into the mouth of a black chicken. Mention the one who gave you the *suman* and ask it to overcome all challengers. Sacrifice the chicken, cook an egg over the fire and eat alone. The string is pulled with the above-mentioned plants while praying.

I was informed by Yaw Mensa that the knowledge of a plant called *Akyeampɔn* is very recent in the history of plant knowledge among the *Bono* and not much is known about it. What is known is that it can be used for cutlass wounds; the juice of the plant is squeezed on the wound to facilitate healing. It is also used for women whose menses fail to appear. You grind the leaves and put them in boiling water, add salt, and drink, and she will never miss. According to Kofi, this plant only clots the wound, but does not heal it. Lastly, it is used to preserve dead bodies and repel mad dogs.

I noticed a while ago that someone fell at the Ɔboɔkyerewa shrine, and this person was beaten, so I became curious as to why, so I asked Yaw Mensa, "why do they beat you if you fall at the shrine in Traa?" He said if they do not you will die in one year. He went on to add you fell because of something that may injure or kill you, so they beat that individual to destroy that thing. According to Nana Effa, it is taboo to fall there, and that is why they beat you. You fall because of something not right with you, so they beat it out of you.

Kofi and I resumed our conversation about the difference between *sunsum*, *ntɔn*, and *kra*. He said they are all the same and the different names refer only to the stages or transition the spirit goes through. He stressed that the *sunsum* and the *kra* are the same and it is the *sunsum* that goes ahead of the body. Perhaps this is how some people can sense or see someone who is coming to visit them before they arrive. In essence, they may have felt the *sunsum* of that person.

Man and woman relationships have always been a very important topic when it comes to understanding the process leading to marriage, so Kofi and I engaged in an enlightening conversation. He said it is essential that a husband give his wife, whom he truly loves, waist beads. These beads symbolize what is called the last love he has for her. They can be strung from any expensive beads, but two of the favorite and most expensive are called *Gyabunu*, which ɔkɔmfoɔ uses for making the *suman* by the same name, and *Bodom*. They also represent sexual love. When the wife desires her husband, she will jingle her beads with her hand, making beautiful music that will stimulate her man. At times, her husband will play with them to let her know his desires and arousing her passion. When her husband presents her with these beads, she will notify her parents that her husband has performed the last love for her, so when she dies, they do not have to ask him about it. She will also show them off to her girlfriends. It is important for the family of the wife to know this, before performing the funeral rites because she will be buried with them, and her spirit will not feel neglected by her husband and become angry with him and disturb his future relationships. She, in turn, when her husband dies, will present her husband with a pair of shorts, a handkerchief, a blanket, and a pillow for his funeral rites so that he may rest comfortably in the spiritual world. If these things are not given, his spirit may annoy her and any future relationships. We also discuss what is called *Kra su*, which is the broth of the chicken that is cooked for soul purification. It can also be water and salt. When praying to the soul, you offer it the hot soup, saying something hot has happened and it should cool it down, since the soul does not like hot things.

It is important for *akɔmfoɔ* not to keep things that worry or disturb them too much in their heart, for this disturbs the soul and leads to a spiritual illness called *sipe*. *Sipe* is a serious illness that, if not taken care of, can lead to death. When this illness comes upon you, the soul connection can become broken, making the *ɔkɔmfoɔ* vulnerable to further attacks, and by then even prayers will be to no avail. When a husband quarrels or has issues with his wife, he should not keep this matter too long in his heart. He should talk to her about this problem in order to let it go, because if he does not, his soul will retreat and desert his body, and if he dies like this, no one may know the cause of his death since he did not say anything that was troubling his heart. An understanding of the principle is important for spiritual independence.

*Sipe* is also a spiritual disease caused by the *ɔbosom* or spirits when you keep thoughts in your mind and heart. When you have a problem, for example, with your wife, and you are so upset with her that you do not eat her cooking, the *ɔbosom* dislikes that, and you will begin to lose weight, which is the beginning of the disease. If you keep problems in your heart and mind and you do not say anything to solve them, the problem will begin to trouble your spirit and lead to *sipe*. In essence, *sipe* is caused by a behavior that is not corrected. The okra becomes disturbed by your thoughts or ill feelings not corrected. If you know better and are doing something that you should not do and pretend that what you are doing is okay or that a problem does not exist or does not worry you, then later on you will see something, and this too will cause *sipe*. It relates to what is called your conscience.

*I was somewhere in a room lying down on a bed. I separated my neck from my body with my left hand and my head with my right hand. Even though I held them, I could still see around me. I place them both on my body and they fitted nicely. I took them apart again, and this time I was standing up. I placed them back on my body, but they did not fit properly. I could still see a gap all around the seams as if I had a mask on as I was looking in a mirror. I went and pressed my head against a wall to close in the gaps, but no success. I thought of sewing it together. I wondered about the bones. After this, I saw Nana Kwabena Mensa, Taa Mensa ɔbosomfoɔɔ, and* Nana Kofi Kyereme, *Taa Kwasi ɔbosomfoɔɔ coming towards me.*

*I also dreamed about food. I was somewhere back home, and they prepared food for me; one type was for me and another for other people. I was looking for my food to eat. I went into a refrigerator and saw food for other people (white) and said that was not for me, then I located my own. I believe the person who prepared my food was a man.*

*This afternoon I had a dream that I was living in a house somewhere back home. I went down to the basement to secure the house and noticed that the bars on the windows were off. I tried to fix them back on. The bars that protected the windows consisted of one single bar that protected two windows. I realized the upper hinges were off too, so I fixed them. I now realized someone had tried to break into my house. I went upstairs, and there I either possessed my* ɔbrafo *or it was he all along. The* ɔbrafo *caught the three persons who were involved in trying to steal my ntoma. I recall something about a car, but anyway I do not remember. These individuals were the woman from Nkoransa and the elder son of* Yaw Mensa *whose room I occupied last year, and* Yaw Mensa *himself. The* ɔbrafo *caught them all. He put* Yaw Mensa *on a bed to stand or some platform. I believed* Ɔbookyerewa ɔbosomfoɔɔ *was there. The* ɔbrafo *went and slapped* Yaw Mensa *with his left hand for being foolish and involving himself in such a scheme. I do not think that he himself had anything to do with the theft, but* he was aware and tried to cover it up the ɔbrafo *wanted to just teach him a lesson. I recall looking out of one of the top floor windows before or at this time, offering drinks to people.*

I had another enlightened conversation with Yaw Mensa about Ɔboɔkyerewa. The history of this *ɔbosom* indicates that this *ɔbosom* appeared by himself. No one brought him to the area or caught him. They found the *ɔbosom* sitting on a stone called *pin* near the Tanɔ River. The other Ɔboɔkyerewa *ɔbosom* in the town near the *ɔbosomfoɔɔ* residence came first and is the younger of the two. The main one near the Tanɔ River or what they call the bush is the elder. The elder *ɔbosom* is the one who instructed them to build his house near the river, which they did. The younger stated that he would no longer live in the bush and that they should build his house in the town, and they did.

When the *ɔbosom* first appeared, they saw a *nkamere* (bracelet) on the *ɔbosom*, so the *ɔbosomfoɔɔ* wore it and when he travels and comes into contact with Ɔboɔkyerewa cases, he can do all the rituals with the *nkamere*.

The *ɔbosom* Ɔboɔkyerewa became a brother to Asubonten for the following reasons. The *ɔbosomfoɔɔ* for the Ɔboɔkyerewa *ɔbosom* was called *Tito*, and the one for Asubonten was called Kwadwo Asubonten, and they both became fast friends. When Ɔboɔkyerewa *ɔbosomfoɔ* visited the Asubonten *ɔbosomfoɔ* he would allow him to carry his *ɔbosom* and vice versa, so as the two *ɔbosomfoɔɔ* became closer than friends and eventually as brothers, so did their *ɔbosom*.

When Ɔboɔkyerewa Kwaku kills anyone, his knives have to be washed with the blood of a ram by the family of the deceased. The number of knives is seven and is referred to as *sekan mmare*. *Duafofi* or *Asonam* is used to repel the ɔbosom after he has caught you. They both have a strong smell, and *famwisa* is added and ground to bath and drink. *Odom* and *Mae* are ground to smear on the body, but they are not meant to be eaten.

*I dreamed I went to my mother's house and saw chickens in a room. I was catching them to put them in boxes, but they were so many of them I could not catch them all.*

Yaw Mensa interpreted this dream, saying that I would get lots of money when I went back home. Kofi's take was that I would have many children, saying that chickens, eggs, and fishes are all symbolic of childbirth.

*I went to Bonkwai to celebrate Nana Kwaku Badu's Buruma festival and was sleeping in his shrine room and dreamed of old man. He was sitting on a chair wearing ntoma. I was kneeling, laying my head on his lap. He was taking an object from a dish and rubbing or pressing it over my body. Some items look like the fargo worm shells that I have seen in the marketplace. One was the beak for the kra, and I saw cowrie shells, but I could not make out the rest. There were some other shells he used first before the two I recalled. Those reminded me of the* sedeɛ ɔkyeame *he had given me for divination.*

*I also dreamed of lots of babies, six to be exact. They were lying on a bed, and I was looking at them; they were all naked.*

I traveled to a place in the North called Ampoma. In this town resides an *ɔbosom* who is called Gyambibi. There is another Gyambibi, one in *Nkoransa*. To distinguish one from the other, the town or area is attached to the ɔbosom. For instance, I visited Ampoma Gyambibi.

The ɔbosom caught a witch, and a ritual was being performed to release her; she was dressed in red-orange and pregnant. I am not sure if it was the ɔkyeame or the assistant who was attending, but he made the witch kneel down outside the shrine room near the entrance and purified her with a broom and then gave her something to drink. After that he took three eggs and smashed them on her head. I was told that the *aduro* she drank was to repel the ɔbosom, so that it may no longer act upon her, but if she continued in witchcraft, the ɔbosom will kill her. Then she was told to walk down and back on a path from and to the shrine. I do not recall how many times, maybe three or seven times, but as she paraded, she was mocked and hooed by children running alongside her singing and dancing. Others were banging on anything they could pick up, shouting at her ɔbayifoɔ/witch, tugging at her clothes, and again hooing at her several times. After this humiliation, she was given an *aduro* to wash her head and face. She put on her headscarf and her slippers and went home with a man whom I presume to be her husband or a family member. I have the incident recorded on cassette, and I took a photo of her.

I visited Nana Kofi Kyereme; he is a nice man and very wise. I have developed a deep respect for him as a human being. As always, we spoke of Nana Dɔnkɔ, whose father Yaw Bodu(?) he said was an ɔkɔmfoɔ, and that (the people I know) Nana Kofi Ankoma, Yaw Mensa, and Yaw Manu are from his direct lineage. I inquired more about Kɔmpan Adepa, which he said in past was associated with a cloth that lasted a long, long time. This name was even printed on the cloth. I am not sure which came first, the cloth or the name, or whether ɔkɔmfoɔ use this name today and if it was taken and represented on a cloth or the cloth and name existed prior and ɔkɔmfoɔ took it up. What I do know is that name became synonymous with ɔkɔmfoɔ. Nana went on to say that only good ɔkɔmfoɔ should be associated with Kɔmpan Adepa, and they should not drink or do bad things. Anything that would last a long time is Kɔmpan Adepa.

*I dreamed that I was going to Asubonten shrine room to possess him. I sat on the stool to carry his pan, but Yaw Mensa did not want me to do so. He said nothing openly, but his manner told me so. They decided then that I would not carry Asubonten, but they would drum, and I would possess him that way. As they started to drum, I began to possess, and I woke up with that same feeling.*

Kofi and I talked about the special padding worn by women called *Atufo*. This is worn by women on top of their buttocks and is considered very beautiful and powerful at the same time. It is said that in the past, women wore beads around their waist and attached a loincloth to protect their modesty, and they also wore their sanitary cloths this way. Their clothing had no pockets, and therefore they stored their personal possession behind their buttocks. Eventually, the priestesses began to put their *nsuman* behind them. Since they could see what was in front of them, they needed something to watch their back. When these women accompanied their husbands on the hunt, the husbands would hold on to this padding to give him extra power so that when he shot his gun, he would not miss. I myself have seen young women doing cultural dances wearing this padding behind them, and they would dance with their backs to us, displaying their prowess and, at times, sitting on our laps. They would not leave us alone until we gave them some money, and you pity the man who had no money or admired him. Sometimes someone laughing would give you money to give to her. Some men enjoy the experience and would have fun with the dancer, touching and playing with her padding, connecting to its sexual overtones.

In rare circumstances, the beads and sanitary cloths were used to spoil powerful things; they were put into the barrel of a gun to spoil gunshot *aduro*. In this case, the owner of the gun would die when he discharged it, even if he had a powerful gunshot *aduro* himself. So, this is why we fear and respect some women more than others. Knowledge is true power.

In a conversation that took place yesterday, I was informed that *Gyambibi*, who is known as a witch catcher, was primarily a war *ɔbosom*, and if you bathe his *aduro* you could catch bullets in your body and take them out. A chicken was used for this ritual. They would bathe *aduro* with a chicken beside them and when the day came, they would shoot the chicken. If it did not die, then you had the *aduro*.

When you petition the ɔbosom *Gyambibi* to catch a witch, the shrine was shot with a gun to signify that the *ɔbosom* would take on your case. For example, when you were troubled by a witch in your family and you came to this *ɔbosom* for help, you bought bullets from the shrine and fired them at the shrine. Sometimes you might miss it, but when you hit it the *ɔbosom* would kill the witch. Now, this practice was soon abandoned since they had to always repair the shrine. They took to shooting a wall, and that, too, was abandoned due to the constant wall repairs. Now they shoot at a tree. This I witnessed. I found it interesting that the death of the witch could fall upon the one who fired the gun and not the *ɔbosom*; psychologically, you were the one using the *ɔbosom* to kill the witch.

*I saw the ɔbosommerafoɔ kyinaman in a dream. We were somewhere and I saw his* ɔkɔmfoɔ(*whom I met in Bonkwae). The ɔbosom gave me his knife and put it on my left waist and I possessed the spirit. I had eggs around. I would in possession talk with this knife. The ɔbosom would move the knife, and it fell to the ground, and I too became unpossessed and fell, then Kwabena Bena came upon me. Next the ɔkɔmfoɔ did the same thing and he, too, possessed the ɔbosom the same way. The ɔkɔmfoɔ had mpɛsɛmpɛsɛ (locked hair).*

On a visit to Tanɔboase, the *ɔhene*, *ɔkyeame*, and I engaged in a conversation about *Atufo*. He said that women in the past used this cloth (pounded from a certain tree) by weaving it in the sky to command power so that when their husbands went off to war, they would be victorious.

The *ɔhene* confided in me that the *ɔbosomfoɔ* of Taa Kora have sexual difficulties, or their sexual ability will be taken away. This is mainly due to the fact the *ɔbosom* is old, and old men do not have desires or concerns about sex, and that is why the current *ɔbosomfoɔ* complains about his inability to please his wife or wives. I have taken a photo of the *ɔbosomfoɔ* in possession, and you can see that he is not a young man himself. The *ɔhene* went on to add that sex and women are something that should be feared. It is considered something unclean as far as the *ɔbosom* is concerned. It affects his proper function. Most *ɔbosom* taboo sex and, on their special days, you should abstain completely and sleep alone so you can have visions. He went on to say that after the visions come and you wake up, you are free to do what you want. This is not what was taught to me when I was training. Maybe it is because he, the *ɔhene*, is old and not a priest.

I visited a *mmoatia ɔkɔmfoɔ* in Kenten; it is unfortunate that I do not recall his name. He reminds me so much of my father; I have taken a curious liking toward him. I was happy to see him, and he seemed happy to see me, too. I went through the usual protocols; I offered him a drink and 42,000 cedis. We made small talk for a while, and he said he wanted to give me a *suman* called *Penya*. He said this *suman* can call things for me, like money, work, or anything I desire. When I go to *akɔm* and there is drumming, I won't fall. He mentioned that I should give it lavender alone, no alcohol, only sweet-smelling things and to speak while rubbing it on. When I finish, rub the rest of my face, hair, and arms. That is all. I can keep the *suman* on the wall. I gave him 45,000 cedis more, not for the *suman*, but because I just like him.

Last night Kofi and I chatted about a *suman* called *Gyinaye*. This *suman* is used to pull or bring something good to you, like customers, if you have a business. The *ɔbosom* also sits upon it. It will support all work, bring money and clients for help, training, building my shrine, stopping all illnesses, witchcraft, bad people of any kind, and expose all evil intention, keeping all evil away from the home. You can keep it in your shrine room or put it in the home. You can also bury it in the ground at the entrance of your property. The ritual is done naked. As a side note, you need a pyramid or cone-shaped mound over the *suman*, and make sure that it is cemented to waterproof it. Afterward, you need to sacrifice a chicken and feed its wings, legs, and intestines to the *suman*.

Nana Kofi Boɔ told me he had a dream three days ago about Kwabena Bena asking for *emo* (rice) and chicken as sacrifice being given him. The food was shared with the children. All this was done on Taa Ho. Kwabena Bena was asking for emo. He is not sure if he just saw the rice sacrifice being given to Kwabena Bena or if it was just being shared with him and the other *ɔbosom*. Perhaps the dream is saying I can use Taa Ho to do rituals for Kwabena Bena. Taa Ho is the one who gave Tigare his clubs and to possess upon humans. He also uses him as his *ɔbrafoɔ*.

*Nteso* is the power of a spirit that is passed on when it is duplicated. For example, if you possess a *suman* and someone wants one like it, you would take part of it and make another. This new one does not only have a physical part of the original/old one but also repeats its spiritual capabilities. This passing on is what we call *nteso*. I can do the same if I want to make another pan of Kwabena Bena to keep somewhere else and do work. This is at the heart of all *Tigare* in the Bono region.

Kofi and I discuss *kunkuma* and how it should only be given to graduate *ɔkɔmfoɔ*, and that we will use it for baptism (his word, not mine) for other initiates. When a new *ɔkɔmfoɔ* graduates, I can add my *kunkuma* to the one being made for the new graduate. In the *Bono* area *kunkuma* is the power all graduated *ɔkɔmfoɔ* must eat. We can also refer to this *ɔkɔmfoɔ* as *kunkuma*. If they have not performed this ritual, we do not believe they have the true power to function as such. I will do the same for all *akɔmfoɔ* whom I train, linking them back to Nana Dɔnkɔ and Nana Effa, who gave me my *kunkuma*.

I observe when the *ɔbosom* is being fed ram after the sacrifice, the neck bone is an important part of the sacrifice. The tongue is cut and placed on top of the opening of this bone; the *ɔkɔmfoɔ* speaks and places it in the pan. Kofi said that this represents life and truthfulness, so whatever is said will be truthful. I will inquire further about this bone. I also saw while eating it I can use it in my divination.

Last Friday I did divination for *Bonkwai ɔhemmaa* (Queen-mother) concerning her problems. There were four things I saw, actually three. The fourth was her inquiring about her son. She was informed about stool *asɛm* and was advised to go and consult and make an offering to *Buruma* to sit on the case since the *ɔbosom* was involved in the matter. She also wanted to start a daycare project and was told to give a broken knife, a drink, and chicken to Kwabena Bena. She should go to her ancestors to ask for assistance in her business. Lastly, she should go to Asubonten and give three types of palm wine, and a chicken to ask for her son to make money during his travel and one day return.

I wanted to get more information on *nteso*, so I spoke with Nana Effa about this power. *Nana* said this is the power that is left over after you made the original, for example, a *suman* or *ɔbosom*. When you gather all the ingredients, you need to make the *suman* or *ɔbosom* and some are left over; you keep this in case someone comes for a similar *suman* or *ɔbosom*. You cannot give the original, but you can give its *nteso*. Maybe you are not able to find all the ingredients to make one, but you have the *nteso* that it was leftover, so you use it to make the home for the spirit for that person in need.

At Tanɔboase, *Ahunu dufa* was given to me by Taa Kora *ɔbosomfoɔɔ* and the chief. The ingredients for the *dufa* included *Abroma* (dove), *Akokonini* (a cock), *Sika futuo* (gold dust), *Nsa* (alcohol), *Mmraha* (plant call hundred law), *Odum*, *Humatre bene*, and *Nokwa*. I recall the sacrifice given to *Amoa*. Everything was ground up, made into a *dufa*, and left to dry. The chief said that Taa Kora is an *ɔbosom* that repairs things, anything that needs to be repaired, Taa Kora can do it, very much like what Rattray documented in his book *Ashanti*.

*I had a dream that my divination sedeɛ ɔkyeame can also be called ntrama.*

Yesterday, on December 4, Kofi and I had a dialogue about the protocol for when someone or the *ɔbosom* wants to help you, but taboos are associated with it. Kofi said since my stomach is troubling me, he can help me. Can I obey the taboos? I replied I don't know; tell me what the taboos are. He responded I must first say yes to the question. I, in turn, said I don't know if I can obey the taboos, so I must know them before I can say yes. We went back and forth and got nowhere fast. He asked *ɔkyeame* Nana Kofi Boɔ who said if the *ɔbosom* said he can help you, can you do what is required, your response should be *me tumi kyere me*, in other words, I am able to teach me. Then the *ɔbosom* would say the taboos of the help he offers. For example, if the *ɔbosom* says to drink *ampatekyi* and you are Muslim, you can say *Nana me pa wo kyew wo, me ye kramo*, then the *ɔbosom* would change it till he tells a taboo you can agree with. The key point here is to tell the *ɔbosom* you can do it and can he teach you how to do it. If you say no first, then the *ɔbosom* would not force you and he would stop.

*I had a dream of an ɔkɔmfoɔ I know distantly. I believed she was one of Nana Dinizulu wives. She had possessed her ɔbosom Asubotopre and I possessed Kwabena Bena. Kwabena Bena went to this ɔbosom and said that he and him were one. Kwabena Bena touched his chest with both hands and then touched the ɔbosom chest then pointed his left hand as if up to the sky. When he said they were one Kwabena Bena also touched or crossed his two index fingers as well. I recall that Kwabena Bena and Asubotopre were there alone, and I did not see anyone else.*

I had an enlightening conversation with Nana Effa concerning spirituality and the *ɔbosom*. *Nana* said it is important that you first do your job as an *ɔkɔmfoɔ* well, so that those you help will tell others and they, in turn, will come to you. He also said if you break your taboos, and the *ɔbosom* do wish to kill you, this offense will show up in your blood as a sign of boils, especially if they appear more than one under the armpits and groin area. This is the *ɔbosom* telling you that you have done something wrong and you should purify the *ɔbosom*. Normally a ram is required, and if you cannot give one and give only a chicken and the *ɔbosom* sits back and does nothing, it is not the *ɔbosom*'s fault because you did not give the *ɔbosom* what he wanted. You may not know why the *ɔbosom* asked for the ram, but he needed it for something. Not only is the *ɔbosom* to be purified, but your blood as well.

Nana instructed me about *aduro* baths and the different ways you can bathe. For some of them, you put an egg in it, so when the egg breaks you will know it is time to stop the bath. Some *aduro* baths are hung from a tree, some are in a basket, and so forth. *Nana* also told me the tree called *dufore* is also called *nokabo*, and I did not know that.

Kwame Agyeman, a friend and fellow *ɔkɔmfoɔ* gave me this *suman* called Akua Boadwe. If I need something, this *suman* can go and get it—money, people, whatever. I can use it for difficult cases that are hard to solve. Use only the egg yolk, not the white, plus *mɔtɔ* to feed the *suman*.

Nana Effa and I are talking nicely these days. He encourages me to believe more in my *ɔbosom* that they will provide and protect me, so I need not fear anything. He gave the example that if someone is going to beat him, he fears not, for that person might end up hitting a tree or someone else instead. This would lead that person to another set of troubles. He indicated that when someone dies (in the family?) the *ɔbosom* sings death songs, so people will come to witness why the *ɔbosom* is singing such songs.

He informed me that ɔkɔmfoɔ taboos being frozen after death because they throw the body down to break the ice. After the body is frozen to thaw out the ice, they throw the body down to break up the ice and it is this throwing down of the body that ɔkɔmfoɔ taboos. When ɔkɔmfoɔ falls, he must sacrifice a ram, and since no one knows or is there to see if the body was abused, this is not a good thing. If they offer no such sacrifice, this will lead to problems.

Nana taught me about *nsuman* that are worn. He said it is better to have the *aduro* inside your body than that which is worn on the outside. Those *nsuman* worn on the body can be easily contaminated, but that which is inside the body cannot. The eating and bathing of *aduro* are superior to wearing them. I think perhaps they can be worn until enough *aduro* is built up in the body. Now, I understand why some ɔkɔmfoɔ here do not wear *nsuman*. Nana added that some of the *aduro* inside the *nsuman* which are worn are sometimes burned as in the preparation of *kunkuma* (graduation *aduro*) to be eaten, so you have the power within you. I know ɔbosom like Taa Kora taboo *nsuman*; I have never seen the ɔbosomfoɔɔ wear anything except one ring before possessing the ɔbosom. Nana always tells me that he wants me to spoil my skin; he wants me to bath some *aduro* one hundred times, so I should take more *aduro* baths. I hope to write more about *kunkuma*; I know it taboos nothing and can destroy all taboos.

*Back in Miami I had a dream. I saw Asubonten and Nana Anane (Asantewaa). I possessed Kwabena Bena, and Nana Anane was on the ground and Kwabena Bena was helping her up.*

*I am not sure if it was an ɔbosom or an ancestor or a sunsum I do not know* that came toward me and put the string of nnufa around my forehead. It was red like nkrawo. I also had what look like bells hanging in front of my eyes, and they were long in the back. After the spirit put this around my forehead, I fell to the ground. I am not sure if I had possessed.

I dreamed I saw Boɔ Yaw ɔkɔmfoɔ, but he did not look like himself, perhaps it was his ɔbosom on him. I was singing his songs, and the spirit was doing something with me. I recall seeing a woman, and I stood up or was I already standing; anyway, I greeted her by touching my check against her cheek. She was fair in complexion.

*M'anansesem a metooye yi, se eye de o, se ennye de o, momfa bi nkɔ momfa bi mmera*

At Poma.

Sacred tree.

Buruma yam festival.

# CHAPTER SIX

## 1998

I arrived in Ghana on January 18, 1998, a Friday night and traveled all night, finally reaching Takyiman around 6:30 a.m. I learned a lot about the death of Nana Kofi Effa, but still everything is sketchy. Everyone said he died quickly; he took ill and was taken to the hospital and died in one week. Amoako added that he turned his face to the wall before he died. Some insisted that Nana Effa died from meningitis while others say because of Ɔbookyerewa. I am not sure where to go.

The story I am told was that he was involved with two women, one whose name whose names I will not mention. I knew both of them. These two women got into a physical altercation, one biting the hand of the other over who would be the dominant woman in Nana's life. I recall back in 1996 One took a cutlass to the other woman over who would get Nana. After the family held court over this incident and told both of them to go, the one who was bitten cursed Nana, saying if he goes to the other woman and not come to her side Ɔbookyerewa should kill him. I recall Nana telling me about this curse back in 1996. He said it was all over a watch of his which the *pito* woman took and he wanted it back. She would not give it back to him and one thing led to another; she cursed him with Ɔboɔkyerewa and he in turn cursed her back. All this led to a big problem for Nana for which he was fined a ram by Taa Mensa. Nana should have known better than to get into such a predicament.

Now, perhaps this new problem with one woman biting the other over Nana took place in my absence, because it does not take Ɔboɔkyerewa one year to kill. After Nana took ill, I was told the family asked Nana, what is wrong? Nana would not talk. Nana Akua Asantewaa related to me that Asubonten said that he would die. Yaw Mensa carrying Asubonten said because he thinks too much about his wife and money, he will become ill and he will die. It was mentioned that he told members of his shrine that he plans to travel to America to help me have a big festival. I also stated that my wife and I too talked about him and Kofi as his *ɔkyeame* visiting us.

So many people attended Nana Effa's funeral that it rivaled Nana Dɔnkɔ and Nana Akumsa's funeral. Kofi said it was because Nana knew so many people, he traveled to so many places that people from all over attended. Take me, for example. I came from America, by far the farthest place to pay my respects and say goodbye to Nana.

I never fully realized how powerful Nana Effa was, his problems and drinking clouded my judgment. I am truly sorry for my lack of insight. I knew he was a powerful and important person, but by no means to this degree. He did so much to help people. He helped so many, so many women to get children, people to win the lotto so that they may get money, cured so many diseases, and caught so many witches.

I recall hearing that one reason why Nana drank so much was due to his looking in the mirror when he divined and seeing so many bad things about himself (such as his death) that it worried him so much that he took to drinking. I have spoken to Nana about his drinking, and he confided in me many times that the family never knew his problems and he took to drinking. I always believe that when he mentioned problems, he meant that the family never fully accepted his *ɔbosom*. This of course may have been one of many issues he had with the family. He told me when he was born he came out with a closed fist, and the family tried in vain to open his hand, but he never would. They took a stick that was put into fire and burned his hand, and when he opened it, something flew away. Nana had a lot on his mind and not a lot of people to confide in. I was one of not too many people Nana would confide in.

I would spend my lifetime continuing the work Nana prepared me for, to be an international healer. I remember hearing *Nana* always saying to me, "we are international healers."

I was told that Asuotipa was upset with him for not properly celebrating his yam festival. I regret not being here to assist and celebrate it with him. *Nana me pa wo kyew*; maybe he depended upon me. I will never know. I always gave him money to celebrate his festival. I wonder if I could have done more.

I lost my *suman Akommere*. *Ɔkɔmfoɔ* do not wear it to funerals. I must remember to ask why. I took it off and placed in inside my pocket, but for some reason or another it fell out of my pocket and Ɔbookyerewa *ɔbosomfoɔɔ* found it. He originally thought it was Akua Asantewaa's, and placed it in the room. After I told Yaw Mensa I lost my *suman* he told me it was found. Ɔbosomfoɔɔ gave it to me and informed me that if anyone else found it they might have kept it and sold it or something. Yaw Mensa said that when you worry or think too much, you lose your *nsuman* or they will break. Nyame is wonderful, Akua Asantewaa told me thank Asubonten and put the *suman* down, which I did. I reflected that while I was on my way here from Kumase, *gyabunu* broke. Hey! Kofi Effa!!!

Looking back now I can see when I lost all my *nsuman* each time I was agitated. An *ɔkɔmfoɔ* must be of one mind, one body, and one spirit. Everything an *ɔkɔmfoɔ* has is a part of his/her universe in which constant balance and order must be maintained. Now, I know why some *ɔkɔmfoɔ* make it difficult for you to get these things, and you do not give it away freely. I know I can charge anyone what I want when I give them a *suman* freely and they lose it or spoil it.

*Yaw Mensa told me he had a dream last night about a certificate and behind it was a suman. He sent the certificate to Nana Kofi Kyereme. I laughed and told him I too had a similar dream back in December 1997. In told him my dream was about gyabunu, he also had a good laugh. We chatted about a certain ɔkɔmfoɔ from America whom we both considered to be an opportunistic person. That person is not viewed as an honest and nice person. I do not wish to continue in this vein except to say that this person is very dishonest and pompous.*

Today they purified Taa Mensa, Asubonten, and Asuotipa. They will purify Ɔboɔkyerewa on Friday. Kofi and I had a pleasant conversation on how *ɔkɔmfoɔ* is a servant and should not be too proud and a seeker of money. Even though money is a necessity, it should not be all there is for an *ɔkɔmfoɔ*. He tried to advise me that I should give my *ɔbosom* a ram and ask him to change so that I can work with him on Sundays. I told him I do not desire to do such a thing. I wish to keep things as they are, even though it has its challenges, and America is different from Ghana. We did agree that I should do more work with the *ɔbosom* in the evenings, like more consultations. He reminded me of how I consulted Nana Effa's *abosom* many times in the evenings. The evening times are good, Kofi added, because the excitement and competition of the day is not as intense, so the *ɔbosom* can come and use us freely without competition. The energy is cooler in the early morning and evening times.

I should also ask the *ɔbosom* to assist me with my business and all those who owe me money should pay me; everything that is for me should come to me and not go elsewhere, and when I prosper, I will thank the *ɔbosom*.

Concerning the death of Nana Effa I spoke to the elder Kofi Manu who inherited Nana Effa and Amokoten, a friend. They said Nana Effa would not talk, and when he did, he said, "I know the law, I know the law." Now, this is very interesting. Before I left America to come here, I went to the *ɔbosom* to inquires why Nana Effa died and my *ɔbosom* said, "When you obey the law, you are one with the law; when you are one with the law there is nothing to fear." Kofi Manu told me that he and Nana Effa made plans to visit Liberia around January 20th. I am beginning to realize the potentiality of the mind and spirit, that when you put your mind to something it can be realized. I came here to find out more about the events surrounding the death of Nana Effa and it is happening.

Kofi Manu said since Kofi Effa is not here, he will support me; he will lift me up higher. He will give me lots of medicine to bathe and to have in my possession. He said that Kofi Dɔnkɔ is gone, Kofi Effa is gone, so he is here. He went on to say he will give me a *suman*, and that I should fear nothing, even if a gun is fired at me nothing can harm me. Since a gun is fired somewhere in the world what is there to fear. He mentioned also that he will give me a *suman* that calls bees to beat anyone who challenges me.

Ɔbookyerewa *ɔbosomfoɔ* informed Yaw Mensa that he talks too much and too long when pouring libation to the *ɔbosom*. He said that he talks as if he is talking abroad. The *ɔbosom* understands the problems more than we do, so he does not have to say too much. Keep it simple; the *ɔbosom* are not stupid.

Sometime ago during the summer months at my mother's house I saw a bird nest in which an egg was laid. I decided to take it, thinking I may need it in the future for something for the *ɔbosom*. Recalling from a book I read by Eliade, he said that a nest represents a house, flocks, and children. In a word, it symbolizes the family of a society. So when I get back home, I will sit the *ɔbosom* on the nest.

Today Kofi Manu (a.k.a. Agyan) came by to visit me. He has taken a good liking to me. He advised me that *ɔkɔmfoɔ* should never eat food that is cooked one place and traveled to another place. He said in essence a path, i.e. road, should never be crossed. There are things in the atmosphere that are bad and people with no good intentions can spoil the food, so when you eat it can cause you lots of trouble. He said he advised Nana Effa about eating such food, but his mother brought him food three times. Agyan reiterated you do not know if the person traveling with your food has spiritual power to protect, or cover your food and a witch can do something to it and kill you. He said *ɔkɔmfoɔ* should always eat food at the spot where it is prepared. Even if he/she is in a market or station, sit down at that place and eat. So I will change my eating habits from now on. He also cautioned about telling your wife all your taboos, saying I should keep them in your mind.

Agyan said he would like to give me something before I travel back home. This spiritual thing will make whatever I say come true; even if people challenge me they will see something. He mentioned I should take water and put it beside my bed and sleep alone. I must get up during the night and wash my face and mouth, saying whatever I say will be like fire and spit into a bucket. I should do this three times during the course of the night. Collect the spittle and put it in a bottle and give it to him. He will also provide me with a spiritual bath. Kofi and I should go to seven markets and put something down and collect anything that strikes my mind, one from each market. Bring these things to him and he will make something for me to take back home.

He said when someone comes for divination or work I will see everything before they sit down. I should at this time use caution and not say everything I see, but go through the process of divining before I speak. Sometimes I may travel and see a lot, but again I should not say everything I see, just small things and mainly speak when I am working at the shrine.

Thinking back on the last conversation Kofi and I had, he stated that the compound word *akɔm* in
*ɔkɔmfoɔ* refers to hunger, suggesting that a priest goes hungry or fasts a lot.

Yesterday Kwasi Komfo told me a dream he had about me. He said he saw Kofi Effa, Taa Mensa *ɔbosomfoɔ*, Nana Kofi Kyereme and I all dressed in white *ntoma*. I was in the center at the Tanɔ River pouring libation.

More stories on the death of Nana Effa came to me. Nana Akua Asantewaa said that a witch killed Nana Effa, not Ɔboɔkyerewa. Kofi said that when an *ɔkɔmfoɔ* makes a mistake, a witch can stand on it and kill him/her, so *ɔkɔmfoɔ* always have to be very careful. Agyan too supported the idea that a witch killed Nana Effa.

He had no wife. They sent his two wives away, and so he had no one to cook for him. Maame had to travel at times to his house with his food. Agyan informed me that before Nana died, he walked around town telling everyone, *me to kwan, me to kwan, me kɔ baabi*, meaning, "I am leaving, I am leaving, I am going somewhere."

Agyan had a lot to say. He told me an *ɔkɔmfoɔ* should fear women and never tell his wife his deepest secrets. He stipulated not only should we fear women for what they can do to us, but they too should fear us for what we can do to them.

So many people have died since I arrived from this outbreak of meningitis. I heard that Ɔboɔkyerewa *ɔbosomfoɔɔ* Nana Kofi Asamadu is in the hospital. He was admitted for symptoms. They said he was vomiting and vomiting for about fifteen minutes.

Reflecting on my conversations with Agyan, I was encouraged to utilize my *suman* on the pan more purposefully. It has the seven *dwene nnua* (thick branches) which I plan to tie a rope onto and bind thoughts with sacrifice to the *ɔbosom*.

I saw Yaw Mensa and inquired about a bath kept in the *suman* room call *dudo*. This *sumam* has seven roots added to make it. I told him I made some back home but it spoiled. He said if I sacrifice to it, it will not spoil and if I cannot change it at my annual festival offer it another chicken and tell it in one or two more years I will change it.

Yaw Mensa asked me if I knew what the name of the cooked ram's blood. I said no, and he told me it is call *kyim* and it is made with salt and shea butter. Thinking back, the word *kyim* seem to resonate with me when I was eating it with Nana Dɔnkɔ.

After the ram is sacrificed the hands of the person who presented the ram is placed right on top of left with the words *yaa yaa ya, hyira* and the name of the person. Then *kuse* is mentioned.

A few days ago *ɔkyeame* Kofi Boɔ was talking about the Tanɔ *ɔbosom* and I told him about a dream I had about the *ɔbosom* Taa Kramo. He said to me Taa Kramo is Taa Ho's *ɔkyeame* and that Puroo is Asubonten's *ɔkyeame*. Taa Ho was very big at one time, he was even bigger at one time than he is now. He eats palm oil, but because he is in Asubonten's room and Asubonten taboos it, it is not given to him. Taa Ho also eats rice. I was surprise to hear of a Tanɔ *ɔbosom* eating palm oil, and *Nana Boɔ* confirmed that some Atanɔ *abosom* do not taboo palm oil.

Now I am thinking that Kwabena Bena has to get his *ɔkyeame*, perhaps it is Taa Kramo. Yesterday, I fed Ɔboɔkyerewa.

Today Kwabena Bena showed everyone who he is. I had the feeling earlier that the *ɔbosom* wanted to come upon me while I was listening to *adowa* songs, so I left to avoid it. I was feeling too sad listening to the music and did not want to possess the ɔbosom in such a state. Yaw Mensa visited me and inquired why I left. I was also call by ɔbosomfoɔɔ and asked why. I explained why and was invited to eat. While eating I felt sad again with no appetite, then suddenly the ɔbosom possessed me. I was informed later on by Yaw Mensa that Kwabena Bena was upset, for he had got nothing from me to eat since he traveled from America to here. I had chopped food but he had not. He said, ɔbosomfoɔ beg the ɔbosom on my behalf and promised a chicken: the ɔbosom ask for drink and left. Yaw Mensa brought the chicken and I the drink. When offering the ɔbosom the chicken he would not accept it, saying he wanted to punish me, for he was angry with me. We begged the ɔbosom for a long time and still he would not eat. Ɔbosomfoɔ pleaded yet nothing. The Kurontihene came to assist someone with work also beg on my behalf and yet the ɔbosom did not respond. Yaw Mensa took a break and did the Kurontihene work and continued with me and still nothing from the ɔbosom. Yaw Mensa decided to offer two chickens at once and elicited no response from the ɔbosom, even when he changes the chicken. There was nothing. Finally a ram was sacrificed, and we will try again on Tuesday. I was told not to worry, that the ɔbosom wants to show that he is in town and will act as such. Yaw Mensa said the ɔbosom was angry from back home, that I am more interested in making money than the ɔbosom. I became disturbed by this news and removed myself to my room for a while, took a nap, but I was awakened because they were sacrificing a ram to clean Ɔboɔkyerewa's knives.

Yaw Mensa teased me saying that I am not a man. I have changed because of what has happened, and I should not think too much about it. He went on to ask me, do I think the ɔbosom will kill me? If I thought so, then I wanted death, so I have to cheer up, and I did. Incidentally it rained for the first time. Yaw Mensa said Kwabena Bena came and so did the rains. But he said if it had rained at the nighttime it would be a blessing, but since it is in the daytime something will happen.

Yesterday I carried Asuotipa. Yaw Mensa said that Asuo ask for the elders, but none was there and so they sent for Amponsa to stand in as a proxy. Yaw also said Asuo told Maame that she worries too much about the family and if she continues, so she will fall ill. She worries about Sewa and Amponsa; if she becomes ill who can she take care of.

Asuo said that the family is not of one mind; some are here and some are there. This is all I recall form what Yaw told me. If I remember anything more I will make note of it. Later on that night Nana Akua Asantewaa visited me and informed me that I should not carry Asuo on Sundays. Saturdays, Tuesdays, Wednesdays, and Fridays are fine, but never Sundays. She reminded me that she does not possess Asubonten on Sundays or Thursdays.

On *Kurudapaawukuo* I carried Asuo again. After carrying Asuo, Yaw Mensa said Asuo advised the family to come together. He was asked about taking a new priest and Asuo said that the family should select three young men and he will chose his priest from among them. Agyan asked him to help with his problems concerning his wives and he stated that this is not an *ɔbosom* matter, but a family matter, yet Agyan insisted and went to pick two leaves and place them on the ground to represent the wives and asked Asuo to choose. Asuo asked for an egg and threw the egg on the ground and pushed one away; the other Agyan took up and pressed to his heart. I was told more but do not recall.

Kofi suggested that I get two bells and with brass chains hang them on the *ɔbosom*'s stool and ring them on *dabone*. On Kuru I ask Yaw Mensa what Nana Effa meant by saying, "giving the *ɔbosom* a stool." Yaw said the giving of the stool is to symbolize giving authority to the *ɔbosom* and to do work. A knife is presented along with a ram and drink, saying that he should help people in need and punish the bad ones, bring money, things etc.

Kwasi Komfo gave me some good advice saying that if your mind is not correct you will suffer in *akɔm*. I will leave for the United States and return to Ghana in September for yam festival.

Today is September 15. They put the markings on the pan. I arrived late to Takyiman from the United States, missing the ritual. I am not sure if they only use clay and water, or herbs added to the water and clay. These markings were all different. I will inquire about their meanings later.

Asubonten has a vertical line, then seven dots, then another vertical line, and seven dots followed by another vertical line, sitting on a horizontal line.

Akumsa has one vertical line followed by three dots, and then another vertical line followed again by three dots and a vertical line all sitting on a crescent.

Taa Ho has a checkmark followed by three dots; then an arrow, followed by three dots, and lastly, a checkmark that is the reverse of the first.

Puroo has four vertical lines sitting on a horizontal line.

I did not see any marking on Taa Kramo.

Last Wednesday, Dada gave me a pair of *nsuman* called *Gyeme*. He said this *suman* would help me to stand when challenged. If someone or something challenges me and I feel I am about to fall, I should call *Gyeme* and I will not fall. Instead, the challenging person will fall. I wear the one with smaller shells on my right arm and the one with larger shells on my left. I pour powder on each shell and libation with sweet-smelling oil. Dada also gave Kwabena Bena a bottle of gin in a box. I feel that he was also instrumental in the elders welcoming my *ɔbosom* with a chicken and drink. I recall that he tried to feed Kwabena Bena repeatedly in vain and he would not eat until Nana Akua Asantewaa was present.

We also went to greet the *ɔkɔmfoɔhene*. He told me to greet the *abosom* when I noticed that the markings on the *ɔbosom's* pan were different.

Sometime later, Kofi came by and during a conversation, he spoke about *akɔm twe*. This is a serious problem for *ɔkɔmfoɔ*. When possessing the *ɔbosom*, sometimes it does not fully possess on the *ɔkɔmfoɔ*. If this happens and someone tests or challenges the *ɔbosom*, it can lead to the disgrace of the *ɔkɔmfoɔ*. This *akɔm twe* problem may exist due to a number of factors. Maybe the *ɔkɔmfoɔ* is thinking too much or has personal problems, like drinking too much, too much preoccupation with women. I think other important factors may be improper training of the *ɔkɔmfoɔ* and not having enough *aduro* in his/her body to attract or make connection with the *ɔbosom*, or not following the instructions of their teacher. *Akɔm* means to possess, and *twe* means to pull or stalk-like a hunter. In this sense, the *ɔbosom* is stalking the *sunsum* of the *ɔkɔmfoɔ* but does not fully capture it.

I have been sick for the past few days with malaria symptoms. I took *aduro*, but still, my stomach and the dizziness bother me and all I want to do is lie down. I possess the *ɔbosom* today and he said two witches are trying to kill his *ɔkɔmfoɔ*. Ɔbookyerewa *ɔbosomfoɔɔ* told me this and we poured libation at Asubonten and asked Ɔbookyerewa and Kwabena Bena to kill those witches. Ɔbookyerewa *ɔbosomfoɔɔ* also said I should go to Traa and bath three times in the river. I do feel a little better after the possession. I feel I will improve.

I learned from Nana Kofi Boɔ that women do not eat the *eto* set aside for the *ɔbosom*. The eto is separated into two, for those given to the *ɔbosom* and men to eat and that which is shared for women, since they cannot eat the food given to Asubonten. The same for Kwabena Bena.

I was informed that you can feed Asubonten on Thursdays and Sundays. This of course, is done indirectly through the *mmoatia*, the children of the *ɔbosom* at the clubs. They will take the food to the father. Even though the *ɔbosom* is fed this way, they do not uncover the pan.

There is serious litigation going on between Ɔbookyerewa *ɔbosomfoɔɔ* and his family members.

Libation is poured by the *ɔkɔmfoɔ* to announce why you are here and to cool the hotness of the *ɔbosom* down. Water is also used because that person will drink water and if they do, the *ɔbosom* will catch them. When the *ɔbosom* is invoked, he rises out of the river and goes to work. By saying

*Nana kɔ tria* three times, you are asking him to lie back in his river or lean against a wall. In essence, you are asking him to stop and not to continue working. The offender throws the egg and if the shell lands facing up, the *ɔbosom* has listened. The *ɔkɔmfoɔ* now pours gin as libation. After this, we go inside to the shrine room to make sacrifices. The thanking person will present their chicken first and thank the *ɔbosom* before the ram is sacrificed. You never give a ram before the chicken; it is always the chicken first.

I recall last Sunday Nana Kofi Boɔ told me when you want to keep your *ɔbosom* or *suman* busy at work you make a pad out of nettle, and you sit the pan or a *suman* on it. Every time they come to rest, it will make them feel itchy and they will get up and work hard to finish so that it is removed.

Kofi told me that I could give *kunkuma* to my children as a *suman* to eat. This will cool down any trouble they might have. When I get back home, I will divide my *kunkuma* in half and mix it with the other *mɔtɔ* I have. I will put it in a gourd I received from Kofi Nimo, Nana Dɔnkɔ's second wife's relative. I will call this *suman kunkuma* and sacrifice a chicken for it. This will be my most powerful *mɔtɔ*, to be used for when the most difficult problems or any serious cases come before me.

In a conversation, Kofi told me that the *abosom* and *nsuman* could all be categorized as *abosom*. I beg to differ; I told him that the *ɔbosom* comes directly from Nyame, not the *nsuman*. He agreed but still insisted that they all can be called *abosom*. I said that a *suman* that catches witches is called *sumanbrafoɔ,* not *ɔbosommerafoɔ.* To me, there is a difference. Later on that evening, I asked Yaw Mensa if there was a difference between the two. He said yes, *nsuman* is *nsuman* and *abosom* is *abosom*; most *abosom* comes from a river, stones, etc., and *abrafɔ* comes from the bush.

Kofi and I talked about how Tanɔ originally put into place the traditional court structure and the ɔkyeame was originally called *tekrema*. I initiated this conversation when I asked him about the meaning of the word *ntrama*, when I had a dream about my divination. Kofi thought and thought for a little while and then began to laugh. Then he said it was the word *tekrema*, which means tongue. I dreamed of this in relation to my divination; I still questioned his definition of the word since I saw the word *ntrama* in an old Twi dictionary that said that *ntrama* was an old word for cowrie, which meant to measure or count. Anyway, Kofi went on to link *tekrema* with ɔkyeame. He said when Tanɔ instituted the court system and the function of the ɔkyeame the ɔbosom changed. When visitors come to greet a chief, they may not understand the protocols and to avoid their embarrassment, the ɔkyeame is the one who advises them before making the introduction on the procedures. Kofi said the word ɔkyeame comes from two compound words *kyea* to greet and *me*, which means I or me. You greet the ɔkyeame before you greet the ɔbosom or chief. We can see now that the ɔkyeame is one who you greet first and will hear all your requests or complaints and decide if you should present it there or some other court. The ɔkyeame will respectfully lead you to the ɔbosom, chief, and all in attendance by performing all the formalities and introductions. Most important is that if the visitor has any bad intentions, the ɔkyeame will be the first to absorb it before it gets to the ɔbosom or chief.

Yesterday, Asubonten advised me to keep the ɔbosom's eating table with me whenever I travel, so that the ɔbosom and I are never separated. This problem arose from me packing the ɔbosom's table in my suitcase. Regrettably, my suitcase did not arrive with me at the airport, and I had to travel to Takyiman without my luggage. Fortunately, for me, it arrived days later. Even though I did not have the *ɔbosom* eating table, I fed Kwabena Bena the ram anyway and Asubonten asked me who ate since his eating table was in Accra. I eventually went to Accra to pick up my luggage. After I had everything, I gave the *ɔbosom* a chicken, and he accepted. Asubonten also said I should give Kwabena Bena a chicken so that he can bring something for me.

Asubonten possessed on Nana Akua Asantewaa advising a male family member on his personal life. Asubonten used a simile about women being like bees. He told him that women are like bees and can bring you sweetness like honey and then can cause you trouble like the sting of a bee. The bees have this function: they make honey, which we all can enjoy due to its sweetness, but they will protect their honey and sting us if we bother them.

In order to reconcile the problem, the *ɔbosom* advised him to make a sacrifice with an egg, shea butter, and a bee. He must catch a bee, make a hole in the egg large enough to put the bee in and cover the hole with shea butter, then give it to the *ɔbosom* to sit upon it. When putting the egg for the *ɔbosom* to sit on, you must make sure that the pathway from the *ɔbosom* to the door is clear and everyone is off to the sides. This sacrifice tells the *ɔbosom* that you do not want something good that will bring you sorrow later on. You do not want this to bring you joy and sorrow. If you want someone's eyes and mind from wondering, you get their eyelashes and hair and put it in an egg and cover the hole with shea butter and sit the *ɔbosom* on it.

It is considered taboo for anyone to hit or sweep an *ɔkɔmfoɔ* with the broom while sweeping. The broom is used for sweeping away unwanted things and an *ɔkɔmfoɔ* does not want to be considered as such. If and when this should happen, the *ɔkɔmfoɔ* should lay the broom down and step upon it three times with the left foot to neutralize its power upon him/her. We use three pieces of the mouth of the broom to tie to *nsuman* to sweep away the bad things that are disturbing the client. We bathe children standing upon the broom to sweep away or neutralize the power of the sickness or harmful things that are bothering the child. We do the same when we place *nsuman* upon the broom.

I was told by Kofi that women can use the broom to make a man impotent. A woman can use spiritual power in her vagina to also spoil a man. The broom that can sweep all kinds of filth and bad things away from you can also sweep good things into heaps for you.

*Akommeren* is special place is set aside for the *ɔbosom*. Normally, spiritual plants are grown in this area. This is where the stone for the *ɔbosom* is placed.

I keep thinking about writing about the event surrounding the death of Ata Kwabena, nephew of Ɔboɔkyerewa *ɔbosomfoɔ*. It is one of the most tragic stories I have ever witnessed in Takyiman. It involved the *ɔbosom* Ɔboɔkyerewa, but I hesitate every time to do so.

Yaw Mensa and I spoke about why the pathway from the *ɔbosom* to the door is cleared whenever we put an egg or anything under the stool for the *ɔbosom* to sit upon. The reasoning behind this is that the *ɔbosom* will sit upon the soul of whoever is on the pathway of the *ɔbosom*. When this happens, the person will become ill and, if left untreated, will eventually die. I recall something similar back in 1991 when Nana Dɔnkɔ was doing work at one of his *suman*. I was told I should not attend for that very same reason. This is a very serious situation. He said the same for when you are tying up a *nsuman*. The soul of that individual will be tied up, especially if they have the same name as you. The *suman* will work against you. Yaw Mensa also informed me you do not always have to sit the *ɔbosom* directly on the egg, you can put it in between the stool.

I am now beginning to understand why people have such fear and respect for the *ɔbosom*. That is why *ɔkɔmfoɔ* must bath lots of powerful *aduro* and wear *nsuman* to protect and strengthen their soul.

Today I asked Kofi about Agya Kofi Nimo, the one who gave me *Asabre* and added *nsuman* to my *fugu* back in 1994. Kofi said he died. I felt deeply saddened by this news, for I wanted to visit him.... all the elders are leaving.

I saw a woman bring three colored eggs to offer to Asubonten. I inquired as to why these three eggs were so different from normal egg sacrifice. I was told one egg was put into saltwater so that the *ɔbosom* will give her sweetness; the other was covered with black, red, and white dots. I cannot remember why. I can only guess that it represented the phases of the day, noon, and night, and the last one, a certain insect, was put into it. This insect has pinchers and makes a hole like ants. It hides curled up in the hole and awaits its prey. The hole of the egg was covered with dirt from the bath area. This is so whoever wishes to box with you will be defeated. This egg was put in between the stool. This woman has a son who has a court case and was told in divination by the *ɔbosom* what to sacrifice for success.

I had a visit from a friend, Kofi Owusu, who has an herbal cure for malaria, jaundice, and typhoid fever. We had a serious conversation about the state of Africa, Ghana in particular, and the impact of Christianity, which has such a stronghold on the people's mind in Ghana. He says the whole problem with Ghana is poverty, and because of this dreadful situation, people do extremely bad things to each other. People are suffering due to poverty and for this reason, they cause their neighbors to suffer. The government officials are corrupt and "chop" (i.e. consume) the money. They always want more than they have. Traders have a hundred percent markup, charging more for their products by lying to their customers, saying their goods cost more than what they really pay for them. All in the name of fearing poverty. People want their family members to die so that they can inherit their possessions, in the name of want. Doctors refuse to give proper treatments to their patients who are poor. The rich will not help the poor for fear that if they give one day, they too will not have and suffer. Everyone is trying to cheat others so that they and their family may prosper.

All this talk from Kofi Owusu seems so pessimistic and flawed. Since I have been coming to Ghana, I have met wonderful and compassionate people with good moral character who are not solely interested in what they can get from me. I am not saying there are not people like what he described, but that is everywhere: you can always find people who fit within that classification.

Christianity, he says, is a stabilizer because of its inherent doomsday or Judgment Day concept. If you do not do good, you will not get into the kingdom of God. So, this forces one to do good for his/her neighbor because they will have to give account one day. I asked him why do they not believe that their ancestors live in a good place, even if we do not call it heaven? He said that they do not know, but since I am more advanced and think better, I may have a better idea than they would about this. All he knows is that their pastor's constant preaching forces them to do good by reminding them of heaven. He emphasized that if people know or have *aduro*, they would use it against their neighbor to die so that they may succeed him. This is why Christianity tells them that if you do badly, God will punish them.

I do not see any changes or differences in people's behavior because of this belief. The *abosom/ɔbosom* will punish evildoers if you ask them for help. All these misunderstandings about the *ɔbosom* are due to western propaganda education, compounded by poverty, which creates improper thinking and doubts about the value of traditional culture. This is what Africa is suffering from.

Kofi Sakyi and I were talking about the history between the *Bono* people and the *Asante* people. He said that the *Asante* people are known for following up on the things that they hear without hesitation. He broke down the meaning of the word *Asante,* which is a compound word, *Asan* from *Ason* to hear and *te* to tell or understand. These people, if they hear about anyone or anything important, they act quickly to secure it for themselves, so that they may benefit. Akwasi Owusu, also known as Kwasi Komfo and who is *Asante,* confirmed this. He added that if Ɔbooky̨erewa was in *Asante*, he would be more important, and you will suffer to see the priest. It would cost you a lot. He said there is a sacred river in *Asante* you cannot easily access. It seems that *Bono* takes a lot for granted or perhaps the *Asante* are too arrogant.

The name Robert Rattray came up, and this was the first time I ever heard it mentioned in all my visits. Kofi Sakyi knows some of his histories. He said that Rattray supported *Asante* very much and wrote about their culture. When he visited Takyiman, they did not reveal much to him. The *Bono* people do not readily trust people and as a result hold back a lot. They did not know Rattray very well. They must first observe your character before they open up and reveal things to you. This reminds me of Nana Akumsa and Bɔngan.

I have often heard Diapemhene say *biribi a baabi* and it instantly reminds me of Nana Akumsa, when she sang the introduction to one of the first songs. She sang for me:
*Me ma wo adwo*
*Biribi a baabi*
*Me ma wo adwo*
*Asubonten ka ne ho, aye*
*Me ma wo adwo*

I am learning more and more about what I already know. I guess believing that you believe takes time to understand. I knew the importance of the mind and spiritual work. When the mind is calm, free, and pure there can never be any problems, but as soon as the mind becomes agitated, problems arise, and you become a servant to your thoughts and become possessed by that which occupies the mind the most.

I am learning more about how to center the mind and heart to be free and bold. I am seeing the significance of its importance daily. It is like taking off a shirt that has become contaminated and putting on a clean one.

There is a special chicken called *Tunsun ɔkokɔ*, which blacksmiths uses for their deity called Tunsun Kofi. The feathers of this chicken are ashy gray. There is another type of chicken called *prae ɔkokɔ* whose feathers look like a broom or a woman who perms or presses her hair. This chicken is used for sweeping away negative things.

Dada has given me another *suman*. I do not know how to thank him enough. He is doing so much freely for me, and I am surprised that no one has been this giving to me since Nana Dɔnkɔ, Nana Akumsa, and Nana Effa were alive. Dada made a *suman* called *Gye to me*; it is like the first one except this one eats chicken and drinks *akpeteshie*. If I am going to an *akɔm* I can send it and it will protect me from all challenges. I hope all my *nsuman* do not compete to do the same work. This *suman* can assist me in court cases or anything having to do with being victorious. It eats eggs and taboo pigs and will drink any extremely hot alcoholic liquor. I will inquire about how it is made later on.

I learned from Yaw Mensa that one of the *suman* I wear is called *nyin kyire*, and it will help me to grow old, and nothing will stop my progress. This *suman* has five small brown beads with black stripes interspaced with *gya bunu* gold/brass. I received this *suman* from Nana Dɔnkɔ some time ago. He went on to add that this *suman* has the hair of a very old person and will tell me later the skins that are added to it.

Nana Kwabena Brown came to Takyiman. I must note that this is the first time we have ever met each other in Ghana. He arrived yesterday, and I was so happy to see him. In our conversation, he suggested that we should do something good together, and tomorrow we plan to travel to *Aboabo*.

Fiema Abudwo ɔ*hene* visited me today, and we chatted a little about the history of the ɔ*bosom* of the town, whose name is *Abudwo*. The name *Abu/Abo* means many, a lot of, and *dwo* means cool. The chief said the ɔ*bosom* is an *Atanɔ* ɔ*bosom* from the river; it is related to Taa Mensa and Taa Kora. It was this trinity that gave Ɔboɔkyerewa his knife to use. Abudwo, like the others, is a father to Ɔboɔkyerewa, who is also his ɔ*brafoɔ*. Abudwo will not touch blood or alcohol except for *nsa fufuo* (palm wine), and he eats only the yolk of eggs. If any blood sacrifice is to be given to him, the stool and the pan are covered so that no blood may fall upon them, and the blood is given to his *ɔkyeame*.

The chief said that anyone can seek refuge from being killed at this *ɔbosom* by saying. I have touched the feet of Abodwo and no chief or *ɔbosom* can kill you. Even if you are cursed, the same and no curse can kill you; not even Ɔboɔkyerewa can kill you.

The chief cautioned that the *ɔbosom* taboos pepper; if you take pepper and curse anything, then put the pepper in the river. In two days, you will see something. This means that something bad will not only happen to the curse, but to the individual who made the curse. This *ɔbosom* Abudwo is a very cool *ɔbosom*, one who is *fitaa*, meaning clean and pure.

I recall today something interesting Fiema *ɔhene* told me. He said that he can never eat if the sun is not shining. This relationship between the *ɔbosom* and the sun I have never heard of before in all my visits to Ghana. Abudwo taboos this because the sun represents life and so does the *ɔbosom*. The priest prays for sunshine whenever it is not shining.

The *ɔbrafoɔ* is a servant of an *ɔbosom* who punishes and administers justice for that *ɔbosom,* such as a Tanɔ.

When you are asleep and you feel held down and cannot move or speak, it is a *sunsum bɔne* that is doing this deed. When a woman dreams of sleeping with another man other than her husband, it too is a *sunsum bɔne*. She is given *aduro* to repel this kind of spirit so that it may no longer trouble her or visit her when she is asleep. The same thing is also done for men.

Yaw Mensa informed me that it was Taa Ho who gave Tigare his knife and is therefore considered the father of Tigare. When this *suman* first was brought from Yiripala to Takyiman, it was brought to Taa Mensa first, then Taa Ho and Asubonten. It was Taa Ho who sprinkled clay on the clubs, and the *suman* possessed for the first time soon after. The owner took this and showed it to the people of Yiripala. So, Tigare can act as ɔ*brafoɔ* for Taa Ho.

I have often heard Kofi say that *Akumsa* is female, but I always questioned this and took the matter to Yaw Mensa, who confirmed that the ɔ*bosom* is male.

I have observed that when you are giving *kola* to a *suman*, you always ask first which one does it want? You will cast it while divining and if both are upright, that means it agrees; if down, it disagrees. The one that is upright, you first pinch a piece off with your nails and place it upon the *suman*, then that one on top of it. The one that is down is for men to eat.

I was invited to Astar FM radio to talk about STDs, not too long after reading a book that said a woman's fertile days begin 11 days after the end of her menses, and her fertile period will last for eight days.

Dada and I continued our conversation about the *suman gyeme*. He added that when tying, use the red string first because when someone comes, they come because of red eyes, which is to say something serious. Next, use the black and last the white string in that order. I saw Dada add a tie to the *suman*, with the fiber that covers the palm tree, along with pepper and the mouth of a broom. Use only the white for myself.

It is important to remember that when someone comes for help, it is because they are trying to get something and perhaps another is also trying to get that same thing, so they want the support of the *nsuman* or *ɔbosom* to help them. This is where the sweeping broom comes in. We use the mouth of the broom to sweep away any obstacle that is in the mind of the adversary so that they will give it to you. In essence, if you want something and someone else puts their mind to get it, or claim it to be their own, the broom will sweep away that thought of theirs and they will concede it to you.

You could imagine my surprise when I found out that Yaw Mensa also has *Hurudwo*. I inquired about him, and Yaw said that it can do anything, and put down any difficult situation. *Hurudwo* works like *kunkuma*, since they both cool down hot and foaming situations. If troubled by a witch, the *suman* will cool them down. The only difference I see between his *Hurudwo* and the one I have is what is used in tying it up. I use pepper, tobacco, *mae* plant, bamboo, and its tail, all tied between my legs. I saw Yaw only use what I indicated above, except for its tail and tying it between his legs.

I can see now with all the *nsuman* I have I do not need any more. I only need the knowledge on how to use them to their fullest ability. With that in mind, I can accomplish any kind of work, no matter how difficult it may appear.

I recall Yaw Mensa saying that if I am going to an *akɔm* or somewhere that makes me concerned for my safety, I should collect the leaves of plants and pour libation with it on *Hurudwo* to cool down the concern I have about that place. This reminded me about a time Nana Effa and I were on our way to a *akɔm* in Forikrom. He instructed me to grab any leaves from both sides of the path and pick up pebbles to toss behind our backs to safeguard us from any unforeseen danger from the unknown.

Kofi informed me that he inquired and received some information on Bɔngan. He said he was told that this *suman* comes from the Gyaman area, and it was an old man, a family member who got the *suman* there and gave it to Nana Akumsa. Kofi went on to say that Bɔngan is something hard to break, something very hard to overcome.

Yaw Mensa followed up and passed on the information to make the *suman nyinkyire*. He said the *suman* will make you grow old even if you are weak and dying. You will not die unless you remove the *suman* from your leg. Use herbs mixed with egg yolk to pull the string for purification. Pour libation on the egg with herbs to cook on the fire and eat.

I recall when Kofi, Nana Brown, and I went to Aboabo to feed Nana Brown's *Tigare* and during the feeding of the *suman* a conversation about odd numbers and why they are more significant than even numbers. This all took place after the cooked yams are poured out so we can count the yam that was stuck to the bottom of the pot. A helper said it is good for one extra to be left to represent that when anyone comes later, there is one leftover for him/her. The odd numbers represent that which is never finished. When you divide something evenly, that is it. And if someone comes, there is none to share, but when there is one leftover, we share it with the unknown one who has come.

I was told by Akumsa *ɔbosomfoɔɔ* that I should bathe with a plant called

*Atome hire.* He is going to give me *ahunu aduro* and when I see things I will not shake (in fear). The plant will spiritually protect me and when I see anything bad, like witches, spirits, and even death, I will not be disturbed.

I have learned from Yaw Mensa that when you pour libation or do sacrifice and if anyone comes after you are finished, this is a sign of good fortune.

I narrated to Kofi a dream I had about the *suman* Kasa bi the brain of a chicken. He said yes! It was given to the *suman* when I was first given it. I told him I did not recall; he said it was done after I left the room. Kofi went on to say that Kofi Nimo said that if I am away from Kasa bi and experience trouble, I should call my wife and tell her to give Kasi bi a drink and to use the red string to tie up my problem. If any person is involved, she should say their name to the *suman* before tying and taking some of the butter and bringing it to me. When she is finished, she should place Kasa bi back on the butter.

Today, October 17, we went to a festival at Forikrom, and toward the end of the *akɔm*, there was a big commotion concerning two *akɔmfoɔ* challenging each other, which all led to a big dispute and it sort of spoiled the event. Everyone eventually sat down with the chief of the town and made comments and solutions. The whole problem began with Kwame Agyeman, Kofi Ofori, and Kwame Adu, something happened between Kwame Adu and Asubonten cook. They all got into some sort of dispute which almost erupted into a fight.

I now reflect back to this morning and the difficulty I had with *Bɔngan* taking so long to eat an egg, which fell and had a dent in it. I thought it was because my mind was too preoccupied, which caused the *ɔbosom* not to possess upon me even though I tried to possess him. I failed in that effort to possess the ɔbosom and now, looking back, I know why Bɔngan would not eat.

I had the opportunity to see an ɔbosom I dreamed about, Kyinaman, at the festival. The ɔbosom carried the exact same knife. I saw him in my dream, and he greeted people with a slap on the back and side with this knife like in my dream, except I was thinking he placed it on them, not a slap. This was the way the ɔbosom greeted people.

Today I also visited Atta for the third time, and he does not look good. I prayed that he survived this illness, which they say is due to Ɔboɔkyerewa and a woman. His mother told me he does not eat, which is never a good sign. I do not know what went wrong with Atta. I helped him back in 1994 to get a car so he could make his own business. Ever since then, I was so pleased to see him whenever I visited Takyiman driving his taxi, and now he is deadly ill and may not survive. He truly does not look good. He is a very young man, perhaps in his twenties.

I can see Dada is trying very hard to support Kwabena Bena. He goes out of his way to look after and protect me more than anyone since the time of Nana Dɔnkɔ, Nana Akumsa, and Nana Effa. He is like a watchman and is always helping me to gain power.

Today Dada used cobwebs to tie the mouth of a broom around a *suman*. The broom represents sweeping all challenges and the cobweb will catch anything bad or good. This ritual reminds me of the binding principle I wrote down. Now I see how they are coming into use.

Dada visited me yesterday and today and he demonstrated the use of gunpowder very similar to how I have seen it used before. He placed a *suman (*Dɔnkɔ) on the ground and put gun powder on both sides of it and on its front and then asked me to light it. Yesterday I was not successful, but today I managed to do it. It seems like there are no limits to what things in nature you can use to manipulate circumstances.

I traveled to Dumase to visit Akumsa *ɔbosomfoɔɔ*. I have taken a liking to him because he reminds me of Nana Dɔnkɔ; he is as much an *ɔbosomfoɔɔ* as Nana Dɔnkɔ but in a very different way. I do not take anything away from him. He made three *nsuman* for me: *Hwee*; *Anyinam;* and *Afram* (aka *Akua Bodwo* or *Ntwerema*) to help me do good spiritual work.

The *sumanbrafoɔ* Anyinam is smeared with shea butter, and the *motɔ* is made from any wood found on the main path. When this *suman* catches you, you will become insane. Akua Bodwo is not given blood from now on; it sits on shea butter and lavender is poured on it for libation.

I fed Anyinam today, and it accepted the sacrifice; the chicken flipped and landed on its back, so everything went well. Blood got on everyone present, on my pants, chest, arms, on Dada, Adu, and Akwam. We collected two clubs called *nkotoba* from the *namprane* tree for the *suman* to sit on. When we fed the *sumam*, we gave it these parts of the chicken: The head and feet; gizzard; liver; and the spinal column and coccyx.

Kofi made some inquiries about *Burokuma* and found out that this *suman* was used when all other things failed. He was informed that with this *suman* you could hunt and catch wild animals and witches. All I have to do is put on the *Fugu/Batakari* and go. I recall Nana Dɔnkɔ telling me you can take the *suman* to war and be victorious. He also advised me not to fight or beat anyone while wearing the *suman.* They could be spiritually injured.

There is a lot of talk floating around and inquiring since Dada and Adu took me to Nkoransa to receive the *nsuman.*

I awoke to the sound of people talking and knocking on doors around 2 a.m. I eventually discovered all the commotion was due to the passing of Atta, who died between 11 p.m. and midnight. I did not expect his death so soon.

Yaw Mensa and I spoke about twins. He told me all twins have a spirit called Boame; they wear white clothes when making sacrifices of yam and chickens. On *Fofie* they also dress in white clothes before they eat. Yaw Mensa also informed me that it is important whether twins are born both male or female, or a combination of either. When both are male or female, this is considered good, but if one is male and the other is female, they will worry about the parents who raise them. He may be referring to the demand placed upon the parents. He also stated that, in the latter instance, they are like witches.

When one dies, the other will come to take the living one, so they use *nsuman* to split them apart spiritually and the dead one is told to go and live in the cemetery and let the living one stay. All this, of course, takes place when the living one possesses the dead one.

On October 24th, I noticed yesterday they did not uncover the shrines of Taa Ho and Taa Kramo, and so I asked Kwasi Komfo and Yaw Mensa as to why? Yaw Mensa said it is because Taa Ho taboos *Fofie*, and he went on to add that he also taboos *Kurupada Wukuo*.

In another conversation, sometime later, the subject of *dufa* came up. Yaw Mensa said the reason why we lay *dufa* on its side while it is drying is because its power would leave if you sat it upright. He further revealed that when we want its *aduro*, we grind it in an upright position, though we lay it on its side when we are not using it.

This morning, Dada (Akwasi Effa) gave me a comprehensive list of the *nsuman* and their ingredients I got from Akumsa *ɔbosomfoɔ*. My original mind was not to document all of it again due to redundancy since I did that earlier, but I decided to stick to my journal as written.

Today a chicken was given to my *ɔbosom*, but he would not eat. At one time, the chicken ruffled its feathers with its beak, and I believe I heard Yaw Mensa say something about *Ntoma*, or cloth, which from this I concluded that the feathers refer to the cloth of the chicken which it wears. So, in the future, whenever the chicken does this, I will bear in mind that the *ɔbosom* is referring to cloth.

I have been meaning to visit *Nana* Kwam Froɔ, whose real name is Kwame Opoku. He is still very strong. I told him about a dream I had about Kofi Fofie *akoroma* wanting to be up high above all other *nsuman*. He quickly responded that he told me so. Which I did not recall, he did not reveal anything else other than he would not tell me anything about the *suman* because it will speak to me and tell me all I needed to know about it in dreams, and if not the other *nsuman* would inform me. He advised me that when I consult *sedeɛ*, I should place *Amaneno* in front of me. He also wanted to know if I see anything when I use *Hweɛ*, and I told him yes!

Later on, I managed to ask him for some of his hair, but he said that was hard for him to do so because his master gave him some of his hair and within three days, his master died. He did say he would tell his family to give me some of his hair after he dies. He also instructed me that if I come back to meet him, I should give him cloth and a ram. I said, I will. I presented to him 20,000 cedi and half a bottle of drink.

Nana Kwam Frɔɔ said to me that he spiritually visited my town and saw a big river there. He poured libation and thanked Nana Dɔnkɔ, telling him that because of him, he met me. I also thank Nana Dɔnkɔ, because of him I too met Nana Kwam Frɔɔ. Nana Kwam Frɔɔ said when I get back, I should give the *ɔbosom* a ram. If I cannot get any ram, I should give a red chicken.

The first person on my list to visit this morning was *Nana* Kofi *Nimo*. I did not meet him, so I visited Nana Kwame Ntwi, Akumsa *ɔbosomfoɔɔ*. I inquired about the ring he wanted to give to me. Somehow, *Dada* did not interpret what he meant, and he was referring to an ankle bracelet, not a *kawa* (ring). The ankle bracelet did not fit, and he said he had it made for me, but he did not know my foot size. Somehow again, there was a misunderstanding due to Dada's interpretation. He decided to give me one of his rings, which he took off his finger. He cooked *moto* for the ring and gave me incisions. The rest of the *moto* was given to me in alcohol to drink. He cautioned me never to hit or beat any of my children with my hands, for this will spiritually injure them, causing them to fall to the ground and drool. He said when this happens, I should put the ring in water and give it to them to drink. Nana Kwame Ntwi's ring is the most distinguishable ring I have been given to date. It is not open like the other *kawa* that was given to me and this area, which is normally open, seems to be covered in either gold or brass. It seems much brighter than brass to me, but I could be wrong. All this will be put to rest when I eventually get the ring to inspect it personally.

I must admit ever since I received the *suman* Akua Boaduro I have to notice the slightest change in myself. I feel a little bolder, more confident and assertive. Even if I seem to hesitate before acting, still active, go ahead. One person I know who is full of this power is Yaw Mensa.

This is my last night here in Takyiman, and how I do love this place and its people! I will always miss being here, no matter how difficult things may have gotten. Yes! There are some people who are selfish, but where can you ever find people who are not? I went to Atta Kwabena's funeral, even though it should not have been celebrated, and since everyone went, it would not look proper if I did not attend. The reason is when the ɔbosom Ɔbookyerewa kills you because of an offense and you attend the funeral, it can be interpreted that the ɔbosom did something regrettable.

On November 1st, back in the United States, reading a book on the ɔbosom of Ancient Egypt, I came across a section on the ɔbosom Hathor which reminded me of a conversation I had in Takyiman either with Nana Kofi Boɔ or Kofi Sakyi. The discussion was about the parts of the animal, in particular the legs, which are given to the ɔbosom when feeding after a sacrifice. I was told that in ancient times the chief was the owner of the land and all the game upon it. This was to make sure no overhunting or abuse was done to the land or animals. And if anyone killed an animal, it was an offense, so hunters had to seek permission from the chief before they hunted, and a portion was given to the chief.

The ɔbosom being also a chief had the same rights. So, when any sacrifice is done, certain portions of the meat have to be given to the ɔbosom, which chiefly consists of the left side of the animal. This is generally when four-legged animals are sacrificed.

I find it interesting that the Egyptians always put their left foot forward, which had to do with putting their heart forward.

*M'anansesem a metooye yi, se eye de o, se ennye de o, momfa bi nkɔ momfa bi mmera.*

After akɔm, at Poma.

After akɔm, at Poma.

Having fun, greeting Nana Mensa and wife Auntie Kate.

Nana Kofi Owusu at yam festival, Poma.

ɔkɔmfoɔ Kwasi Owusu and me during festival at Poma.

Women singing songs at Poma.

More serious moment with Nana Mensa and wife Auntie Kate.

Nana Mensa and me during festival at Poma.

www.ingramcontent.com/pod-product-compliance
Lightning Source LLC
Chambersburg PA
CBHW040251090526
**44586CB00041B/2745**